HEAVY HORSES

HEAVY HORSES

An Illustrated History of the Draft Horse

Grant MacEwan

The publisher gratefully acknowledges the support of The Canada Council for the Arts and the Department of Canadian Heritage. We acknowledge the financial support of the Government of Canada through the Book Publishing Industry Development Program for our publishing activities.

Printed in Canada

01 02 03 04 05/ 5 4 3 2 1

NATIONAL LIBRARY OF CANADA CATALOGUING IN PUBLICATION DATA

MacEwan, Grant, 1902-2000
Heavy horses

Previous ed. has title: Heavy horses : highlights of their history.
Includes index.
ISBN 1-894004-74-4

1. Draft horses—Canada—History. I. Title.
SF311.3.C2M33 2001   636.1'5'0971   C2001-911160-6

Front cover painting, *Diggin' In*, by Adeline Halvorson
Back cover photograph: Shea's Brewery team, Winnipeg
Design by Articulate Eye

Published in Canada by
Fifth House Ltd.
A Fitzhenry & Whiteside Company
1511–1800 4 Street SW
Calgary, Alberta, Canada
T2S 2S5

First published in the U.S. in 2001 by
Fitzhenry & Whiteside
121 Harvard Ave.
Suite 2
Allston, Massachusetts
01234

Contents

About the Author

Grant MacEwan at Belgian Field Day, Lynnwood Ranch, Aldersyde, Alberta.

Grant MacEwan was born in Brandon, Manitoba, on August 12, 1902. Educated in Brandon and Melfort, Saskatchewan, he went on to graduate from Ontario Agricultural College in 1926 and Iowa State College in 1928. He was a professor of animal husbandry at the University of Saskatchewan and department head from 1928 to 1946, and dean of agriculture at the University of Manitoba from 1946 to 1951.

He began his political career in 1951, when he stood as the Liberal candidate in Brandon's federal by-election. He moved to Calgary soon after his defeat and served as an elected alderman from 1953 to 1959. Elected as an MLA in 1955, he served as leader of the Alberta Liberal Party from 1958 to 1960. He was elected Mayor of Calgary in 1963 and served in this capacity until 1966.

Grant MacEwan served as lieutenant-governor of Alberta from 1965 to 1974 and was made a Member of the Order of Canada in 1975. Grant MacEwan Community College in Edmonton was named in his honor. He published four agricultural texts and close to fifty books on historical subjects, averaging close to a book a year between 1970 and 1990.

Grant MacEwan's wide-ranging experiences in academic, political, and literary circles often put him in the public eye. He won the hearts of thousands of people across the prairies with his engaging personality, accessibility, and the hundreds of entertaining stories he had at his fingertips. He died in June 2000 at the age of ninety-seven.

Foreword

Grant MacEwan needs no introduction to horse lovers across Canada, for few people achieved greater respect in the equine fraternity. Given his background, this is no surprise. As a youth on the family farm in Saskatchewan, MacEwan learned to love and appreciate horses, especially Clydesdales, given his Scottish heritage. Heavy horses remained a passion throughout his life. As a college student and a university professor, draft horses were foremost among the agricultural topics that commanded Dr. MacEwan's interest. It was rare for an academic to have such a good eye for these animals, and this gave him added credibility as a writer. Cognisant of breed character and appreciative of structural soundness, he favored draft horses that could wheel their freight with extra flash. Breeders of the Belgian, Clydesdale, Percheron, Shire, and Suffolk were his friends.

I first learned about Grant MacEwan when I was registered in the Faculty of Agriculture at the University of Alberta. Students of agriculture who studied Animal Husbandry as a major were required to read *The Breeds of Livestock in Canada*. The textbook, written by a Professor Grant MacEwan of the University of Saskatchewan, covered sixty breeds of horses, cattle, sheep, and swine. It is significant to note that Clydesdale, Percheron, Belgian, Shire, and Suffolk respectively, were the subjects of the first five chapters.

The textbook remains a classic in the seed-stock world.

Grant MacEwan and I first met when he was mayor of Calgary. I will always remember the occasion. I had business in Calgary with Hardy E. Salter, secretary of the Canadian Percheron Association. When the business was concluded, Salter suggested we visit City Hall to say hello to Grant MacEwan. I felt this was neither the time nor the place, but Salter was adamant.

I entered Calgary's City Hall with mixed emotions. When Salter approached a receptionist and asked if we could see the mayor we were informed that we had no appointment. However, the receptionist took our names and asked that we take a seat. Seconds later a door opened, and Grant MacEwan himself welcomed us. Salter introduced me, and then we were escorted into the mayor's office.

When I look at that occasion in retrospect, the real essence of Grant MacEwan comes to the fore. Here was a man who placed great emphasis on friendship. Spontaneously, the conversation that day turned to horses, Clydesdales and Percherons in particular. The spirited dialogue centered on Baron of Buchlyvie, Craigie Masterpiece, Monarch, and Chief Laet; on past heavy horse shows at Calgary, Brandon, Toronto, and Chicago; on sidebones, stringhalt, and curbs— topics certain to spark debate in heavy horse circles. Questions, comments, and anecdotes that surrounded a legion of horsemen well known to MacEwan and Salter fueled expresssions of concern, recollections, and repeated laughter. I was the recipient of an education no amount of money could buy.

Each time I reflect on that afternoon in Calgary, I realise that more than a door to MacEwan's office was opened. The considerable romance that surrounds the draft horse had blossomed into a personal love of breed history. Anecdotes shared on that occasion can be found in MacEwan's book *Heavy Horses*, a book that is so much more than history. It is a compelling story of great horses, colorful characters, and memorable events. It is told with authority, wit, and style. It is Grant MacEwan at his best.

Bruce A. Roy
Editor of *Feather and Fetlock*
May 24, 2001

Preface

This is my salute to equine friends of other years—Clydesdales, Percherons, Belgians, Shires, Suffolks, Canadiens, and those of ancestry unknown—and the horsemen who fed, watered, cleaned, and harnessed them at 5 A.M. and ended each day with a shakedown of straw bedding at 9 P.M.

If familiarity breeds contempt, users should have hated their horses. But it would be difficult to imagine anyone hating the faithful and generally beautiful big creatures that gave all they had, asking no more than feed and merciful treatment. There were instances of carelessness, neglect, and even cruelty but there was nobody who wouldn't offer an affectionate pat on the nose or a bit of scratching under the mane where horses always get itchy.

The fact was that horses of the heavy breeds were nation-builders as much as humans were, but being silent builders they were too often ignored and too quickly forgotten. Moreover, they were leading actors in one of the most spectacular agricultural and industrial dramas when mechanization was being accepted and later, when the going price for a purebred mare could fall from $500 to a cent a pound and then bound skyward to $5,000. It was tragic but dramatic.

When heavy horses went out of style like button boots and plug hats, most people believed they would never come back. Light horses gained in popularity and numbers as those of the draft breeds declined. Many lovers of heavy horses, fearing they were backing a lost cause, took to promoting pleasure horses, but it was not a case of abandoning sentiment and admiration for the drafters to which the Canadian debt of gratitude will never be paid.

The idea of writing the story of the draft breeds in Canada was in my thoughts for years but it needed the encouragement of public interest. When opportunity did appear, I seized it with what must have seemed like reckless haste.

As is commonly the case when a book of this kind is written, there is the help of many individuals and organizations to be acknowledged with thanks: Mrs. Cathie James, secretary of the Canadian Percheron Horse Association; Albert Hewson, secretary of the Clydesdale Horse Association of Canada; Keith Brady, president of the Alberta Belgian Association; Mrs. Fran Anderson, secretary of the Canadian Shire Horse Association; Gordon Marks of the Royal Agricultural Winter Fair; R. J. Coleman of the Horse Industry Branch of the Alberta Department of Agriculture; Glenbow-Alberta Archives and Library and all the accommodating people employed there. Finally, my thanks to all those who answered my letters—and my forgiveness to the ones who did not.

How Well They Served, Suffered, and Survived

Horses of draft type and breeding were the engines that powered the wheels of agriculture and transportation for generations before being displaced by motorized machines. They were the obedient slaves, not always treated with gratitude and mercy. Emaciation, harness galls, overgrown hooves, and shortened lives too often betrayed neglect, abuse, and silent suffering when there should have been appreciation and compassion.

Frontier homesteaders and farmers in backward parts of the world might be grateful for oxen as sources of power because of their ability to live off the land. But they dreamed of having horses and probably realized that if agricultural people never owned and used anything more serviceable than the indifferent and uninspiring oxen, progress would have been seriously retarded. Farming practice would have been slow to graduate from flails and sickles and walking plows. All history would have been different and decidedly more dull.

The long and amazing story of ups and downs that can be told about the workhorse and his ancestors is often taken for granted. In some ways, the story is glorious, in others sad. With the possible exception of the turkey, the horse surpasses all members of the barnyard fraternity in length of residence on this continent. If horses were conscious of their history and could relate it they would, quite properly, be the proudest critters of them all. And if humans were more conscious of their ancient and current debts to their slaves and companions, there would be more expressions of concern and more acts of mercy.

For millions of years, wild horses were at home on these North American plains. The fossilized proof is there, "written in ageless terms on the pages of the rocks." It makes clear that much of the horse's evolutionary rise from a miniature ancestor no bigger than a wire-haired terrier, to varieties the size and shape of the modern draft horse, took place right here.

The wild horses must have been present in great numbers. Some scholars believe that horses were at one time more numerous than any other North American mammals. They were still here when the first humans entered the continent 20,000 or more years ago, coming, no doubt, by way of an Ice Age land connection between the land masses now known as Siberia and Alaska.

But the horses of the wild North American strains, once so abundant, fell upon bad times and died out completely in these parts. The exact reasons for the tragic loss will never be known, but scientists will not rule out the possibilities of disease, an increase in natural enemies, a major shift in climate, or a change in the balance of nature due to the presence of a new species such as man.

The doomed horses might have taken their race with them to extinction had it not been for earlier escapes to Asia. Some of the North American stock moved out over the same land bridge by which humans, mastodons, mammoths, and some other new forms entered.

Horses are believed to have been domesticated in China a few thousand years ago. After spreading widely in Asia and Europe, they were taken across the Mediterranean to Arabia and North Africa where type improvement took place and a branch of the refined strain appeared later as the highly regarded Arabian breed. Cavalry forces aided by the same superior Arabian and North African horses drove westward, victoriously, in the eighth century. Crossing into Europe, they triumphed in Spain but, weakened by the mounting distance from their home base, they suffered defeat in France. In their retreat, the Moor invaders lost or abandoned many of their superior horses which were taken joyously as prizes of war by the French and the Spaniards. The captured horses proved valuable for breed improvement in both countries and doubtlessly contributed greatly to the creation of new breeds, especially in France. There was instant enthusiasm for horse betterment in Spain and when Columbus was about to set sail, horses of the best lines were supplied from the Spanish royal stables.

As part of an expansion program in the New World, the Spanish conquistador Hernando Cortez landed sixteen or seventeen of the good horses on the North American mainland in 1519, the first of the race to be returned to the native land after its long spell of horselessness.

After thousands of years without horses, the North American Indians forgot that there were such creatures and when they saw representatives of the equine family again, they were filled with fear as though the animals might be man-eating monsters. But in spite of their initial forebodings the native people were quick to forget fears and pursue the benefits of owning these animals that had become servants of man.

By capturing strays and stealing from the Spanish newcomers, the Indians very soon became proud possessors. Ownership of horses was to change completely the way of life of the Indian people, making them more skillful in warfare, more effective in the hunt, and more dashing in courtship. It became instantly obvious, also, that with one tribe in possession of horses, neighboring tribesmen had to have them at any price. Hence, the new horse strain spread north and west, mainly through what became a leading pastime or game—stealing.

The Comanches were probably the first of the North American Indians to see the horses brought by the Spaniards and the first to acquire their own mounts. This would explain why these Indians became superior horsemen. Anybody about whom it was said that he could "ride like a Comanche" was being paid a high compliment. By 1715 these tribesmen were well mounted and the Kiowa and Missouri Indians were riding soon thereafter. The Crows, the Snakes, and Mandans followed in rapid succession. Horses of the new strain were moving ever closer to what is now Canada.

Horses from France were brought for the benefit of colonists in the St. Lawrence River Valley as early as 1665. The west of present-day Canada had to wait another sixty-five years for Indians to ride their first horses into the area. Understandably, the process of passing horses from one tribe to another through theft, took time. Noted historian Arthur Silver Morton maintained that the first representatives of the new race appeared in the valley of the Bow River in the possession of an invading war party of Snake Indians in 1730. The Blackfoot of the southwestern prairies were the first of the region's residents to obtain horses—also by stealing—and then it was only a matter of time until the Crees had them and then the Assiniboines. By that time all the aggressive Indians on the plains were mounted.

This Indian possession of horses held advantages for the first European settlers in the West. The Selkirk settlers who began arriving in 1812—the majority of whom were from Scotland—felt an urgent need for livestock, especially horses. Having known the specialized breeds of Scotland, England, and Ireland, they were unimpressed by the Indian horses they saw. Although they traced to the high grade Spanish stock, these seminative Indian horses had deteriorated greatly and were now small and scrubby in appearance. The settlers longed for the imposing breeds of their homelands and failed to recognize certain characteristics of great importance in the horses they were able to obtain from the tribesmen, characteristics such as hardiness, adaptation to climate, and sure-footedness.

The fact was that these cayuse horses were better than they were judged at first appearance and infinitely better than no horses at all. The settlers obtained them by barter and then discovered a problem they had not anticipated: it happened too often that the native from whom a horse was acquired during daylight, returned at night to recover the animal by theft. It took time to convince the native people that stealing horses was regarded as a crime; they preferred to think of horse stealing as a game or pastime and reasoned, almost convincingly, that if they steal your horse tonight, it is your privilege to steal it back tomorrow night, "if you're smart enough to play the game."

But not many of the settlers were ready to play and losses by theft were wholly discouraging, whether the thievery was perpetrated by Indians or non-Indians who liked to drive their ill-gotten gains north, or south to cross the international boundary. The Selkirk settlers in 1816 had twenty-one horses in the colony and then, suddenly, horse thieves came by night and lifted all of them.[1]

The man in charge of the Hudson's Bay Company trading post at Qu'Appelle reported losing twenty-four horses at one time, and the traders at Fort Edmonton who needed horses for freighting lost over a hundred in one night.

After a succession of horse thefts, William Laidlaw, who was in charge of the Hayfield Experimental Farm at Red River in 1818, was reduced to hitching three horses, two cows, one bull, and a buffalo heifer in order to make up two plow teams.[2]

The Red River settlers proved their resourcefulness but they did not lose their longing for horses possessing both size and quality and most of the settlers, being Scottish, thought of Clydesdales. They dreamed of and may have prayed for a carefully chosen stallion of a British breed. Hudson's Bay Company officers in London were aware of the desire and the need for horse improvement and in a moment of unusual generosity, resolved to make the handsome gesture of a gift of a good stallion. The purchase would be made in England and shipped to Red River via York Factory.

George Simpson, the company governor of Rupert's Land, received the first intimation of the gift horse in a communication from London dated February 23, 1831: "We shall send a stallion of a proper breed by the ship to York Factory. We should think the Experimental Farm at Red River the best place to commence raising horses for the service."[3]

George Simpson, later Sir George, issued an order for the collection of the best mares on the prairies, most of them to be placed at the experimental farm, a short distance back from Red River, in anticipation of the next breeding season.

Hopeful settlers were excited about the prospect of an imported stallion of "a proper breed," but tempered their optimism by concluding cynically that company officials in London wouldn't know "a proper breed" if they saw one. They were nonetheless eager to see this mystery horse and determine if it was a Clydesdale, Shire, Suffolk, Hackney, Thoroughbred, or something else.

The stallion was shipped from London early in 1831 and at York Factory, after almost two months on the ocean, transferred to a canoe or York boat for the precarious journey of some 700 miles to Red River. Nobody has explained the problems of transporting a mature stallion as a passenger in a canoe on northern waters, but doubtless they would be immense. To the everlasting credit of those in charge, the stallion was delivered safely at Point Douglas—now at the heart of Winnipeg—and received a welcome befitting a king.

Immediately, the mystery concerning "a proper breed" was brushed away: the horse was a Norfolk Trotter, a breed of minor prominence even in England and one of the breeds from which the Hackney horse was produced. His name was Fireaway and what was immediately more conversational than the matter of breed, the horse was magnificent and nobody from the settlement was trying to hide his delight.

Fireaway was of a utility or general purpose type which should have been highly acceptable at Red River. When he stepped from the canoe to the riverside, he stood like a statue, with head held high, ears erect, and tail carried with a flourish. He was a bright bay in color, standing sixteen hands in height and was said to be able to trot fifteen miles an hour.

George Simpson could report gleefully to the company officers in London: "The stallion sent out reached the settlement in perfect safety and in high condition. He will soon give us a better breed of horses. He is looked upon as one of the wonders of the world by the natives, many of whom have travelled great distances with no other object than to see him."

Having such a handsome horse at the second experimental farm at Red River obviously caught the attention of the horse thieves and an armed guard was placed with him. And, mated to the best of the Indian mares, the resulting offspring were, in both size and quality, far ahead of anything seen in the country.

Fireaway was indeed a blueblood, a purebred registered in the *Norfolk Trotter Studbook* of England. He was the first horse brought to the West for improvement purposes and he fulfilled the highest expectations. His offspring, for many years after his career ended, were conspicuous as the best buffalo runners, the best racing horses, the best farm horses, and those commanding the premiums when sales were made.

Then, with lingering memories of the Fireaway successes, the Hudson's Bay Company, in 1848, moved to repeat the gesture, sending an English Thoroughbred stallion, a grey Thoroughbred mare, an Ayrshire bull, and two Ayrshire cows. This was the second shipment of pedigreed stock on record. The idea was excellent and the five purebred animals deserved to be recognized as the first of their respective breeds in the country. But this time luck wasn't with the project; the Thoroughbred mare produced a promising foal the following spring but before the summer ended, both mare and foal were dead. The stallion, Melbourne by name, kicked his groom and broke his arm and before long, the five bluebloods were all but forgotten.

Settlers in the St. Lawrence River community were the first in the East to see heavy horse improvement by the importation of superior breeding stock. But improvement by breeding came slowly because an accelerating influx of settlers—in both the East and West—caused the demand for work horses to rise faster than the supply, and people needing power urgently often settled for small and inferior horses, aging horses, or bronchos. Even lame horses seemed better than nothing and for a time, horse numbers appeared more important than quality.

All Canadian settlers wanted horses, good horses, but when the supply was inadequate and the cost high, many turned to oxen, either buying trained work stock or following the simple expedient of carving a hardwood yoke to proper size and shape and breaking young steers to work in it.

Work oxen served their owners moderately well and with their natural advantage of large stomach capacity, were able to consume enough roughage feed in the form of pasture grass or hay to meet their energy needs for at least half a day at a time. This avoided the necessity of supplying concentrated grain feed like oats or barley, which most newcomers to homestead country didn't have anyway. Hence the bovine ability to live off the land in the summer seasons. They did not perform as well in the winter when grazing land was blanketed with snow. Horses on the other hand, with a background of millions of years on the North American plains, knew how to paw their way through the snow to the dead grass below.

Oxen had their place and earned more gratitude than they ever received. One of their misfortunes was a sulky disposition, and nobody loved the poor critters. Owners promised themselves they would acquire horses as soon as circumstances justified purchase, at which time the oxen would be converted speedily to winter supplies of beef, albeit tough.

By the year 1900, Canada had about 1.5 million horses, mainly of draft type and breeding, and importing purebreds of four or five draft breeds was becoming an important business. Importers and dealers maintained big sales stables in many Canadian cities. Brandon had the self-imposed title of Horse Capital of Canada. The principal items of sale were purebred stallions brought from the United States or overseas, thousands of them, to be offered for sale at one or another of the busy stables operated by Colquhoun and Beattie, Trotter and Trotter, J. B. Holgate, Vanstone and Rogers, Alexander Galbraith, and many other importers and specialists. Beecham Trotter could report that by the first decade of the twentieth century, the horse breeding and selling business was so brisk that his firm paid out over three million dollars for horses brought to the Brandon stable for sale.

It was a time, of course, when every Canadian farmer was a horseman and the ambition of every farm boy was to be an expert horseman like his father. Most horse owners could have been considered specialists, with a good understanding of feeds and feeding, a practical knowledge of disorders and unsoundnesses, and an artistic touch in preparing a team of horses for the showring or a trip to town on Saturday afternoon. They could drench sick horses, file teeth, break the wild ones, roll mains, trim hoofs, read ages from the teeth, and drive big outfits with four reins. They talked about sweat-pads, colic cures, snorting poles, catch colts, stringhalt, buck straps, bellybands, spreadrings, tie chains, martingales, and smooth mouths. Their vocabulary was their own.

The heavy horse judging ring was, at that time, the acknowledged beating heart of every fair or exhibition, and assisting and promoting governments were anxious to have a financial stake in anything as popular. The Dominion Department of Agriculture not only paid prize money but gladly subsidized horse breeding by paying part of the service fees for every foal that came from an approved stallion. It was reasonable to presume that every one of the operators of Canada's half million farms wanted and needed at least two horses for work in heavy harness and hoped to breed his own replacements. So great was the Canadian public involvement in horse breeding that Isaac Beattie of the firm of Colquhoun and Beattie could report 607 mares bred to one or another of five stallions kept at the Baubier Stable on Brandon's Eighth Street in a single season.

Feeding work horses at 5 A.M. and working with them almost continuously until they were fed and bedded down for the night at 8 or 9 P.M., was tedious enough to drive some young people from farms, but horsemanship was not without glamour aplenty. Young farmers of the period had no Cadillacs but they found satisfaction and pleasure in placing polished harness with Scotch tops and ivory spreadrings on their most stylish team of heavies for a mission to town where they might drive down the main street with horses prancing and pedestrians on the board sidewalks pausing to stare. There was also the incomparable joy of harnessing and driving a well-groomed and well-trained four- or six-horse team into the local showring and skillfully guiding the powerful outfit as it was called to walk, trot, back up, and cut the figure eight before the judge. The crowning glory would be to qualify for a prize ribbon before a crowd of admiring spectators.

Altogether, it was a glamorous chapter in horse history, also made distinctive and exciting by strong and often bitter breed prejudices. Every horseman in those years when draft horses ruled or at least influenced most Canadian lives, had a favorite breed

Breaking sod in the early years of the century on a Saskatchewan homestead.

and was ready to argue or fight in support of its good name. For a few decades before the Belgian had become established, the main quarrels were between the adherents of Clydesdales—many of them speaking with thick Scottish accents—and those with equally strong feelings for Percherons.

Differing denominational loyalties could divide a rural community. Opposing political party affiliations could do the same. But in some districts, where breed prejudices seemed to get out of hand, Clydesdale supporters sat defiantly at one end of the judging ring bleachers and Percheron supporters with the same serious scowls sat at the other. It was told of at least one rural church that friends of the Percheron breed sat on the left side of the central pew and the conscientious believers in Clydesdales sat unbending on the other side.

It would be folly to allow breed animosities to soar to such heights again, but as evidence of the enthusiasm and loyalties that were a significant part of horse history in Canada, that early rivalry should be good for a laugh and certainly worth remembering.

By 1911, the Canadian horse population had risen to 2,664,000, an increase of a million head in one decade. And in 1921, after another ten years, the Canadian horse population reached 3,610,500, the highest figure to be recorded either before or since. The overwhelming majority were farm horses of draft type and the total number would represent about five for every Canadian farm. Saskatchewan alone had about a million head, almost all on farms and showing some degree of Clydesdale, Percheron or Belgian breeding.

But by this time, the horsemen's principal competition was not from another breed but rather from mechanical power which made its initial threat in the form of the slow, heavy, and cumbersome steam tractors. The big steamers gave way gradually to big tractors driven by internal combustion engines. Still, the horsemen laughed at the utter improbability of their draft horses ever being displaced on farms by tractor power.

In 1918 the Government of Canada, motivated by the continuing wartime demands for greater food production and the shortages of farm help, sold and distributed the first of a fleet of small tractors, Ford-built and known as Fordsons. From that point onwards the horseman's position became steadily more insecure. The new tractor presented an entirely new concept; it was a two-plow unit with four cylinders, relatively light in weight, fast on the road or trail and fascinatingly maneuverable. It was being delivered at a price of $795. Moreover, the Fordson was instantly popular and many small farmers who bought Fordsons at what seemed like the going price for four average farm horses, sold or retired forthwith two or three or four of their usual stock of horses.

As the small tractors of many makes grew in popularity, horse breeding slumped, but the actual number of horses on farms did not fall sharply because horses have long lives and

A four-horse hitch of purebred Clydesdale mares making a delivery of grass seed at the University of Saskatchewan, circa 1930. *Photograph by Leonard Hillyard.*

HOW WELL THEY SERVED, SUFFERED, AND SURVIVED

many retired and idle horses, unsalable, remained on pastures and ranges to be counted as usual at census time. But, clearly, more and more of the surviving and unmarketable horses were unemployed. By 1944, farmers and ranchers were losing patience with the idle animals eating valuable grass and showing no return.

At a meeting held at Val Marie, Saskatchewan, in March, 1944, for the express purpose of considering surplus horses, the Western Horse Marketing Co-operative was organized; the double purpose was to realize some return from the surplus animals and make more grass available for the readily salable cattle and sheep. Seven months later, the organized horsemen had one slaughtering plant at Swift Current and were acquiring another at Edmonton. They were in the meat business in a totally new way, with eyes fixed upon the inevitable markets for canned meat in postwar Europe.

In 1952, the co-operative could report the removal of a quarter of a million otherwise unmarketable horses and meat sales amounting to roughly $19 million. Most of the sales were of canned meat shipped or about to be shipped to Europe where the need was great and horse meat was a generally acceptable item of diet. It was then announced that the two meat processing plants at Swift Current and Edmonton that had operated on behalf of 36,400 shareholders in Saskatchewan and Alberta were for sale. They had served their purpose.4

A few horse meat stores opened in Canada during those war years but most Canadians wanted no part in making horses a permanent item of the nation's diet. Of twenty-three shops licensed to sell horse meat in

Winnipeg and west of there in 1951, only three were operating in 1953. For the majority of Canadians, eating horse meat was too much like eating their friends and they were not going to do it.

From that time on, the horse population continued to fall, largely from natural causes because the country's horses were growing old and the death rate was climbing. There was practically no replacement of the lost heavy breed horses. By 1971—fifty years after the Canadian horse count stood at 3,610,500 and Saskatchewan had a million head—the Canadian numbers had fallen to about 325,000 and Saskatchewan's to 65,000.

Following the liquidation of the thirties and forties, some observers predicted—not very wisely—that the horse heavies would completely disappear, like the dinosaurs, and some stuffed specimens should be recovered for museum needs in future years. The drafters did, indeed, fall to shockingly low levels of popularity and interest. Breeding of their kind came to a standstill. A tourist driving from Winnipeg to Calgary in

One of the last binder teams seen on the prairies was on the farm of James Wyatt, Longview, Alberta, in 1963. Adding interest is the fact that these horses—Kate, 35, Scotty, 31, Red, 31, and Bess, 32—with an aggregate age of 129 years, were possibly the oldest team ever hitched for work on a prairie farm.

June, 1952, reported that he did not see a single foal following a heavy mare.

But the draft breeds did not disappear. Although they experienced more extremes and reverses in fortune than any other domestic animal, purebred draft horses leaped from a point close to extinction to appear with a nucleus of good breeding animals and then command all-time record prices and widespread public admiration.

Now, it's a completely new order for Canadian draft breeds. The good purebred mares of Percheron, Belgian, and Clydesdale breeds that might have sold for $500 each prior to 1921, would have brought one cent a pound in the thirties, but their counterparts could have commanded several thousand dollars in the seventies and eighties. A certain six-horse team of geldings that won extensively in the 1980s was said to represent a $100,000 investment with their show harness.

It raises questions, of course, about the place of high class show and breeding horses of the draft types in the years ahead. Will those recent showpieces that were partly a reflection of depleted numbers, retain their popularity? Nobody is qualified to answer the question but it must be extremely doubtful if good representatives of the heavy breeds will ever again sink to the pathetic depths experienced in the years of the Second World War.

It seems reasonable to conclude that almost every Canadian farm could employ to advantage at least one two-horse team of heavy horses for routine and special tasks when mud and snow forbid the use of trucks and tractors. There are progressive Canadian farmers who are determined that they can perform daily barnyard chores more economically with two heavy horses than with a tractor. The rather common sight of an expensive tractor doing a two-horse job makes little sense. And more than a few business leaders with products to sell in nearby urban communities are admitting that a team of good and proud horses hitched to a show wagon offers the best and most economical advertising they can get. Said one man: "Those heavy horses can capture more human hearts than any other advertising attraction I can offer. And I have my horses' companionship as a bonus."

How much does a team of purebred draft mares have to offer in return for a place on an average mixed farm in either eastern or western Canada? A search for the answers suggests the following:

1. Either member of the team can pull a row cultivator in garden, orchard, shelterbelt, or wherever there are rowcrops.
2. Both members of the team can reproduce to provide replacements or cash revenue from sales of purebred stock or geldings.
3. Singly or together, the horses can furnish power for farm chores with the maximum of efficiency and economy—and with power to spare.
4. Singly or as a team, the horses can furnish entries for local fairs or exhibitions and fill places of distinction in urban parades and other similar events.
5. They can keep alive some of the finest traditions of the Canadian mixed or family farm.

2
The Clydesdale

"Oh, what a bonnie sight!"

Scotland's pride appeared in many shapes and sizes. Land of rugged grandeur and home of robust sons and daughters, "Auld Scotia" was the birthplace of useful animal breeds that encircled the agricultural world. From what had to be seen as an international nursery of improved livestock came an amazing number of types and strains with familiar names: Ayrshire, Aberdeen Angus, Scotch Shorthorn, West Highland, Galloway, Blackface, Cheviot, Shetland, Highland pony, Clydesdale, Collie, and more. What a contribution from a small land with restricted resources of soil and wealth!

For many years Scotland's best known exports to Canada were settlers for Canadian homesteads, Scotch whiskey, Scottish stories created in Aberdeen, and Clydesdale horses—all fiery and distinctive. Time changed many things; the supply of homestead land became exhausted and work horses of draft type were largely displaced by mechanization. But Clydesdale sentiment survived and so did some of the horses, ample to make Scots and other admirers gasp as always upon recognition of one of their beloved and stylish drafters: "Oh, what a bonnie sight!"

It was the kind of sentiment that Ben Finlayson of Canadian Clydesdale fame was heard to utter at times, especially when making a pitch to sell a purebred mare: "What is home wi'out a Clyde?" His point did not seem to be lost because his favorite breed dominated the Canadian draft horse scene for many years before the Percheron and then the Belgian breeders answered the challenge to overtake and then surpass the Scottish breed in numbers and popularity.

Breed origin is never very clear but, as with other draft breeds, legend gives the big Flemish horses from the European mainland a founding role. William, earl of Douglas, is said to have obtained a permit from King Edward III of England to bring ten of these big stallions to the valley of the Clyde in 1352. Understandably, detailed breeding records for that period do not exist. Better records begin about 1750 when John Paterson, a tenant farmer at Lochlyoch in Lanarkshire imported a black Flemish stallion from England. The unnamed stud proved prepotent and when crossed with the local mares, left big horses, mainly bays and blacks with white markings, and may have

earned the right to be regarded as the breed's principal foundation.

Regardless of the selection for founding sire, the valley of the Clyde River that waters Lanarkshire for most of its length and brings life and vigor, must be seen as the cradle of the breed. The undulating countryside is picturesque, enlivened by well-managed farms and marked by coal fields, industry, including shipbuilding, and Scotland's biggest city, Glasgow. Farm work was the primary task for the early Clydesdale horses although carrying coal on their backs might have been considered almost as important.

Following the union of England and Scotland in 1603, a lively droving trade sprang up between the two countries, making for many exchanges of breeding stock, most of them unrecorded but effective to some degree in shaping neighboring breeds. In spite of such interchange of blood lines, however, the influence of Paterson's black stallion was coming through without loss of identity. This happened largely through one of his distant progeny, a stallion known as Glancer, alias Thompson's Black Horse, foaled about 1810 and owned by a Mr. Somerville of Lampita farm. Glancer, in turn, was the great-grandsire of Broomfield Champion, foaled some time after 1820 and to whom the most famous Clydesdales of later years traced. The Champion was a black with white legs; he in turn sired another Glancer, known also as Fulton's Ruptured Horse, but, rupture or no rupture, he became an important link in the chain of breed progress.

The names of highly regarded stallions became ever more prominent and important in the developing breed. Places of honor were given to Rob Roy, Old Clyde, Old Farmer, Pringle's Young Clyde, Sir Walter Scott, and so on, suggesting strongly that the history of the Clydesdale could be recounted very largely by the achievements of individual breeding horses. Most students of Clydesdale history, for example, are more familiar with the breeding and showyard successes of Prince of Wales and Darnley and other famous stallions that followed—Baron's Pride, Hiawatha, MacGregor, Top Gallant, Sir Everard, Baron of Buchlyvie, Bonnie Buchlyvie, Dunure Footprint, Benefactor, and so on—than with the people who bred them and brought them to fame.

If John Paterson's black Flemish stallion was seen as a figure from the breed's ancient history, then Prince of Wales and Darnley must be the forerunners of modern history.

Prince of Wales and Darnley were the undisputed Clydesdale greats in their generation and were the means of sending the breed to greater heights of excellence. The former was born in 1866, to a mare called Darling, said to be part Shire in breeding. It was probably from the Shire ancestor that Prince of Wales got his heavy bone and a mature weight of 2,200 pounds. He had good feet and legs and moved with the best of action. On the other hand, he had a Roman nose and was criticized for being straight in his hind legs and shallow at the rear flank. But he proved to be a superior sire, of stallions particularly.

His most outstanding offspring was his grandson Hiawatha, foaled in 1892 and a horse whose showring record was never surpassed in the Clydesdale breed. He won the championship at the Highland Show in 1899 and the Cawdor Cup—the most coveted

trophy offered within the breed—in each of four years. The Cawdor Cup, incidently, has been offered annually since 1892. At first the contests were at the Glasgow Stallion Show but after 1925, they carried on at the Highland and Agricultural Society Show.

At the age of eighteen years, Prince of Wales was bought by David Riddell of Paisley and lived to be twenty-two.

Prince of Wales was known as an outstanding sire of males, Darnley as an outstanding sire of females. Foaled in 1872, Darnley was six years younger than Prince of Wales and traced to Broomfield Champion six times. At three years, he was sold by his breeder Sir William Sterling-Maxwell to David Riddell, mentioned previously. Darnley, too, was a big horse, weighing 2,240 pounds. Like Prince of Wales, he may have inherited his size, in part at least, from a Shire ancestor on his dam's side. Canada's well-known early horseman Alexander Galbraith told of seeing the excellent mare who was Darnley's mother, Kier Peggy, as a four-year-old at the Highland Show in 1864 and seeing her again twenty years later. Said Galbraith: "I would describe this grand mare as resembling the best of present day Shire mares. She weighed 1900 pounds."[1]

Among Darnley's most famous sons was Top Gallant who sired Sir Everard. Sir Everard sired Baron's Pride, foaled in 1890. Baron's Pride was the most inspiring horse of the breed up to his time. There were those who said he was overly refined but most observers saw him as the Clydesdale that breeders had been hoping for. He was tall and stylish and his feet and legs were said to be flawless. At the age of four, he was champion at the Highland Show; about that time he was purchased by A. and W. Montgomery in whose hands he remained until his death at twenty-three years. His get dominated the showrings and brought the highest prices on both sides of the Atlantic for years.

The universal admiration for the handsome Baron's Pride brought recollections of how he almost escaped existence. His sire, Sir Everard, was among the colts marked for castration at one year of age because of his mediocre appearance. The first of the yearlings were emasculated as planned; it was only at the last moment that a decision was made to leave Sir Everard for another year to see if he would look more promising. He did and the decision was to spare him for breeding. It was a fortunate decision for the breed.

The most famous son of the great Baron's Pride, Baron of Buchlyvie, made even more history than his sire. Foaled in 1900, Baron of Buchlyvie, a rather slow maturing colt, won neither championships nor much praise in his first year. But at two years of age, he attracted James Kilpatrick and William Dunlop, two of Scotland's most successful horsemen, who paid £750 for him.

In the first years after his purchase, the Baron stood at Kilpatrick's Craigie Mains in Ayrshire, then at Dunlop's Dunure Mains. The partnership continued until 1909 when a dispute arose. Dunlop insisted that he bought Kilpatrick's interest on a certain date, giving him £1,000; and Kilpatrick was just as determined that he had asked £2,000 and had not agreed to accept the lower sum. In support of Dunlop's claim, hotel attendants testified that a celebration had taken place at the time of the alleged sale and that on the following morning, large sums of money were found on the floor among empty champagne bottles. The first court decision was given in favor of Kilpatrick in 1910 but the judgment was reversed and the case went ultimately to the House of Lords.

The final judgment was that the ownership could not be established and the horse should be sold by auction and the returns divided between the two litigants. Consequently, Baron of Buchlyvie was sold by James Craig Ltd. at Ayr, on December 14, 1911, amid scenes rarely matched in breed history. Five thousand people attended. The opening bid was £3,000. At £4,000, Kilpatrick entered the bidding and Dunlop appeared to drop out. At £5,000 a stranger began bidding and continued until he had secured the horse for £9,500. It was then discovered that the stranger was bidding on behalf of Dunlop.

The sale at the equivalent of $45,750 in Canadian money, was the highest price paid for a horse anywhere in the world up to that time. Baron of Buchlyvie died in 1914 and was buried in the rose garden at Dunure Mains, near Ayr. Four years later, his skeleton was exhumed to be set up as a permanent display in Kelvingrove Museum in Glasgow.

Outstanding among the sons of Baron of Buchlyvie were Bonnie Buchlyvie, Dunure Footprint, The Dunure, and Craigie Litigant. Bonnie Buchlyvie, a Cawdor Cup winner in 1909, was sold at the Seaham Harbour dispersion in 1915 for 5,000 guineas and as explained later, almost came to Canada at that time.

For William Dunlop of Dunure Mains, Ayr, one of the dividends from his investment in Baron Buchlyvie was the Baron's son, Dunure Footprint, foaled in 1908 from the great mare, Dunure Ideal. Following the tradition of Baron's Pride and Baron of Buchlyvie,

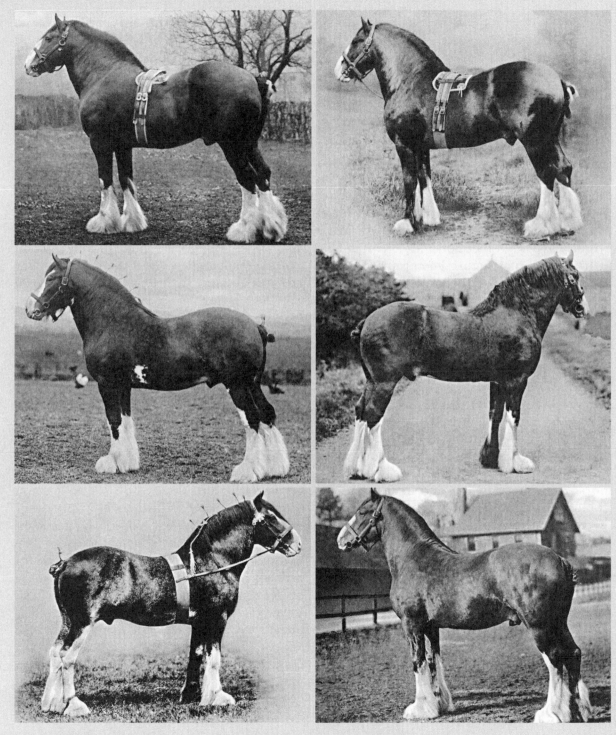

Scotland's famous Clydesdale stallions. Clockwise from top left: Hiawatha, Baron's Pride, Baron of Buchlyvie, Bonnie Buchlyvie, Dunure Footprint, and Apukwa.

Dunure Footprint in his time was regarded as Scotland's best.

Even in the name for the young stallion there was a deep sentiment, as Mr. Dunlop revealed later. He had reserved that name for the ideal colt he hoped to breed, one that would leave "footprints in the sand of time." Thinking that he saw his ideal in a certain son of Baron of Buchlyvie, he registered the colt with the name Dunure Footprint. Then, regretting his decision, he sold the colt to Robert Brydon. Strange as it must have seemed, Mr. Brydon wrote to ask if Mr. Dunlop would have any objection if he changed the colt's name from Dunure Footprint to Bonnie Buchlyvie. Dunlop, more pleased than he admitted, agreed, and Brydon's young stud was renamed, releasing the name Dunure Footprint for Mr. Dunlop to use on another colt, possibly a better one.

When the foal from Dunure Ideal arrived in 1908, Dunlop was convinced that it was the one about which he had dreamed and registered him as Dunure Footprint. He was right this time; Dunure Footprint became the new Clydesdale sensation, both as a show horse and as a breeder. The young horse won the Cawdor Cup in 1910 and in prolificacy, he came to be seen as the greatest ever. After establishing a reputation, Dunure Footprint's service fees were set at £60 at the time of breeding and £60 additional when the mare proved to be in foal. And even at that very high price, mares came in record numbers. It was told that the stallion was being used at the rate of one mating every two hours, night and day. There must have been some basis for the report; volume 42 of the stud book confirms the registration of 121 foals born from him

in 1919. Evidently, the old sire's diet was being supplemented with milk at that time and Mr. Dunlop was keeping two extra cows to supply his needs.

Neither Dunlop nor Kilpatrick was lacking in sentiment. A reader can weigh Dunlop's words about the best mare he ever owned or saw. She was his own black Knox's Rosie, four-time winner of first prize at the Highland. "To see her walk," said he, "was a joy. To watch her trot was a three-fold delight. To me she was the most momentous monarch of the breed I have ever seen on the female side. Her great volume of weight when trotting made one feel as if the ground under her was all alive with an earthquake. Rosie was the heaviest, most compact, biggest, best looking matron that ever graced an exhibition, Shires included."

Happily, it can be told that the two old horsemen, after many years, agreed to forgive and forget. Of the reconciliation arranged by friends of both men, Kilpatrick wrote: "Twenty-two years had elapsed since we last spoke to each other. Our reconciliation was made the occasion of quite a celebration by our friends and we remained on good terms until Mr. Dunlop's death . . ."[2]

After Dunure Footprint, there were other stallions to lead the Clydesdale parade in Scotland. One was Benefactor by Fyvie Sensation, bred by William Meiklem of Kirkaldy and later owned by A. M. Montgomery of Netherhall. Then there was Craigie Beau Ideal by Craigie McQuaid, foaled in 1929 and bought by James Kilpatrick for use at Craigie Mains. The latter was never beaten in his class and won the Cawdor Cup in 1930; for four years in succession he won the championship at the Glasgow Stallion Show.

The system of hiring stallions was a strong force in Scottish horse improvement. Hiring societies were organized by mare owners from 1837 onward, with many of them conducting annual stallion fairs in home districts. To these fairs the stallion owners would bring their entries to compete for cash premiums, perhaps as much as £80, it being understood that the winning stallion in each case would be travelled in the district at fees stated in the fair rules. Glasgow was conducting stallion shows before the middle of the nineteenth century and a big hiring fair from about 1870 that displaced the earlier shows.

The Glasgow Agricultural Society began to demand right of first choice from stallions exhibited. The society choice in 1882 was Lord Erskine, already hired for breeding elsewhere. But the society membership insisted upon the enforcement of its rules and got the horse. The next year the district that lost out previously made another contract to get the same horse, inserting a condition in the agreement that the horse in question would not be entered at the Glasgow Stallion Show.

Organization and a stud book were essentials in breed building. The Clydesdale Horse Society of Great Britain and Ireland was organized in 1877 and the first volume of the stud book was published in the following year.

Unlike England, Scotland remained a one-breed country. In 1939, of the 468 pedigreed stallions of draft breeds licensed to travel in Scotland, 459 were Clydesdales.

Much of the Clydesdale drive at home was due to the brisk overseas demand which began about 1840, the year in which the first of the breed was brought to Canada, and continued until mechanization in all trading countries brought horse sales almost to an end. As indicated by export certificates issued from the breed society, 514 Clydesdales were shipped overseas in 1885. The number dropped to 15 in the depression year of 1895 and rose to a record of 1,617 in 1911. Australia, Canada, and the United States were the leading importers. Exports numbered 103 in 1925 and then moved steadily downward to almost disappear.

THE PIONEER CLYDES IN CANADA

When Scotland's sons and daughters emigrated to Canada, their dearly beloved Clydesdales were not far behind. Not only did these equine friends perform the slavish parts in pulling homestead plows and farm wagons but, like bits of heather, haggis, kilts, and Burns poems, they brought sentimental comfort and inspiration.

Once circumstances permitted the ownership of a Clydesdale with official-looking papers confirming the purest of breeding, that registration certificate was sure to be admired, studied, and filed for safe keeping along with family birth certificates in the big family Bible. Then, as the proud proprietor of a progeny of Baron's Pride, the horseman presumed license to take liberties with Shakespeare and shout: "A Clyde! A Clyde! My kingdom for a Clydesdale!"

Because of its British connection, the Clydesdale was comparatively early in arriving on the Canadian scene and then clung tenaciously to a place of interbreed domination for many years before being overtaken and then surpassed in numbers by the two European mainland breeds, Percheron and Belgian.

The first purebred Clydesdale with the qualifications for registration in Canada appears to have been the stallion Cumberland. There must have been unusual difficulty and uncertainty in that pre-stud book period in identifying the horses with the best claims to pure breeding. Even among the first Clydesdales admitted to registration, there were some whose sires and dams and birth dates remained in doubt.

About the stud, Cumberland, however, there was more available information than in many cases. He was imported in 1840, still more than forty years before the first organized efforts to collect stud book information. Even in his case there were points of record book information which had to be given the benefit of doubts. On his mother's side, for example, the registration certificate was marked "Dam unknown." Nevertheless, Cumberland was big and beautiful and nobody could say that he did not deserve the distinction accorded to him.

Cumberland was a bay with a star on his forehead. His sire was Glenelg and his importer was David Rowntree of Weston, Upper Canada. Bringing any horse across the Atlantic in the years of sailing ships which had to carry enough feed and fresh water to last for a five to six week crossing was not a small matter for either the animal or the man in charge. Shipping risks were high and coupled with freight charges of up to $300, were enough to discourage most horsemen. But testifying to the hardiness of the stallion Cumberland, he stood the voyage well and after his arrival in the hardwood bush country of Upper Canada, he travelled regularly over long routes in the cause of greater Clydesdale population. He left many superior offspring but none that were admitted to the Canadian stud book except through the grading-up route, for the simple reason of total absence of mares with stud book qualifications.

In only one respect were the Scottish horsemen disappointed with Cumberland; as a representative of Scotland's darling breed, the horse, though bred in England, should have had a Scottish name. For over a hundred years the name Cumberland was unpopular in Scotland. It was inevitable. The name was a bitter reminder of the Battle of Culloden.

Three other Clydesdale stallions followed Cumberland to Canada during the forties: Grey Clyde, Sovereign, and Marquis of Clyde, although still no mares with stud book qualifications. Sovereign was imported in 1845 and Marquis of Clyde in 1847.

Of the three, Grey Clyde was outstanding, both as a showring winner and as a breeder. He, like Cumberland, was bred in England and foaled "about 1837." His importation to Canada was by Archibald Ward of Markham

Grey Clyde, foaled about 1837 and imported to Canada in 1841. He was travelled in Ontario districts for many years before being sold to American agents in Kentucky where he died in 1852. The exaggerated contrast between the two horses reveals not only breed favoritism and pride, but is also an attempt to impress potential buyers with the size and power of the breed. *Canadian Clydesdale Stud Book, volume IV, 1892.*

where he was travelled in his first season in the country. As the artist saw him and painted him, he was a rich dappled grey with a massive frame, near-perfect feet and legs and a small head. The original painting by a Thomas Ireson of Markham was acquired by the pioneer importers, Graham Brothers of Claremont. A striking photographic reproduction appeared in volume IV of the *Canadian Clydesdale Stud Book*, 1892.

Grey Clyde won first prize at the provincial exhibition at Toronto in 1846 at which time seventeen of his get, all greys, were paraded with him to leave spectators with unforgettable memories. In the next year, the great grey was led from Markham to Hamilton for the provincial exhibition where he again won first prize. In 1848 he was sold to Joseph Thompson of Columbus, Ontario, who showed him at the New York State Fair at Buffalo where he won both class and championship. Grey Clyde continued to win but in 1851 he was sold to Kilgour and Cushman of Kentucky, where he died about one year later.

Many students think of Grey Clyde, after being shipped to Kentucky, as the first horse of his breed in the United States. Be that as it may, he certainly was the first in Canada to leave a bright and lasting mark on the breed.

William Miller of Pickering, remembered as an importer and breeder of Shorthorn cattle, imported the Clydesdale stallions Rob Roy, foaled in 1853, and Black Douglas, foaled in 1856. They shared the regional limelight with one of the best Canadian-bred stallions seen in the fifties, Tam O'Shanter, foaled "about 1850" and sired by Grey Clyde.

A substantial number of eastern breeders who became prominent in the importation of Shorthorn cattle at that period were also importing Clydesdales. John Miller of Thistle Ha', Hon. M. H. Cochrane of Compton, Quebec, Simon Beattie of Markham, James I. Davidson of Balsam, and John Dryden of Brooklin, all found Scotch Shorthorns and Scotch Clydes to complement each other in a breeding and importing program.

Between 1850 and 1860—still long before there was a Canadian stud book—eleven Clydesdale stallions were shipped from Scotland to Canada. The number was small but the movement was growing and some of the animals were being resold to United States buyers. As the number of importations and resales increased, the trade began to resemble that of the Cruickshank or Scotch Shorthorns at the time. A big percentage of the cattle from the Sittyton herd of Amos Cruickshank was being forwarded to James I. Davidson of Ontario who in turn was supplying breeding stock to many American breeders. The arrangement seemed to suit everybody. In the case of the Clydesdales, the key man in Canada was Joseph Thompson of Columbus, one-time owner of the great Grey Clyde.

Thompson, as the most important single figure in Canadian Clydesdale affairs during the fifties, deserves attention. Born in England, he came to Ontario by way of the United States. Arriving in 1840, he was soon dealing in and breeding horses and, in time, importing. Although he suffered some serious losses at sea he did not quit. His ownership of Grey Clyde did about as much to enhance his reputation as it did for the horse's. After selling Grey Clyde, he imported Loudon Tam, a big rough horse, but one that came to have an excellent sire record. After Loudon Tam's death, Thompson maintained his reputation for judicious, even uncanny, selections by purchasing and importing Netherby. Although not the greatest show horse, his success in populating the country with halfbred Clydesdales, seemed to be about what the country needed. Netherby was credited with 250 foals from 365 mares in a single year.

Highlights of the Eighties

Importation from Scotland gained momentum although many of the incoming horses were soon purchased by American horsemen who would rather buy Scotch Clydesdales from Canadians than travel to Scotland for them. The percentage of mares among the imports was higher, indicating a growing intention on the part of Canadians to meet Canadian needs in Clydesdales with Canadian-bred stock.

In the opinion of many observers, the real highlights of the decade were first, the stallion MacQueen; second, the emergence of the firm of Graham Brothers of Claremont, responsible for bringing MacQueen to the country and years later, recovering him from the United States for use near home; and third, the twin achievements of organization and the first stud book.

The story of Graham Brothers that assumed an international character must begin with the father, Richard Graham, on whose pioneer efforts the sons built. The elder Graham, the original master of Cairnbrogie, began importing in a modest way about 1870 and did much to improve the public appreciation for Clydesdales. But in volume of trade and in the excellence of horses bought and sold, no individual or firm up to their time made as much Canadian history with and for Clydesdales as the Graham sons. Fastidious buyers, American as well as Canadian, made paths to the Cairnbrogie farm gate and many of the horses imported and sold won international championships. But the horse that brought the most publicity and fame was the stallion MacQueen. Because of his numerous successes, his admiring public gave him the name "Matchless MacQueen."

He was sired by MacGregor, one of the widely known sons of Darnley, and was foaled in Scotland in 1885. The Grahams bought and imported him as a two-year-old and won with him at the American Horse Show on the Water Front at Chicago in the year of importation. Shown annually for a number of years, he was never defeated in his class. At the Columbian Exposition in 1893, he stood at the top of a class of sixteen aged stallions and then won the Columbian trophy for stallion and get. One of the few sweepstakes awards he did not win was when he met a stallion, Prince Patrick, said to have been selected in Scotland and shipped to Chicago expressly to beat the Canadian horse.

MacQueen was sold a short time later to head the Blairgowrie stud owned by former Canadian Robert Burns Ogilvie, at Madison, Wisconsin. Mr. Ogilvie was for many years the secretary of the American Clydesdale Association.

MacQueen's breeding worth was made clear from the day in 1889 when he and three of his offspring—Lass O'Gowrie, Lass O'Gowrie 3rd, and McHappy—appeared at the American Horse Show in Chicago and won the Grand Challenge Shield against horses of all breeds and all ages.

The Grahams wanted the "Matchless" one back and persisted until they bought and returned him to their Claremont farm in 1899. He was then fourteen years old and there he remained until he died at twenty-six years of age. His popularity never diminished. In the first eight years after returning to the Grahams—which would take him to the age of twenty-two—he bred 1,717 mares and left 1,079 foals. Service fees during that period exceeded $21,000.[3]

Editors at the time of his death said that no stallion had been as successful in stamping a "pattern of excellence" upon the breed in America. His most famous son was Young MacQueen, bred by R. B. Ogilvie and owned, used, and exhibited by the Graham Brothers.

It was not to be overlooked that the Grahams of Cairnbrogie were quite properly part of the Markham community, giving further support for the view that if the Clydesdales of Canada had earned the right to their own national capital in those early years, Markham, northeast of Toronto, would be the logical choice. It was the home community of Archibald Ward who imported Grey Clyde, of John Sanderson, importer of the stallions William Wallace and Wonderful Lad, and Mrs. A. Ward who imported Merry Farmer. It was also the home base of John Torrance who brought Clydesdale Jock to the country, and Simon Beattie—one of the most skillful stockmen in Canadian history—who was responsible for introducing the stallion Lord Clyde and others. All this is quite apart from Graham Brothers and the Matchless MacQueen. Just as the Upper Fraser offered the best spawning beds for sockeyes, and Indian Head became the prairie source of shelterbelt trees, and Halifax was the nation's

mill for successful bankers, so Markham deserved to be remembered as a community of distinguished horses and horsemen.

The best of MacQueen's stallion contemporaries in Canada included MacBean, sired by MacGregor by Darnley and imported by Graham Brothers; the Granite City, sired by Lord Erskine, foaled in 1885 and imported two years later by R. Beith of Bowmanville; and St. Gatien, foaled in 1883 and also imported by Beith.

Each of these stallions made fine showyard records. MacBean won first and sweepstakes for horses of any age at the Clydesdale Horse Show at Toronto in 1889. The Granite City won his class at the Highland and Agricultural Show at Perth just before being shipped to Canada, and added to his winnings at Toronto and Portage la Prairie. And St. Gatien won the medal for the best Clydesdale stallion of any age at the Toronto Industrial Exhibition in 1888.

The twin achievements of organization and the stud book deserve special praise. The supporters of Shorthorn cattle were earlier in organizing their breed association but the breeders and importers of Clydesdales were the first Canadians to publish a record book. The Clydesdale Horse Association of Canada began in 1886 and the publication of volume I of the *Canadian Clydesdale Stud Book*, a monumental production under the circumstances, occurred later in the same year.

Preparation for that first stud book began four years earlier when members of the Agriculture and Arts Association of Ontario recognized the need to collect the pertinent stud book information about Clydesdales in the province before more of it was lost. According to Henry Wade who was the moving spirit and editor of volume I, "the registration of Clydesdale horses in Canada commenced in September, 1882, by the Agriculture and Arts Association, mainly at the request of the present secretary . . . At the commencement of this record, there was only one volume of the *American Clydesdale Stud Book* published. It contained a number of Canadian bred animals. So the standard was made the same as that of the American Association, admitting occasionally a Shire cross, as in early days they were not known as being any different to the pure Clyde. When enough animals were recorded to make a fair sized volume, at the request of the secretary of the Agriculture and Arts Association, the Board called a meeting of the breeders of Clydes in Canada to confer with them as to the establishment of an association for Canada, to assist in the completion of the first volume and to consider the question of standards. The meeting was well attended and an association formed which comprised a large number of the breeders and importers of Clydes in Canada."[4]

Thus, in March, 1886, the Clydesdale Horse Association of Canada was born and the immediate task facing the new officers consisted of producing the first stud book with the least possible delay, notwithstanding the necessity of reassessing the standards for admission to registration. Because the American and Scottish Clydesdale Associations had recently raised their standards for entry by excluding Shire crosses, the Canadian breeders believed they should do the same, and the working committee set about to segregate the candidates carrying mixed blood. That seemed fair enough until the next meeting of the Executive Committee of the

Clydesdale Association and the Stud Book Committee of the Agriculture and Arts Association when a deputation of horsemen with a well-signed petition made a plea that there be no changes in the rules governing admission to the first volume at least. It was recognized that many of the horsemen who applied for registration under the old rules had some reason for the protest, and a resolution was passed to register those horses which could have been admitted under the existing rules but not under the proposed changes. These names would appear in an appendix to the stud book, essentially for horses of mixed but predominantly Clydesdale breeding; it would be called the Canadian Draught Horse Appendix. Horses with some Shire blood would thus be eligible for admission.

When volume I of the *Canadian Clydesdale Stud Book* appeared—in time to make it available for purchase at the provincial exhibition at Guelph—it showed 320 stallions and 243 mares registered in the "stud book proper," 227 stallions and mares in the Draught Horse Appendix, and 487 stallions and mares in the Scotch Appendix.

David McCrae from Guelph was the elected president of the infant Clydesdale Association of Canada; William Smith of Columbus, Ontario, was vice-president and Henry Wade, the unfailing public handy man was secretary. When the first annual meeting was held in December, 1886, the president could report ninety-three members as of September 1, 1886. What he probably did not report was that nearly all members were Ontario people. There were a few from the United States, a few from Quebec, and none from western Canada. Two years later, in

1888, there were only two western members, Henry Nichol and John E. Smith, both of Brandon.

The distinction of registration number one for stallions in the stud book went to Blairadam, sired by Young Lochfergus and foaled in 1877. The corresponding honor for mares was for Dolly, about whom the pertinent stud book information was scant. All that was recorded was that the mare was "grey, age and pedigree unknown. Imported by Mr. Spence about 1850." The best reason for including her in the stud book was that she had a daughter with better qualifications. Dolly 2nd, by William Wallace was registered next to her mother with number two.

Nobody had more reason for satisfaction in the achievements of the decade than Henry Wade who concluded the preface of the first volume of the stud book with needless modesty: "It is to be hoped the public will lightly criticize this first volume. It has been a labor of love to the editor who hopes the next will be more satisfactory, especially as to Scottish nomenclature."

THE FIRST IN THE WEST

Clydesdales of pure breeding were relatively late in reaching the Canadian West, arriving at least forty years after the importation of the stallion Cumberland by David Rowntree at Weston.

A new and bigger wave of Scottish horses came to Ontario and neighboring eastern regions following the publication of volume I of the Clydesdale stud book and new names became prominent. Graham Brothers of Claremont retained a position of leadership but were being challenged by Robert Ness of Howick, Quebec, D. and O. Sorby of Guelph, John Gardhouse and Sons of Malton, Simon Beattie of Markham, and William O'Brien of Nova Scotia. There were also Robert Davies of Thorncliffe, Hodgkinson and Tisdale of Beaverton, William Smith of Columbus, the Brandons of Forest, and more.

It is impossible to identify positively the first purebred Clydesdale in the West but there has been a suggestion that it was the stallion Charming Charlie, foaled in Scotland in 1883 and brought to Canada three years later by Alex Colquhoun of the pioneer firm of Colquhoun and Beattie, Brandon. Beattie told that in making the purchase, his partner agreed to pay the Scottish owner one dollar of Canadian money per pound for the horse. When Charming Charlie was weighed, the vendor looked for a settlement of $2,163 and Beattie added with an enforced grin: "That damned Aberdonian refused to 'knock off' the three dollars." But the stallion was undefeated at Winnipeg and Brandon for a period of five years and won his last championship at Winnipeg at the age of eleven years.

Anyone studying volume I of the stud book might find reason to pause at the fourteenth entry in the book. It is for the stallion Prince of Tay, foaled in Scotland in 1880, then brought to Canada by Richard Leaitch of Harriston, Ontario. He is registered in that initial book in the name of James Burnett who, about the time the stud book appeared, was making his way west to settle at Napinka, Manitoba, where he became a prominent breeder of Clydesdales for more than fifty years. The question which remains unanswered is this: Did he bring Prince of Tay with him to become one of the first Clydesdales in the West? Regardless of the horse, James Burnett was one of the earliest breeders in the West and made an additional record by registering another Clydesdale stallion, Glengarry, foaled in 1937, for inclusion in volume xxxvi, published in 1944. Thus, Jim Burnett's first and last stallions were registered in stud books published fifty-eight years apart.

The first Clydesdale in what is now Alberta appears to have been the stallion Carlyle, bred in Aberdeenshire by Amos Cruickshank of Shorthorn cattle fame and imported to Canada by John Miller and Sons of Ontario. The horse was taken to the Alberta area by Ed Quinn in 1888 and was used extensively for breeding in districts south of Calgary. Here Robert and John Turner dominated the Clydesdale scene with the noted show horse Balgreggan Hero and mares bought from the Sorbys of Guelph a short time later.

Some of the other very early Clydesdales in the foothills were stallions brought to the big ranches, notably the Walrond and the Bow River Horse Ranch when the latter evolved from the big Cochrane Ranch west of Calgary in 1888.

And in British Columbia, the distinction of being the first purebred Clydesdale fell to the imported stallion The Boss, brought to the Douglas Lake Cattle Co. ranch in the Nicola Valley in 1887.[5]

When Charles Beake, one of the Douglas Lake partners, was in Scotland in that year, he bought the first prize two-year-old stallion at the Glasgow Stallion Show for $5,000 and sent him to the British Columbia ranch in charge of one John Blackwell. The horse made the long journey around the lower tip of South America without mishap. But it was quickly concluded that with no purebred mares on the ranch, such a stallion was an extravagance. In the next year, six registered mares were brought from the East, having been purchased from the Sorbys, and in time a flourishing horse business resulted, so brisk that stallion colts were sometimes sold before they were born.

GREAT HORSEMEN OF THE EARLY WEST

Canada's biggest market for horses—both work stock and breeding horses—between 1890 and the end of World War I was in the West, and many horsemen who came and gained national and international stature, remained there to the end of their lives. Some of these were Alexander Galbraith, W. H. "Scotty" Bryce, Alex and George Mutch, Ben Finlayson, Dean W. J. Rutherford, and others. There should be no hesitation in writing about them. In an academic sense, leading horsemen should command at least as much attention as champion horses.

If there was such a title as Dean of Horsemen in the West or in Canada in those pioneer years, Alexander Galbraith would have had the best claim to it. Born and raised in Scotland, it was to be expected that Clydesdale horses would have been his first love. Perhaps he never lost his preference for the Scottish breed but he acknowledged good in all breeds, saw weaknesses in all, and commanded, to an admirable extent, the respect and confidence of horsemen everywhere.

Arriving in Montreal in 1883, he went to Janesville, Wisconsin, where he plunged into the business of importing and breeding, mainly the British breeds—Clydesdales,

Shires, Suffolks, and Hackneys. As the representative of the firm of Galbraith Brothers, he sold a thousand stallions in the ten years prior to 1893 when the partnership was dissolved because of the economic depression gripping the United States. He took to farming in Wisconsin but was soon back to importing horses and conducting educational programs for the University of Wisconsin. In 1901, Alexander Galbraith, with his son, opened a sales stable at Brandon and became more absorbed with western Canadian affairs. He was like a one-man agricultural extension department until 1915 when he was appointed superintendent of Fairs and Agricultural Societies in Alberta, notwithstanding his age of seventy-one years. By that time, an inventory of his major public service assignments would have shown him as having judged at three world fairs and more than a score of state and national fairs. He had taken part in five winters of farm courses for the University of Wisconsin, been called by one provincial university and five state colleges to do special lectures, and emerged as the most competent and popular judge of horses—all breeds—on the continent.

Not the least of Galbraith's distinctions was the almost universal respect he commanded in both the United States and Canada. Of him De Witt Wing, associate editor of the *Breeders' Gazette*, Chicago, would write: "Distinctive courtesy, scrupulous conscientiousness, unswerving loyalties and a clean serene life."[6]

Anyone with such talent and character could not fail to be a force for good in his chosen profession, and the horsemen of Canada had a huge debt to Alexander Galbraith.

The Mutch Brothers from Mount Forest, Ontario, came to the Qu'Appelle Valley to farm in 1883 and for many years the names of Alex and George Mutch meant good Clydesdales.

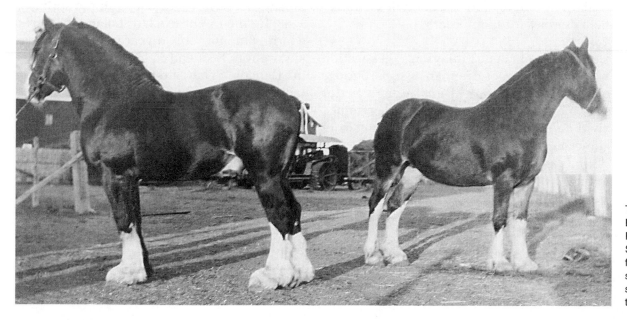

The Bruce and Lady Bruce, owned by R. H. Taber of Condie, Saskatchewan. Two famous Clydesdale showhorses in the second decade of the century.

In 1890 they bought a carload of purebred mares in Ontario—mainly from the Grahams and Sorbys—and in the shipment was Montrave Ceshia, soon to be seen as one of the best show mares in the new country. But the best thing the Mutch Brothers did for themselves was in the purchase of the stallion Baron's Gem, by Baron's Pride, in 1903. Baron's Gem's perfect showring record and his mounting reputation as a breeder were enough to push the Craigie Mains stud of Saskatchewan into a forward position. From the Mutch ownership, Baron's Gem was sold to head another leading pioneer breeding establishment, that of R. H. Taber of Hillcrest Farm at Condie, Saskatchewan, where he preceded the next style-setting sire of the time, The Bruce.

Among other Mutch successes was the breeding of the famous show mare, Eva's Gem, that followed Baron's Gem to the Taber stud.

George Mutch died in 1910 but Alex—not very big but dynamic like a whiz-bang—remained active and influential in horsemen's circles for many years.

Horsemen of Ben Finlayson's generation would never forget the man, a superb judge of heavy horses and, if anything, a better showman than a judge. Many people retained vivid memories of him presenting horses in showrings. Inducing an exaggerated flexion of limb joints in the horse, he matched the animal's performance with his own, giving the pleasing impression of man and horse moving in perfect unison.

Coming from a home farm in Perthshire where Clydesdale horses were raised, Ben arrived in Canada in 1907. W. H. "Scotty" Bryce of Arcola bought Clydesdales from the Finlayson farm in Scotland, among them the good stallion Gallant Buchlyvie. As an immigrant, Ben Finlayson took a temporary summer job as a farm hand near Regina and then went to Arcola where he felt right at home with Bryce and the Clydes. He assisted with the preparation and then the showing of the Bryce horses that went to the shows in the spring of 1908. He then went to Claresholm and bought a farm, but after only a year he sold the farm and went to Scotland to buy horses for resale in Canada. That first shipment in 1909 included twelve pedigreed Clydesdales and it must have been profitable because he made two such shipments in 1910 and was a regular importer for the next twenty-three years.

Alexander Galbraith may have imported more horses of the British breeds to North America, but nobody shipped more Clydesdales from Scotland to western Canada than Finlayson. Nor, indeed, did anybody handle more of the outstanding stallions used in the West, as even a partial list would show. Among these were such distinguished names as Arnprior Emigrant, three times grand champion at the Royal Agricultural Winter Fair; Lochinvar, with a record of five grand championships at the Royal; Golden West that headed the stud of C. C. T. Robertson at Bradwell; Dunure Norman that became the senior herd sire at the Dominion Experimental Farm at Indian Head; Riccarton Landmark, by Bonnie Buchlyvie, outstanding show and breeding stallion for Isaac Cormack, Kenton; Sansovina, by Signet, shown by John Sinclair of Congress to win the grand championship at the International Show in Chicago in 1927 and the Canadian Royal in 1930; First Principal that gained the grand championship at the first Canadian Royal in 1922 for the Manitoba Department of Agriculture; Dunduff Chancellor, by Dunure Footprint, that became the herd sire and show horse for Joe Lorimer of Conquest; and Edward Garnet, by Royal Edward, an almost perpetual champion at prairie exhibitions during his lifetime.

It was a distinguished record that ended abruptly and sadly with Ben Finlayson's death in a motor accident in 1933. He was forty-eight years of age, still a comparatively young man.

When James Kilpatrick of Scotland's Craigie Mains—the most influential individual in the Clydesdale world—travelled across Canada, visiting breeders and importers in 1912, he credited W. H. "Scotty" Bryce of Arcola, Saskatchewan, with having the "best stud of Clydesdales in Canada."[7] No horseman in the country at that time would have disagreed.

Bryce settled at Arcola soon after coming to Canada in 1882 and laid a foundation of carefully chosen Scottish breeding stock in 1888, adding to it from time to time. Twelve Clydesdales were imported in 1905, including the Cawdor Cup mare Rosadora and the

highly rated stallion Perpetual Motion. Twelve more were imported in 1906, thirty-six in 1910, and eleven in 1911. Of Rosadora, James Kilpatrick said she was the first Cawdor Cup winner to leave Scotland.

Bryce was singularly fortunate in the calibre of the stallions he chose. Perpetual Motion and Baron of Arcola were examples. The first was bred by William Motion of Haplands, Scotland, and sired by Hiawatha, four times winner of the Cawdor Cup. Foaled in 1902, Perpetual Motion won first prize for three-year-olds at the Highland Show in 1905, after which he was bought by Mr. Bryce for about $3,750 for shipment to Doune Lodge farm. In Canada the horse had an almost unbroken record of winnings, first for Mr. Bryce, then for W. C. Sutherland of Saskatoon and, finally, for W. J. Young of Griswold, Manitoba. Although not a particularly big horse, he possessed quality and action that nobody could criticize. In the

W. H. "Scotty" Bryce, distinguished pioneer Clydesdale breeder in the West.

Perpetual Motion, imported by Scotty Bryce in 1905. In Canada he had an almost unbroken record of championships.

early years of ring contests in showmanship, every serious aspirant wanted to borrow Perpetual Motion to demonstrate showmanship skills; he was such a showy horse he made it easy for a contestant to win. Ringside spectators were known to remark that the ribbon should have been presented to Perpetual Motion rather than the competing showman.

One year after buying Perpetual Motion, the laird of Doune Lodge made an even better purchase, that of the stallion Canadians came to know as Baron of Arcola. That was not the stallion's name when Bryce bought him. This son of Baron's Pride was registered in the first instance as Keystone but Bryce, with more of sentiment than most people recognized, wanted the horse in which he had great faith to carry the name of his adopted Saskatchewan town of Arcola, and paid £5 to have the name changed in the stud book to Baron of Arcola.

At the Winnipeg Industrial Exhibition of 1907, Baron of Arcola placed second to Sir William Van Horne's unbeaten showhorse, Lord Ardwall, but at Brandon Exhibition the following week, the placing was reversed with the general approval of the horsemen. For the next few years, the Baron and his offspring largely dominated the western showrings.

Clydesdale stallions owned by Scotty Bryce of Arcola. From left: Gallant Buchlyvie, Clive, Baron of Arcola, and Baron Romeo.

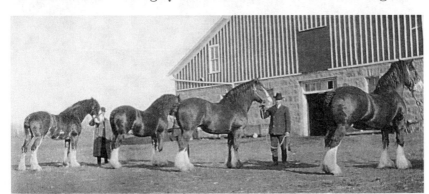

Bryce demonstrated his readiness to go to almost any length to obtain the best in breeding stock. His attempt to bring the great Bonnie Buchlyvie to Canada was a clear example. Travelling in Scotland in 1912 with his friend James Kilpatrick he visited the Seaham Harbour stud and there inspected the famous Bonnie Buchlyvie, which some were ready to call "the greatest living Clydesdale." Scotty Bryce was much impressed; perhaps he was overwhelmed. No doubt he had a vision of this mighty horse occupying a box stall next to his uncle, Baron of Arcola, at the home farm in Saskatchewan. He wanted to buy him then and there but Bonnie Buchlyvie was not for sale.

Before leaving Kilpatrick's company, however, Bryce instructed him that if the famous horse became unexpectedly available, Kilpatrick was to buy him at any price up to £4,000 and ship him to Saskatchewan.

Three years later the stallion was indeed being offered at the Seaham Harbour sale. Kilpatrick bought him for £5,000 and cabled Bryce to notify him of what he had done and advise him that he could have the stallion for what he had been obliged to pay for him. But fate intervened and the message was received at Arcola on the day of Scotty Bryce's funeral. It was the expressed conviction of Peter Taylor, Mr. Bryce's son-in-law, that if Mr. Bryce had been alive and well, the illustrious Bonnie Buchlyvie would have been brought to Saskatchewan.

Of the horse, James Kilpatrick wrote: "Bonnie Buchlyvie proved a good investment to me and lived until he was twenty-one years old, siring, among other noted horses, Craigie McQuaid, which in turn produced Craigie Beau Ideal to head my stud."[8]

Two imported Clydesdale stallions in harness at the University of Saskatchewan, circa 1923. On off side, Bonnie Fyvie by Bonnie Buchlyvie; on nigh side, Kinleith Footprint by Dunure Footprint.

FAITH, HOPE, AND CLYDESDALES AT THE UNIVERSITY

Horse history was made aboundingly at the University of Saskatchewan in the years after 1919. Some of the best Clydesdale breeding in the world, outside of Scotland, was being concentrated there where W. J. Rutherford was the dean of Agriculture. He did not deny that Clydesdales were close to his heart, and when accused of breed prejudice, he replied that he favored any horse possessing true Clydesdale quality. It didn't satisfy the supporters of other breeds who clung to criticism of the alleged creed based on "Faith, Hope, and Clydesdales."

Be that as it may, the dean was largely responsible for the policies and decisions that filled the big university barn with horses of the Scottish breed and left the horse users of the province arguing about the merits and demerits of Clydesdales.

A request from the Saskatchewan Horse Breeders' Association for assistance with horse improvement in the province was submitted to the cabinet in 1919; its reception was favorable. There followed an agreement by the government to buy one or two of the best Clydesdale stallions available in Scotland. They would become the property of the University of Saskatchewan to be used in ways likely to produce the most good. A purchasing committee consisting of Robert Sinton of Regina, William Gibson, superintendent of the Experimental Farm at Indian Head, and Dean Rutherford was appointed and the search followed.

In Scotland, members of the committee encountered strong reluctance about parting with their best animals, regardless of the price,

Rosalind, one of the greatest show mares of her time, won the Cawdor Cup before leaving Scotland in 1916. When owned by the University of Saskatchewan, she won the reserve grand championship at the Royal Winter Fair of 1927. *Photograph by Live Stock Photo Co.*

and the hope of buying one of the truly great proven sires was shattered. The alternative was to buy two of the most promising young stallions. Finally, two royally bred yearling stallions were purchased—Craigie Enchanter by Craigie Litigant and Bonnie Fyvie by Bonnie Buchlyvie—both with excellent show records. The price was £3,000 for each. The two sires were among Scotland's best; James Kilpatrick would buy Bonnie Buchlyvie for use at Craigie Mains and of Craigie Litigant, he told of refusing £10,000 for him, regarding him as "the best Clydesdale alive at the time."

But there was misfortune ahead; Craigie Enchanter died from strangulation of the intestine resulting from a tumor, just months after delivery at Saskatoon, and Bonnie Fyvie developed stringhalt and was destroyed in 1926. To partly compensate for the loss, Craigie Fyvie, a full brother of Craigie Enchanter and known as "the gift horse," was presented to the university by his Scottish owner.

The Province of Alberta, about this time, acted along similar lines by voting a substantial sum of money for the purchase of two stallions, one Clydesdale and one Percheron. Craigie Masterpiece by Everlasting was the Clydesdale choice in Scotland, a truly magnificent specimen, delivered in 1920.

But the most exciting drama was still to come.

Disappointment from the two high-priced imported stallions placed with the University of Saskatchewan left no lasting discouragement with the dean and when he saw an opportunity to give his College of Agriculture a world status in propagating richly bred Clydes, he seized it.

The prologue began in 1918 when William Graham of Ontario's Graham Brothers, was commissioned by two American businessmen, F. L. Ames and George A. Cluett, to buy the best available foundation Clydesdales in Scotland. The mares assembled, in the words of one journalist, were the best to cross the Atlantic at any time.

In the first shipment to Ames was the yearling stallion Kinleith Footprint, said to have cost 6,000 American dollars. But Mr. Cluett wanted this son of Dunure Footprint and bought him from Ames for $10,000. Kinleith Footprint, never a big horse but right in quality and pedigree, was one of thirty-one head of Clydesdale aristocrats delivered.

Postwar depression gripped the country and George Cluett, on February 1, 1923, wrote to Dean Rutherford whom he met and admired when the latter was judging horses at Chicago, offering to sell his entire string of Clydesdales at a fraction of what the animals cost him. Cluett admitted that he was anxious to see the horses he had assembled kept together and go to a good home. In other words, he wanted Rutherford to take all the mares and stallions and continue the breeding program started south of the boundary.

In addition to Kinleith Footprint, the Cluett band at that time included the Cawdor Cup mare of 1916, Rosalind, which had come to Cluett at a reported cost of $15,000; Craigie Sylvia, winner of first prize at the English Royal, second at the Highland, and later, grand champion mare at Chicago International for Mr. Cluett; Eva Footprint, Greenmeadow Muriel, Fyvie Queen, Langwater Jessica, and others with good names.

It should be added concerning Rosalind that she was the mother of Rosabel, the winning filly foal and grand champion female at the Chicago International show in 1921. It wasn't often that a foal won a grand championship and to further enliven the story about Rosalind's filly, she was bought for shipment back to the land of her forebears. It was a nice compliment to Rosalind who was not shown extensively on this side of the Atlantic but was at the Royal Winter Fair in 1927 to win the brood mare class.

In writing to Dean Rutherford, Mr. Cluett said: "I would be willing to sell the entire lot to you for $10,000, which, as you will realize, is only a fraction of their value." Actually, it was the figure that Cluett had paid for Kinleith Footprint alone.

The dean was eager and persuaded the university governors to act. The purchase was confirmed and thirteen of the most richly bred Clydesdales on the continent were delivered at Saskatoon. One member of the group of thirteen, Langwater Jessica, an American-bred mare, was nursing a stallion foal, Green Meadow Footstep by Kinleith Footprint. That foal developed well and went east with the university show herd in 1925 to win the grand championship for Clydesdale stallions at the Royal Agricultural Winter Fair and, days later, the grand championship at the Chicago International.

The university Clydesdales did all that was expected of them. They performed the field work on the university farm, entered regularly into breed competitions at the Royal Winter Fair, were called upon for inclusion in special educational displays, served as study subjects for students in agriculture, and

Langwater Jessica, owned by the University of Saskatchewan, raised two foals in 1930, her own and the orphan of Craigie Sylvia. Both foals went to the Royal Winter Fair that fall and placed first and second, making something of a record for the mare.

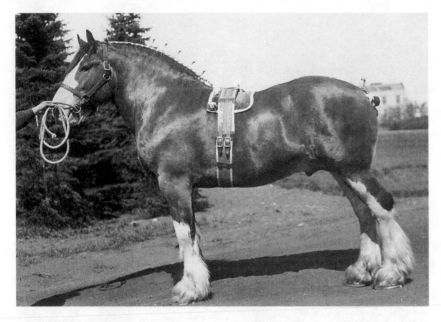

Duke of Argyle, a one-ton stallion that headed the University of Saskatchewan stud for some years after 1942.

contributed a limited number of mares and young stallions for sale in farming districts.

But times were changing. Mechanization was gaining ground. Farm horses were being displaced. Efficiency became the order of the day. Sentiment for horses vanished—at least for the heavy ones—and the university Clydesdales were liquidated. Some were sold as work stock without pedigree certificates. Some ended their days at slaughter plants. Nobody considered the possibility that Clydesdales, Percherons, and Belgians would be wanted again and that prices would soar because of a scarcity of the good ones.

THE TWENTIES

Horse fortunes were changing ominously in the decade of the twenties. Fordson, Titan, Happy Farmer, and Waterloo Boy tractors were making friends and inroads upon what had been seen as the horse's prerogative in farm fields. The Canadian horse population that reached its highest point ever of 3,610,000 in 1921, turned downward to lose an average of three-quarters of a million head per decade for the next forty years.

The breeds of heavy horses were in escalating trouble but the breeders, whether from natural optimism or stubbornness bordering on cussedness, scarcely relaxed in breeding and faithfully continued to exhibit their stock. Strange to say, Canadian Clydesdale exhibitors had some of their best years in the twenties. It was the decade in which the Royal Agricultural Winter Fair had its birth at Toronto and Clydesdale competition was Canada-wide and strong from its beginning in 1922. In the first ten years of the Royal, including 1931, eastern entries won the grand championship for mares seven times, mostly with Canadian-breds, while western entries won the stallion championship nine times, all with imported horses.

The most significant series of showring triumphs for Canadian-owned Clydesdales at the time was at the Chicago International Fat Stock Show where Canadian exhibitors won the grand championship for stallions ten times in as many years, 1920 to 1929 inclusive.

Percherons and Belgians had the bigger shows and keener competitions at Chicago but, nevertheless, there were many good American studs making regular entry in the Clydesdale classes at that time. The Canadian-bred stallion Wee Donald by Hugo's Stamp, bred by R. D. Ferguson of Port Stanley, Ontario, and shown by Charles Weaver, Lloydminster, led the winning parade. He had been brought to the West by the horse dealers Vanstone and Rogers and sold to Weaver. He couldn't have gone to a better home or more devoted owner. Weaver built a small barn for Wee Donald's exclusive occupation and painted across the front: Wee Donald's House.

As Weaver discovered, Wee Donald had superior tastes. He liked music and fresh bread. Music when he entered a showring made him prance and filled him with the will to win. And when loaves of fresh bread from Mrs. Weaver's oven disappeared, she knew they had been filched for Wee Donald's enjoyment.

Wee Donald won the Chicago championship in 1920 and as Canadians were pleased to note, the first five awards in the class for mature stallions were taken by Canadians.

After Wee Donald's first win at Chicago, various horsemen wanted to buy him but the owner, with his Lancashire accent, said: "Ye cannot buy him; there isn't enough money in the world to buy my friend." But after Wee Donald returned to the International to win his second grand award in 1921 and his third in 1924, tragedy brought a sudden end. Attracted by a band of horses in a nearby paddock, he tried to jump a fence, fell, and broke his neck.

The Chicago champion in 1922 was First Principal, owned and shown by the Manitoba Department of Agriculture. He was also the grand champion at the first Canadian Royal that same year.

The next in the succession was the imported Mainring by Dunure Loyalty, winning in 1923 for W. B. Cleland of Troy, Ontario. He was the second stallion to win the grand championship at both the International and the Royal in the same year.

As noted elsewhere, Green Meadow Footstep by Kinleith Footprint won the Chicago International and the Toronto Royal grand championship in 1925 for the University of Saskatchewan.

In the next year, 1926, Forest Favorite by Rannas Print by Dunure Footprint, shown by owners Haggerty and Black, Belle Plaine, Saskatchewan, maintained the winning International record. He was six years of age, having been used for several years by Brandon Brothers of Ontario who imported him.

The year of 1927 saw the big imported Sansovina by Signet becoming the grand champion at Chicago for his Saskatchewan owner, John Sinclair of Congress.

In 1928 the black stallion Lochinvar, imported by the well-known western horseman Ben Finlayson and owned by John E. Falconer of Saskatchewan, won the grand championship at the International after winning the similar award at Canada's Royal Winter Fair. It must also be noted that Lochinvar won

Forest Favorite, imported by Brandon Brothers of Ontario and in the ownership of Haggerty and Black of Saskatchewan, won the grand championship at the Chicago International Show in 1926. *Photograph by Live Stock Photo Co.*

the grand prize at the Canadian Royal not just once but five times.

Completing the famous run of ten consecutive International grand awards to Canadian Clydesdale stallions was the Saskatchewan horse Sonny Boy, shown by A. Johnstone of Yellowgrass in 1929.

The horse business might be sinking into depression but the Canadian Clydesdale breeders were not giving up—not yet anyway.

LEADING SIRES OF CLYDESDALE WINNERS AT THE CANADIAN ROYAL

Canada's Royal Agricultural Winter Fair, held annually at Toronto since its inception in 1922—except for a seven-year suspension related to the exigencies of World War II—has become a truly national institution. It has more of the character of a "Supreme Court" in making showring judgments on livestock than will be found elsewhere. It was reasonable, therefore, that in attempting to identify the most influential sires in the common breeds, the Royal winnings would prove most useful.

A tabulation of winners at the Royal was undertaken for each of the two separate periods in the show's existence, to 1985. The disjunction of seven years seemed to warrant quite separate studies and, as it happened, the analytical technique was changed somewhat between the first and second study periods.

In the early survey, the sire was given five points for each winner of first prize in the breeding classes—including get-of-sire—four points for a second award, three points for a third, two points for a fourth, and one point for a fifth. For the forty-year analysis, however, it was concluded that the method could

be simplified without significant loss of value or usefulness, allowing three points to the sire of a first-prize winner, two points for a second place, and one for a third. In pointing up the really great sires, the amended scale used between 1946 and 1985 seemed quite satisfactory. For only one year, 1969, were part of the winning records unavailable.

The ten high-scoring sires from the earlier seventeen-year period are named in the following lines and the top fifteen from the forty-year period are shown immediately after. [SEE FIG. 1]

Doura Excelsior, the high-scoring sire on the above list, was bred in Scotland, owned for most of his life in the United States, and made the striking showring impression in Canada. The Canadian impact was largely through daughters bred in Scotland and bought for export to Canada before the stallion was purchased by Paul Cooper for shipment to his Wisconsin farm. The biggest single contributor to the Doura Excelsior sire record in Canada was obviously the mare Kirklandhill Queen o'Carrick that was shown to fifteen Royal Winter Fair grand championships.

Although Excelsior was never owned in Canada, three of his sons won a total of eight grand championships at the Royal; Doura Perfect Motion won in 1974, '76 and '77 for the Quebec Clydesdale Club, and Doura Royal Scot won in 1978, '80, and '82 for Wreford Hewson. The third son, Greendykes Excelsior Again, won in 1979 and '81 for Paul Cooper and Family.

Bardrill Castle, likewise imported from Scotland, won no grand championships at the Royal but his son, Aspiration, won in 1973 for the Brandon Clydesdale Club.

FIGURE 1

CLYDESDALE SIRES OF WINNERS IN ORDER OF SCORES, ROYAL WINTER FAIRS, 1922 TO 1938

1	Carbrook Buchlyvie [22039]	by	Bonnie Buchlyvie
2	Forest Favorite [23627]	by	Rannas Print
3	Renown [26948]	by	Benefactor
4	Ardyne Refiner [24841]	by	Dunure Refiner
5	Green Meadow Footstep [23834]	by	Kinleith Footprint
6	Craigie Fyvie [24391]	by	Craigie Litigant
7	Lochinvar [25468]	by	Coronation
8	Brunstane Again [25390]	by	Dunure Footprint
9	Provost Marshal [22735]	by	Premier Baron
10	Bonnie Fyvie [22782]	by	Bonnie Buchlyvie

CLYDESDALE SIRES OF WINNERS IN ORDER OF SCORES, ROYAL WINTER FAIRS, 1946 TO 1985

1	Doura Excelsior [25911]	by	Salchrie Prince Philip
2	Bardrill Castle [30377]	by	Golden Dawn
3	Scotland's Pioneer [30177]	by	Tarraby Pioneer
4	Muirton Sensation [28739]	by	Muirton Tide
5	Torrs Premier [28260]	by	Craigie Capture
6	Windlaw Proprietor [23940]	by	Windlaw Pre-Eminence
7	Drumlanrig Inspiration [29297]	by	Balgreen Inspiration
8	Caradoc Footprint [25960]	by	Forest Favorite
9	Dunsyre Benefactor [24759]	by	[unknown]
10	Craigie Surmount [30201]	by	Craigie True Form
11	Benedictine [30756]	by	Bardrill Castle
12	Broomley Blue Print [24751]	by	Dunsyre Footprint
13	Happy Monarch [30035]	by	Muirton Monarch
14	Dunsyre Footprint [24610]	by	Balgreen Final Command
15	Doura Perfect Motion [30808]	by	Doura Excelsior

Clearly, however, Bardrill Castle dominated the Royal winnings between 1963 and 1973, just as Doura Excelsior did in the next ten years.

Scotland's Pioneer, third-ranking sire on the list, was another imported stallion that demonstrated ability to win in strong competition and also sire winners. He was grand champion at the Royal in 1954 and produced a son, Riverview Pioneer Laddie, that did the same in each of the following two years for Manitoba breeder Fred Dunn. [SEE FIG. 2]

THE INCREDIBLE QUEEN O' CARRICK

The most significant features of the following lists of Clydesdale champions at the Canadian Royal Winter Fair are the striking prominence of the name of one breeder, Wreford Hewson, and the equally amazing sweep of grand championships won by the Hewson-owned mare, Queen o' Carrick or, more correctly, Kirklandhill Queen o' Carrick. By the end of 1985, Hewson entries had won the grand championship for Clyde

FIGURE 2

Grand Champion Clydesdale Stallions, Canadian Royal Winter Fair

Year	Name of Winner	Sire of Winner	Exhibitor
1922	First Principal	Dandy Dick	Manitoba Dept. of Agric.
1923	Mainring	Dunure Loyalty	W. B. Cleland
1924	Arnprior Emigrant	Apukwa	Ben Finlayson
1925	Green Meadow Footstep	Kinleith Footprint	Univ. of Saskatchewan
1926	Arnprior Emigrant	Apukwa	Reston Clyde. Syndicate
1927	Lord Willingdon	Bridgebank Sensation	W. J. McCallum
1928	Lochinvar	Coronation	J. E. Falconer
1929	Arnprior Emigrant	Apukwa	Reston Clyde. Syndicate
1930	Sansovina	Signet	John Sinclair
1931	Lochinvar	Coronation	J. E. Falconer
1932	Brunstane Zenith	Brunstane Again	Ben Rothwell
1933	Lochinvar	Coronation	J. E. Falconer
1934	Craigie Gaiety	Craigie Ambition	R. Duff and Son
1935	Lochinvar	Coronation	J. E. Falconer
1936	Lochinvar	Coronation	J. E. Falconer
1937	Torrs Ambition	Craigie Winalot	Nelson Wagg
1938	Windlaw Marcellus	Scotland's Marcellus	R. R. McLaughlin
1939	to 1945, no Royal Winter Fairs owing to World War II		
1946	Windlaw Proprietor	Windlaw Pre-Eminence	Elmcroft Farm
1947	Happy Monarch	Muirton Monarch	Experimental Farms, Ottawa
1948	Craigie Diplomat	Duntroon Castle	Canada Dept. of Agric.
1949	Uniformdene	Art Union	Ont. Clydesdale Club
1950	Uniformdene	Art Union	Ont. Clydesdale Club
1951	Monarch S Flash	Happy Monarch	Fred Dunn
1952	Craigie Surmount	Craigie True Form	Baxter Wright
1953	Scotland's Pioneer	Tarraby Pioneer	Fred Dunn
1954	Scotland's Pioneer	Tarraby Pioneer	Fred Dunn
1955	Riverview Pioneer Laddie	Scotland's Pioneer	Fred Dunn
1956	Riverview Pioneer Laddie	Scotland's Pioneer	Fred Dunn
1957	Broomley Blue Print	Dunsyre Footprint	W. J. Taylor and Sons
1958	Broomley Blue Print	Dunsyre Footprint	W. J. Taylor and Sons
1959	Bandirran Baron	Bandirran Barrister	Nathan Goff
1960	Muirton Select	Muirton Supreme	Wreford Hewson
1961	Bellmont Ideal	Dunsyre Double Star	Wreford Hewson
1962	Collessie Ideal Print	Muirton Sensation	Peter L. Graham
1963	Bellmont Ideal	Dunsyre Double Star	Wreford Hewson
1964	Bellmont Ideal	Dunsyre Double Star	Wreford Hewson
1965	Bellmont Ideal	Dunsyre Double Star	Wreford Hewson
1966	Bellmont Ideal	Dunsyre Double Star	Wreford Hewson
1967	Dunsyre Silver King	Dunsyre Benefactor	Anheuser-Busch

Year	Name of Winner	Sire of Winner	Exhibitor
1968	Bardrill Vintage	Glenord	Wreford Hewson
1969	Bardrill Glenord	Glenord	Anheuser-Busch
1970	Bardrill Glenord	Glenord	Anheuser-Busch
1971	Bardrill Glenord	Glenord	Anheuser-Busch
1972	Bardrill Glenord	Glenord	Anheuser-Busch
1973	Aspiration	Bardrill Castle	Brandon Clyde. Syndicate
1974	Doura Perfect Motion	Doura Excelsior	Quebec Clyde. Club
1975	Bardrill Glenord	Glenord	Anheuser-Busch
1976	Doura Perfect Motion	Doura Excelsior	Quebec Clyde. Club
1977	Doura Perfect Motion	Doura Excelsior	Quebec Clyde. Club
1978	Doura Royal Scot	Doura Excelsior	Wreford Hewson
1979	Greendykes Excelsior Again	Doura Excelsior	Poor Paul's Place
1980	Doura Royal Scot	Doura Excelsior	Wreford Hewson
1981	Greendykes Excelsior Again	Doura Excelsior	Paul Cooper and Family
1982	Doura Royal Scot	Doura Excelsior	Wreford Hewson
1983	Doura Sensation	Doura Masterstroke	Poor Paul's Place
1984	Doura Sensation	Doura Masterstroke	Poor Paul's Place
1985	Doura Sensation	Doura Masterstroke	Poor Paul's Place

A Royal Winter Fair class of Clydesdales in the showring, 1955. *Photograph by Canada Pictures Limited; courtesy* The Western Producer.

FIGURE 3

Grand Champion Clydesdale Mares, Canadian Royal Winter Fair

Year	Name of Winner	Sire of Winner	Exhibitor
1922	Gleniffer Belle	Lord Gleniffer	Graham Brothers
1923	Bonnie Jean	Bonnie Fyvie	Univ. of Saskatchewan
1924	Crescent Rose	Upperton Prince	W. F. Batty
1925	Crescent Rose	Upperton Prince	W. F. Batty
1926	Deanston Choice	Doune Lodge Revelanta	David Binnie
1927	Doune Lodge Princess	Doune Lodge Sensation	Mrs. W. H. Bryce
1928	Roboline	Ardyne Refiner	A. Cote
1929	Bridgebank Melissa	Dunure Hiawatha	Frank P. O'Connor
1930	Shearington Queen	Graitney Silver	Don Alda Farms
1931	Brunstane Phyllis	Brunstane Again	Don Alda Farms
1932	Brunstane Phyllis	Brunstane Again	Don Alda Farms
1933	Solway Maid	Master Print	Maryvale Farm
1934	Brunstane Phyllis	Brunstane Again	Don Alda Farms
1935	Lady Jean	Renown	R. Duff and Son
1936	Lady Jean	Renown	Don Alda Farms
1937	Lady Lonsdale	Ardyne Refiner	Don Alda Farms
1938	Townhead Anne	Douglas Castle	Windsweet Farms
1939	to 1945, no Royal Winter Fairs owing to World War II		
1946	Peggie Vanguard	Torrs Vanguard	Hon. Mitchell Hepburn
1947	Flora Hiawatha	Hiawatha Refiner	Robert Haining
1948	Lilac Grove Belle	Craigie Elegant	Alvin Taylor
1949	Ratlingate Marigold	Carlyle Castle	Wreford Hewson
1950	Nemesia	Nemesis	Wilson Beaver Stock Farm
1951	Birdhouse Heart's Desire	Boltonhall Ambassador	W. F. Batty and Son
1952	Ratlingate Marigold	Carlyle Castle	Wreford Hewson
1953	Phyllis	Dunmore Fine Art	W. R. Shaw
1954	Ratlingate Marigold	Carlyle Castle	Wreford Hewson
1955	Birdhouse Heart's Desire	Boltonhall Ambassador	W. F. Batty and Son
1956	Bellmont Charm	Doura Obligation	Wreford Hewson
1957	Bellmont Charm	Doura Obligation	Wreford Hewson
1958	Bellmont Charm	Doura Obligation	Wreford Hewson
1959	Balwill Mayflower	Balwill Print	Wreford Hewson
1960	Balwill Mayflower	Balwill Print	Wreford Hewson
1961	Collessie Powerful Link	Muirton Sensation	Wreford Hewson
1962	Clifton Nellie Dene	Balgreen Final Command	Wreford Hewson
1963	Collessie Powerful Link	Muirton Sensation	Wreford Hewson
1964	Clifton Nellie Dene	Balgreen Final Command	Wreford Hewson
1965	Hayston Lucky Girl	Craigie Paramount	Wreford Hewson
1966	Clifton Nellie Dene	Balgreen Final Command	Wreford Hewson
1967	Glororum Maria	Torrs Benefactor	Wreford Hewson

Year	Name of Winner	Sire of Winner	Exhibitor
1968	Clifton Nellie Dene	Balgreen Final Command	Wreford Hewson
1969	Dalfoil Donella	Torrs Renown	Wreford Hewson
1970	Kirklandhill Queen o' Carrick	Doura Excelsior	Wreford Hewson
1971	Clifton Nellie Dene	Balgreen Final Command	Wreford Hewson
1972	Kirklandhill Queen o' Carrick	Doura Excelsior	Wreford Hewson
1973	Kirklandhill Queen o' Carrick	Doura Excelsior	Wreford Hewson
1974	Kirklandhill Queen o' Carrick	Doura Excelsior	Wreford Hewson
1975	Kirklandhill Queen o' Carrick	Doura Excelsior	Wreford Hewson
1976	Kirklandhill Queen o' Carrick	Doura Excelsior	Wreford Hewson
1977	Kirklandhill Queen o' Carrick	Doura Excelsior	Wreford Hewson
1978	Kirklandhill Queen o' Carrick	Doura Excelsior	Wreford Hewson
1979	Kirklandhill Queen o' Carrick	Doura Excelsior	Wreford Hewson
1980	Kirklandhill Queen o' Carrick	Doura Excelsior	Wreford Hewson
1981	Queen of the Shamrocks	Doura Rose Hall Favorite	Paul Cooper Family
1982	Kirklandhill Queen o' Carrick	Doura Excelsior	Wreford Hewson
1983	Kirklandhill Queen o' Carrick	Doura Excelsior	Wreford Hewson
1984	Kirklandhill Queen o' Carrick	Doura Excelsior	Wreford Hewson
1985	Kirklandhill Queen o' Carrick	Doura Excelsior	Wreford Hewson

mares thirty-two times, of which the Queen o' Carrick accounted for no fewer than fifteen, to say nothing of two or three reserve grand championships.

As a Royal record, it surpassed that of any other individual in livestock and it seemed highly improbable that the record would ever be matched in the future.

In addition to her unprecedented list of championships in breeding classes, "The Queen" was driven in numerous hitches, twos, fours, sixes, and eights. Sometimes she was in the lead team, sometimes in the swing, and sometimes in the pole team. "She will take any position and do it well," Hewson said, "and for all the years we have been showing her, I never saw her take a lame step."

She was foaled in Scotland and sired by Doura Excelsior, the stallion presently at the top of the sires of Royal winners list in the 1946 to 1985 period.

Mr. Hewson, on one of his many trips to Scotland, saw Queen o' Carrick as a nursing foal and tried to buy her but the owner would not sell. In the next year, however, after the filly won the coveted Cawdor Cup, Hewson bought her and brought her to her new home. Paul Cooper of Wisconsin tried to buy her from Hewson. Failing that, he bought her sire, the exceptionally successful breeding horse Doura Excelsior.

Mr. Hewson saw Excelsior at the English Royal Show where the young stud placed fourth in a class of four and remarked at the time that he might have the best future of them all. Although tempted to buy him, he realized that with two imported stallions at home he could not justify the purchase of another.

Queen o' Carrick was one of Doura Excelsior's first foals and having bought her, Hewson returned to Scotland expressly to buy more from the same sire. He bought ten more Excelsior fillies which, in large measure,

Kirklandhill Queen o' Carrick, fifteen times grand champion mare at the Royal for Wreford Hewson. *Courtesy Hewson family.*

and won well-deserved admiration. Some of these were Benjamin Rothwell and Wreford Hewson in the East and Robert Sinton, James Burnett, Lawrence Rye, and Alfred Edwin Arnold in the West. There was also Thomas Parker Devlin who, as association secretary and breed authority over many years, served all of Canada.

Of these, Wreford Hewson of Beeton, Ontario, and Eddie Arnold of Shoal Lake, Manitoba, were, at the time these paragraphs were being written, demonstrating that horsemen well beyond the age of eighty can raise and exhibit heavy horses and enjoy doing it. Hewson, who showed his father's horses at the first Royal Winter Fair in Toronto in 1922, and his father's or his own at all other Royal shows to the end of 1985, was unmatched, and Arnold's record was almost as good. The latter exhibited at the Royal Winter Fair in 1925 and could say in 1985 that he had missed only one scheduled show since that time. Such breeders needed nothing more to make their records distinctive.

Robert Sinton was one of the colorful leaders in livestock improvement in the West. He was the frontiersman who, after leaving his home in Beauharnois County, Quebec, arrived at Winnipeg ahead of the rails and drove a horse-drawn wagon to Rapid City, later continuing to the future site of Regina when it was still known as Pile of Bones. Although he settled there to farm he also had the foresight to acquire land that would soon be needed by town developers. The land on which the Legislative Building now stands was once part of farmland for which he paid a pittance. His horse-trading experience proved useful when speculators came to buy land on which

accounted for Excelsior's high rating in the tables shown above.

Seen after winning her fifteenth grand championship at the Canadian Royal in 1985, the eighteen-year-old mare was still the picture of excellence, almost a ton in weight, eighteen hands in height, proud in bearing, and capable of near perfect action. At the Beeton farm she occupied the box stall next to that of the ten-year-old stud header Doura Royal Scot. They constituted a pair that visitors and students of breed history were not likely to forget.

OCTOGENARIAN MAKERS OF HORSE HISTORY

Every breed had its patriarchs, the breeders who by longevity, perseverance, and skill became the leading makers of breed history.

The Clydesdale breed seemed to have a greater-than-average number of octogenarian breeders and exhibitors who defied retirement they suspected the provincial seat of government would be built.

As Sinton told it, the land dealers asked his price and he answered: "$150 an acre." The visitors made a pretense of shock and left saying, "When you decide to take less, we may be interested in buying." After a short time, they were back, asking if he had changed his mind about the price.

"Yes," Sinton replied, "the price is now $250 an acre." The visitors displayed well-rehearsed resistance and made a show of walking away but asked as they were leaving: "For how long will that price stand?" Sinton, taking out his watch, answered: "Sixty seconds." The speculators were eager to get the land and bought 500 acres there and then.

Sinton made his first journey to Scotland to buy Clydesdales in 1908 and before the outbreak of World War I in 1914, he made nine more buying trips. When asked to name the best of the stallions imported, he answered, "Gartly Bonus, champion at the Highland."

When the government of Saskatchewan, in 1920, resolved to do something practical for horse improvement and voted $25,000 for the purchase of the best stallions available in Scotland, Robert Sinton, Dean Rutherford, and William Gibson were the horsemen appointed to constitute a selection committee. As related elsewhere, when the committeemen were unable to buy one of Scotland's outstanding proven sires, they bought two young horses of exceptional promise, Craigie Enchanter and Bonnie Fyvie. When the stallions were about to be shipped, Sinton announced that he was surrendering his reservation for first class accommodation back to Canada because he wanted to travel with the two stallions. And travel with the stallions he did.

Regina's birthday party of the year, 1944, was at the King's Hotel on May 17, marking Mr. Sinton's ninetieth birthday. It was a happy event, looking more like a Clydesdale breeders' reunion than a birthday party. The tall, erect, and still-active guest of honor talked for an hour, relating Clydesdale history and pleading for more humane care for heavy horses that were still man's most faithful and useful servants.

Lawrence Rye of Alberta called himself "the little man with the big horses." He was more than that. Spectators at the ringside of the Royal Winter Fair in November, 1972, were astonished to hear that the little man showing a gelding in the light draft class and then riding high on his heavy wagon in the first team class—placing near the top in both— was Lawrence Rye from Namao, age eighty-nine years. It was his thirty-third year as an exhibitor at the Royal and nobody who knew him was surprised that earlier in the year, this man with unfailing love for Clydesdales and a never-die spirit, was making another Clydesdale importation from Scotland.

Almost exactly eighty years earlier, the nine-year-old Rye arrived with his family from Parry Sound, Ontario, to settle at Namao, north of Edmonton. In coming to the western frontier, the eastern family, as Lawrence Rye told members of the Alberta Historical Society at a meeting in 1960, brought a big stock of what they considered necessities, including flour, tea, sugar, a spinning wheel, a weaver's loom, two sheep, four horses, five cows, "and a black pig."[9]

The lad received his showring initiation at the small fair at St. Albert and then ventured into the stronger competition offered by the Edmonton Exhibition, of which he would some day be the president for two years. But he still had a long way to go. From the Namao farm he seized the opportunity to make a few dollars by hauling hay and green oat sheaves for sale at the Edmonton market, then freighting on the hundred-mile trail to Athabasca Landing. He did not hesitate to say that some of his best boyhood inspirations came when, with an hour or two to spare in Edmonton, he would slip away to the Alexander Galbraith sales barn to study the great horseman's horses and listen to the Galbraith wisdom.

The first purebred Clydesdale mare of importance to Lawrence Rye was Walnut, imported to Ontario about 1910 and soon thereafter bought by Joseph Rye and Son. The new owners bred her and exhibited her successfully and when the Ryes believed they needed a stallion, they bought Sir Valleyview and, a short time later, Esperanto Heir. The latter was a winner at the Edmonton Spring Show of 1918 for the Ryes.

But young Rye was becoming more discriminating and the purchase of the mare Queen Benedict marked the beginning of a long succession of great show and breeding mares. This perhaps reached a pinnacle with the mare Queen of the Roses by Emigrant's Masterpiece, and her daughter, Prairie Rose by Westerton Favorite. The latter mare was the champion Canadian-bred Clydesdale female at the Royal in 1937.

Rye was a firm supporter of the federal government's stallion-loaning policy and a constant spokesman for horsemen who believed they should have more voice in the allocation of the government sires. He praised the provincial government for its purchase of Craigie Masterpiece in 1920 and approved of the horse being kept part-time at Olds College and part-time at the government farm at Oliver.

Lawrence Rye did well showing breeding horses but his heart in later years was in the harness classes in which he achieved a notable triumph at the Royal in 1964. His geldings shown on halter were consistently close to the top in each of their classes. In the team classes he won everything—first for two-horse heavy draft team, first for four-horse team, and first for six-horse team. He won every team class open to him and as he told it with the usual Irish twinkle in his eyes, "My ponies got some extra oats that night."

A. E. Arnold of Shoal Lake, Manitoba, was known to most Canadian horsemen as Eddie, and to many others as "the Clydesdale man." Speaking like a horseman, he said: "People think I've been around horses all my life but that's not so because I was four years old before I had my own Shetland pony."

When he was eighteen years old, he and his brother took their farm horses of unknown breeding to the Shoal Lake fair where they were placed in the general purpose class and won. That modest success was enough to drive the boys to bigger things and in 1924, Eddie Arnold bought a purebred Clydesdale mare, Dora, from an imported dam. That was an important event in the young man's life; in the next year he bought a stallion, Deanston Gallant, from Deanston Farm at St. Charles, Manitoba. The colt had good breeding, sired by Gallant Buchlyvie by Bonnie Buchlyvie and from a mare by Doune Lodge Revelanta.

With mounting ambitions, the young horseman took his small string, including Deanston Gallant, to the East and was encouraged by winning fifth prize at the Royal, second at Guelph, and third at Chicago with his stallion. Better than that, the stallion's offspring were showing up with increasing promise; his first foal, Croydon Ina, won as a two-year-old at Brandon and then first prize and the reserve junior championship at the Royal. Showing at Brandon became a regular performance. He missed it only four times between 1925 and 1984. Competition there was about the strongest to be encountered anywhere except at the Royal. He recalled a 1927 colt class with sixty-five entries in the ring.

The Arnold horses were being seen with the same degree of regularity at the Royal and not many breeders won more championships for Canadian-bred Clydes. Many sales to United States buyers were made at the Royal, among them a colt foal from Croydon Rosemarie that was sold to Paul Cooper of Wisconsin and went on to win the grand championship at the United States National Clydesdale Show.

Arnold would say that one of his best breeding stallions was Commander by Bardrill Castle (imp) and bought from Wreford Hewson. Of that stallion Mr. Arnold said: "I think he was as good a draft stallion as I ever saw but unfortunately, he died with a blood clot before he was four years old."

Eddie Arnold wrote further: "The last horse I owned was one of the best, Torrs Reformer (imp), that I bought at the Highland Show in 1983. He was second and reserve champion at that show and later junior champion and reserve grand champion at the Canadian Royal in 1983. At the Royal of 1984, he was again junior champion and reserve grand champion."[10]

It was Mr. Arnold's last show. He was eighty-six years of age and knew he had to quit sometime. But he had a good philosophy: "Horses kept me busy for most of my life but being busy with good Clydesdales has been a lot of fun."

He was honored on many occasions with scrolls, testimonial banquets, gifts, life memberships, and admittance to the Manitoba Agricultural Hall of Fame. He never married but had a good life and intended to have more of it in the Shoal Lake community where he was born in 1898 and to which he and his Clydesdales attracted national and international attention.

James Burnett of Napinka, Manitoba, bred, exhibited, and judged Clydesdales for some sixty years after his name appeared as the owner of the stallion Prince of Tay in volume I of the *Canadian Clydesdale Stud Book*. In 1940 the Clydesdale Horse Association of Canada was recognizing the hundredth anniversary of the arrival of the stallion Cumberland, the first purebred Clydesdale in Canada. At that point the significant role of two pioneer breeders was noted. Of all the horsemen whose names appeared as either breeders or owners in the first volume of the stud book, only two were still alive and active—James Burnett of Manitoba and Benjamin Rothwell of Ontario. Ben Rothwell was on record as the importer of the Clydesdale stallion Young Topsman, brought to Canada in 1876. And James Burnett, mentioned previously, was shown as second owner of Prince of Tay.

Moreover, as many Canadians recall, Mr. Burnett had a good memory and a good sense of humor. When he arrived at North Battleford to judge the horses at the summer exhibition about 1935, the hotel clerk asked: "Do you wish a room with bath?"

The horseman, then in his seventies, grinned and asked: "Do I look as though I needed a bath? I'm here to judge horses and they are the cleanest creatures in God's world. I'll save the government a few dollars and take a room without a bath. Anyway, it's just a mile to the river."

He liked to draw upon his memory of the spirited days when Clydesdale horses filled the showrings. Thomas P. Devlin, secretary of the Clydesdale Horse Association of Canada in 1945, shared a letter he had received from Mr. Burnett, then in his late eighties, in which the writer was recalling the Brandon Winter Fair in the spring of 1912 and the buoyant state of horse breeding in Canada:

"There were 41 Clydesdale stallions shown in the three-year-old class and in the two-year-old class there were 23 out. The horse that won the three-year-old class that day was Dunure Sparkling Hope (imp), shown by A. and G. Mutch of Lumsden and later owned by Jock Falconer. In the two-year-old class, the first prize winner was Fyvie Stamp (imp), owned by R. H. Taber, Condie, Sask. Burnett was in third position with Baron Rozelle (imp) and McKirdy Bros., Napinka, were fourth with Crowned King."[11]

The pioneer horseman's lingering reaction to those massive classes was stated succinctly in a further quotation from his letter: "Those were the days of real shows when competition was so keen that many a good horse was given the gate as the judging ring was so crowded that they had to weed out a lot to make room for the others to display their paces."

The horsemen of 1912 were making history and Jim Burnett was recording it, probably unconsciously.

Benjamin Rothwell, father of George Rothwell who was an extremely able director of Production Services in Canada's Department of Agriculture, was a source of inspiration to many young horsemen. "The dean of North American breeders of Clydesdales" was the way he was described at the time of his death in March, 1944. He was an enthusiastic horseman to the last when he died at the age of ninety-five years. As one of the two survivors whose names appeared in the first Canadian stud book, he became an object of prime interest to students of horse history when the Canadian Clydesdale Horse Association was celebrating the hundredth anniversary of the arrival of the first purebred Clydesdale on Canadian soil.

The initial Rothwell importation accounting for the stud book entry of Young Topsman, foaled in 1874, furnished the added information that he was "imported September 17, 1876, by Benjamin Rothwell, Ottawa."

Volume XXXVI of the Canadian stud book, published fifty-eight years later, showed eleven new registrations in the name of the same Benjamin Rothwell, most of them filly and colt foals, sired by Craigie Fitz Gallant. His sire had been the most famous Scottish stallion of that period, Craigie Beau Ideal. Craigie Fitz Gallant was imported in 1937, the last foreign purchase by Mr. Rothwell who was then eighty-eight years old. He had been going back to Scotland for sires throughout the years, and the stallion

Brunstane Zenith, an importation of 1932, became his best showhorse. With his ageless owner at the halter shank, this stallion won the grand championship at the Canadian Royal Winter Fair in 1932. The loud cheers from the rows of spectators were as much for the eighty-three-year-old horseman as for the grand champion stallion.

Thomas P. Devlin, a 1925 graduate in agriculture from the University of Alberta, was for many years Canada's most widely acknowledged authority on Clydesdale history, Clydesdale pedigrees, and Clydesdale type. Born in Ayrshire, Scotland, in 1899, he grew up in the heart of the Clydesdale country and throughout his long life was completely dedicated to the breed.

After graduation, Tom Devlin spent some time as livestock editor of the *Nor'-West Farmer*, Winnipeg, and then accepted a position with the Canadian National Railway Department of Colonization and Agriculture, with offices successively in Winnipeg, Saskatoon, Montreal, and back to Winnipeg.

With his enduring love for the Scottish breed, he might have preferred to be breeding and showing Clydesdales, but he was never very far removed from them and nobody knew more about what was taking place in the stables and showrings of Canada, the United States, and Scotland.

He judged on numerous occasions at the biggest shows in Canada and the States, including the Canadian Royal and Chicago International. It is doubtful if anybody since the time of Alex Galbraith received more horse judging calls and assignments, and he did not allow his octogenarian years to end his judging ring activities.

But in direct service to the Clydesdale breeders of Canada, Tom Devlin's best contributions were through the offices of secretary-treasurer, first for the Manitoba Clydesdale Club and then for the Clydesdale Horse Association of Canada. The positions were never financially rewarding and he enriched the organized breeders more than they enriched him.

It was in the early forties that Devlin became the man of the hour for the Canadian association. The horse business was failing. Association revenue was falling. There was a big overdraft at the bank and directors meeting on February 3, 1944, were presented unexpectedly with the resignation of the incumbent secretary-treasurer.

Something had to be done quickly. But, horsemen being generally resourceful and practical, the directors acted forthwith, sending a telegram to Tom Devlin in Winnipeg and then adjourning until the next day. The minutes of the reconvened meeting on February 4 tell everything in a few words:

"In a reply to a wire to T. P. Devlin of Winnipeg the previous evening asking him to be secretary-treasurer at $100 honorarium for a year, a wire in reply was read, stating that if he could help the Association, he would do so."

From that date forward the association had the benefit of Devlin's experience and judgment, and no salary problems arose. At the end of 1944, the directors voted an additional honorarium of $100, or $10 per month, for stenographic services, and in 1945 the executive approved the sum of $100 per year to go toward the secretary-treasurer's expenses. It is doubtful if a secretary, who was more of a counsellor and general manager,

Octogenarian Wreford Hewson driving a team of Clydesdales at the Royal Winter Fair, circa 1980. *Courtesy Hewson family.*

had ever performed more service for less monetary return.

Wreford Hewson of Beeton, Ontario, was the horseman's horseman—practical, forthright, durable, and individualistic. At eighty-three years of age in 1986, he was the only stockman living who could tell of exhibiting purebred draft horses at every Canadian Royal Winter Fair from its inception in 1922.

When a visitor from the West called at the Hewson farm on a Sunday morning in March, 1986, the horseman was found doing the usual chores in a stable where over a hundred purebred Clydesdales and Percheron horses were fed and sheltered regularly on winter nights. Chores on such a scale are a big task and would, quite properly, have first call upon the horseman's time. The visitor, eager to engage the distinguished horse breeder in conversation about his long experience with many of the country's best horses

and horsemen, offered to remove his coat and help clean the stable. The proprietor's reply was short and easy to comprehend: "The way you can help me is to stay to hell out of my way until I'm finished. Then we'll talk."

Needless to say, the hint was accepted without argument and in due course the two men of similar ages settled down like a teacher and pupil to review Clydesdale history in Canada and make the ensuing few hours both entertaining and enlightening.

The distinguished breeder of Clydesdales—and a few Percherons—was born on the parental farm at Malton on July 4, 1903. His father Albert Hewson brought his Cleveland Bay mare, Maud, to the kitchen door and held his newborn son on the mare's back for a moment. If the ritual was intended to ensure a long and successful life with horses, it seemed to bear results.

The Hewsons were Yorkshire people and one of them was said to have signed the death warrant of England's King Charles I who governed without calling Parliament for eleven years. Members of the family performed their full share of toil in converting the Upper Canada bush to cultivated fields. When seven years old Wreford showed his first horse, a Shetland pony mare, at Malton fair and won the class. It was about this time that the boy's father bought his first purebred Clydesdale mare, an event of importance for both father and son.

In 1922, year of the first Canadian Royal Winter Fair, the nineteen-year-old Wreford was exhibiting some of his father's Clydes and participating in the intercounty judging contests, having been chosen for a place on the Peel County team being coached by J. A. Carroll of the provincial Department of

Agriculture. The Peel team won the competition. But there were bigger things ahead. The young fellow obtained his own Clydesdales and as they increased in numbers and quality, he won more prizes at the bigger shows. He showed at the International at Chicago in 1941 and won a junior championship for females and a senior championship for males.

Still more important, he married in 1927 and in 1986, Wreford and Alice Hewson celebrated their sixtieth wedding anniversary. In 1971, they moved to the farm at Beeton where their Clydesdales gained even more fame. To obtain what Wreford Hewson believed he needed for his purpose, he began importing from Scotland and crossed the Atlantic twenty-four times for one purpose or another—always related to horses.

Three times he judged Clydesdales at the Scottish Highland Show, four times at the Chicago International Fat Stock Show, several times at state fairs, and once at the Melbourne Royal Show in Australia. On one occasion he was invited to drive a four-horse team at the Scottish Highland—a team owned by Peter Sharp—and he had the satisfaction of seeing one of his Ontario-bred stallions, Doura Magnificent by Melbourne Royal Ideal, being purchased by John Young for breeding in the homeland. Not only that, but the Hewson-bred stud distinguished itself as a breeder in Scotland.

During one of their last visits to Scotland, the Ontario horseman and his wife were the guests of honor at a banquet, in the course of which the Hewsons were presented with a large silver tray engraved with the message: "Presented to Wreford and Alice Hewson by their Scottish Clydesdale friends."

Not only did Hewson win a lion's share of the Clydesdale breeding classes—ten times

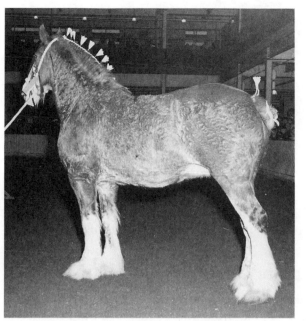

Clifton Nellie Dean, grand champion mare at the Royal Winter Fair, 1962, '64, '66, and '68 for Wreford Hewson. *Courtesy Frank Martin.*

Bardrill Vintage, grand champion Clydesdale stallion at the Royal, 1968, for Wreford Hewson. *Courtesy Frank Martin.*

the winner of the grand championship for stallions at the Canadian Royal Winter Fair and thirty-two times winner of the grand award for mares at the same show up to the end of 1985—but his record in team classes was scarcely less impressive. He won the six-horse-team class for the first time at the Royal in 1938 and then fourteen times thereafter. It was an amazing score, and there was more to it. The eighty-three-year-old who would not accept help for his morning chores believed he had thirty mares in foal, surely a classic demonstration of optimism.

The Clydesdale Today

Clydesdales were the favored horses in pioneer Canada, everywhere except in the Province of Quebec. If there was such a thing as a national breed, it had to be the Clyde. British settlers, bespeaking a Scottish and English ideal, said: "No foot, no horse," and gave the impression that nothing counted for much except feet and legs. Too often, symmetry, muscling, and constitution were overlooked. There were warnings, some of them from loyal friends of the breed like Alexander Galbraith, that farmers would soon demand more thickness and weight, but the entrenched showring ideals were difficult to change.

But the Clydesdale was changed, slowly, and those members of the breed that retained the clean, sharp bone in feet and legs, the best of action, the attractive white markings in feet and face along with heavier and better bodies, were able to consolidate a slight edge of favor for show teams and street use by brewery firms.

Even as late as 1935, the Canadian National Live Stock Records could report 1,220 Clydesdale registrations in Canada, compared with 922 Percherons, 265 Belgians, 18 Suffolks, and 6 Shires. By that time, however, Belgian and Percheron popularity was on the ascendancy and the Clydesdale majority was slipping.

Annual registration totals fell for all the draft breeds, but faster for Clydesdales than for Percherons and Belgians. When interest in the heavies revived in the seventies, the recovery pace was much faster for the Belgians and Percherons than for the Clydesdales. In 1985, new Clydesdale registrations numbered 236, which was less than 13 percent of the total of 1,856 for the three leading breeds.

Ontario was still the best supporter of the Clydesdale, as it had been over the years. To indicate the breed's distribution in Canada, 105 of the new registrations in 1985 came from Ontario, 34 from Saskatchewan, 34 from Alberta, 28 from Quebec, 12 from Manitoba, 8 from Prince Edward Island, 7 from New Brunswick, 3 from British Columbia, and 1 from the United States. The Clydesdale Horse Association of Canada had 228 active members and 39 life members. The registrations and memberships were comparatively low but the scattered loyalties to the old Scottish breed were still strong.

The Percheron

Big and Beautiful

A search for Percheron roots leads to three distinct and powerful areas of influence in the homeland: first, the ancient and unrefined Flemish horses of western Europe; second, the transforming force of the North African and Arabian horses left behind by an army in flight; and, third, and comparatively recently, the united pursuit of clearly defined type and performance ideals by French horsemen in the lovely old district of La Perche, south-west of Paris.

Big and rough Flemish horses bespeaking antiquity were probably common ancestors of all British and European breeds of heavy horses. But the Percheron, more than the others, owed its early improvement to the circumstances of invasion and the unexpected genetic inheritance from the defeated invaders' horses.

The Saracen and Moor cavalrymen from North Africa, riding what must have been the best Barb, Turk, and Arabian horses in the world at that time, triumphed as they drove westward across their own continent and in Spain. Intoxicated by repeated victories, they crossed the Pyrenees to add France to a proud string of successes. But, handicapped by the mounting distance from their home bases, they were soundly beaten by the French resistance led by Charles Martel at Tours and Poitiers in the year 732 A.D.

The victorious French were probably inspired by their new horses almost as much as from the military success and distributed the horses, most of which were stallions, the general favorites for cavalry use at that period. Interbreeding these new stallions with native mare stock brought greatly improved horses and revised ideals about quality and type.

Additional infusions of the so-called Oriental breeding may have been made with stallions brought to France by Crusaders returning from the Holy Land in the eleventh, twelfth, and thirteenth centuries. The use of outside bloodlines was important, but the most spectacular progress in horse improvement was in one particular district of old Normandy, the well-favored province of La Perche which is no longer shown on most maps.

To understand any breed of animal, the student or breeder would do well to begin by gaining a reader's familiarity with the region of origin which, in the case of the Percheron, was that rich agricultural area centered by the City of Nogent le Rotrou, some seventy-five miles from Paris and entitled to be called the heartland of a breed.

The countryside is gently rolling, cut by small rivers and decked with greenery denoting good soil and ample rainfall. Temperatures are moderate and the farm scenes are idyllic with hedgerows separating fields and farms to give a checkerboard effect. Real estate salesmen in the La Perche region should find it easy to sell farms.

This district is old in occupation but it was only in comparatively recent times that it gained its widely recognized and well-deserved distinction in horse breeding. The strains that combined to make a breed were old but the Percheron horse of current size and type is young. As recently as the 1830s the popular horse of La Perche was one of general purpose or diligence type, medium in size, active, tireless, and a specialist in pulling the cumbersome French diligence or public stagecoach at a lively speed over the rough and often wet roads of the time. Weight would range between thirteen hundred and sixteen hundred pounds, and height was commonly at fifteen hands. A bold, straight, and snappy action was demanded and endurance was a similar necessity in horses expected to maintain a fast gait mile after mile. One authority cited examples of road performances in La Perche during the 1860s. A mare, Julie, ran a mile and a quarter in three minutes and fifty seconds in 1864; another one, Sarah, ran two miles in six minutes and two seconds in 1865; and Decidée, harnessed and drawing a load of 386 pounds, made two and three-fifths miles in nine minutes and twenty-one seconds in 1864.

Most La Perche horsemen fancied long manes, and grey or white horses were favored for stagecoach work because they could be seen readily at night. A French writer described as a local historian added that the La Perche horses becoming known as Percherons and used "for the post and messagery service" possessed courage, strength, and longevity, rendering them "extremely precious and though they rarely exceeded four feet and nine inches in height, [14½ hands] they were good for all kinds of work. To their excellent constitution were added perfect legs and unwearable feet."[1]

From the same source came information about changes in La Perche horse breeding policy in the years after 1820. An agricultural committee was formed at Nogent le Rotrou under the chairmanship of Le Comte de Bussy who acted at once to bring in two Arabian stallions, Godolphin and Gallipoli, to stand for service at the government horse farm at Le Pin. This institution appears to have been started in 1714, destroyed during the French Revolution, and restored by Emperor Napoleon in 1806. The two Arabian stallions, according to the early report, brought tone to the Percheron breed and fixed the color "at a dappled grey."

Increasingly, the official emphasis was directed at greater size in horses and more suitability for the needs of agriculture. Fairs offering prizes for the best horses became important instruments in improvement. At the same time, superior breeding horses were

gaining attention, one of the first signs of progress in breed building.

Most notable among the early sires was the white Jean le Blanc, foaled in 1823. He was either a son or a grandson of the imported Arabian Gallipoli and came to be recognized as a cornerstone of the breed. Yet, strange to say, there have been responsible students of the breed who argued that the famous Jean le Blanc never actually lived at all, that he was nothing more than a legend. Until there is better proof that the great grey stud was only the product of some fertile imagination, however, he should be treated as though he were real, handsome, powerful, prepotent, and much alive until he died at the age of thirty-two.

The Percheron was not the only draft breed to be developed in France, although it is generally agreed to be the best and was the only one to gain popularity abroad. There were also the Boulonnais from the vicinity of Boulogne, the Ardennais from Northern France, the Nivernais from the central part, and the Bretonnais from Brittany. The Percheron was the only one to make friends around the world.

The transformation from a middleweight diligence horse to an agricultural draft type was hastened about 1840 when railways were displacing horse-drawn stages. As the market for diligence horses failed, the demand for heavier animals for street use in conjunction with drays and lorries grew, and buyers came to purchase stallions of the heavier kind for export. Being eager to take advantage of the changing markets, La Perche breeders were suspected of taking a short cut to the goal of size by introducing big stallions of the old Flemish strain, still to be found outside of their region. Whether such out-crosses were made or not, there is no reason for believing the main strides of progress in the advance to greater size without loss of quality were not made by the more tedious but safer technique of simple selection of superior types. In any case, the La Perche horse breeders experienced a boom-time market for their stock, so favorable that many local producers sold themselves short of breeding animals and regretted it later.

Horse breeding in the Percheron area over the years was in the hands of two classes of producers: first, the mare owners operating small farms and regularly breeding their approved mares; and second, the keepers of and dealers in stallions, generally on larger farms and ever ready to buy, sell, or lease their goods. To members of this group, the owners of small bands of mares sold their young stallions, sometimes before they reached weaning age.

Stallions standing for public service were required to be inspected by government-appointed officers who could recommend outstanding horses for government subsidies, generous enough to largely ensure against removal from the country. On the other hand, stallions found to have hereditary unsoundnesses or plainly objectionable traits could be denied a permit for public use. It was part of the public policy to prevent the best breeding stock from leaving the country and inferior animals from perpetuating their kind.

The French breeders were most successful in interpreting the requirements of their overseas customers and bred accordingly. It was doubtful, however, if the Percheron producers in the homeland ever became quite as enthusiastic about size and weight as the North American buyers. The United States and Canada became the best overseas markets for the Percherons but Argentina and other South American countries, Russia, Spain, and Austria took sizable numbers too.

Britain, with three breeds of draft horses of British origin, was relatively late in adopting Percherons, but the British experience with horses of all breeds in the South African war and later in World War I, left observers with an enthusiastic interest. In both wars, Percheron hardiness and the versatility typical of the old diligence horses increased the breed's usefulness, and its popularity was not forgotten in postwar years. An English survey conducted soon after the South African war showed that 90 percent of the London bus horses were grade Percherons brought from the United States and Canada. Shortly thereafter, purebred Percherons were imported from France to become England's fourth breed of heavies and one to enjoy almost instant popularity.[2]

As with most breeds, Percheron history recorded many names that became familiar to horsemen everywhere. Members of the Perriot family stood out prominently. Louis Perriot, who died in 1920 at the age of eighty-five, began breeding Percherons in France in 1859. His sons Edmond and Ernest continued to breed Percherons. Ernest was largely instrumental in founding France's *Percheron Stud Book*, became a national figure, and died in 1922. Professor A. B. Cain of Iowa State College reported that M. W. Dunham had estimated his payments for Percherons bought from Ernest Perriot for shipment to the United States at not less than $350,000. Perriot also made sales to American buyers during the Paris Exposition of 1900—at which he won many prizes and championships for his horses—to the amount of $100,000. Among famous horses bred by this horseman were Brilliant, a second Brilliant, Brilliant 3rd, Fenelon, Voltaire, Briard, and Villers.

Other French families of note in Percheron horse history included the Tacheaus and the Avelines. August Tacheau Jr. bred the stallion Seducteur; Charles Aveline, founder of the French Percheron society and for many years its president, bred the noted stallions Dragon and Etudiant.

Charles Aveline's son Louis became well known in Percheron circles in the United States and Canada and was particularly friendly with George Lane of Bar U fame. His grandson, Robert Aveline, was at the time of writing, the very active president of the Percheron Society of France.

As for Percheron horses in contemporary France, an account printed in the Canadian breed publication, the *Broadcaster*, in March, 1978, reported total Percheron registrations for the country during 1974 at 550.[3] That would compare with 157 new registrations for the breed in Canada in the same year.

The report also conveyed some enlightening information on other Percheron matters, including colors. Canada and the United States, where black is the dominant Percheron color, never followed French preferences and France never adopted North American fancies. Greys continue to outnumber blacks by a wide margin in the homeland. Of the 76 stallions registered in the year under report, 66 were greys and 10 blacks. Of the 474 mares registered, the division was 353 greys, 118 blacks, and three bays.

The same source of information conveyed some points of interest about leading Percheron shows. At the Le Pin show and sale, for example, forty-two stallions of the breed were presented for competition. Height seemed to be given more consideration than weight in determining size; height measurements ranged to a maximum of seventeen hands.

Robert Aveline, president of the Percheron Horse Society of France, was among the exhibitors and sold four stallions. The government representative responsible for the administration of the public stud farms bought ten stallions at the sale, paying the equivalent of from $3,550 to $4,400 in Canadian money for them.

To give some idea of the size of the breeding program conducted on and from these government stud farms, the Le Pin farm was reported to have twenty-one breeding stallions, all greys except one; the St. Lo farm

Leroy, one of the best specimens of the Percheron type which will be remembered by older breeders. Owned and shown by Jonathon Fox, Jr. This picture was taken at the Edmonton Spring Show of 1944 where Leroy won the grand championship. *Photograph by Ashdown Johnson.*

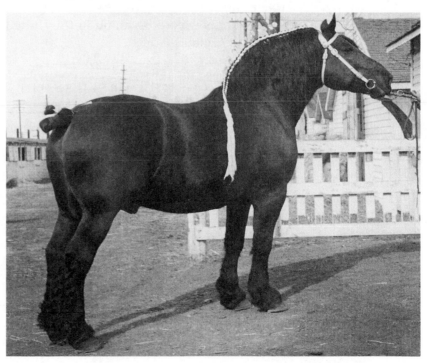

had twenty-two stallions, all greys except two; and the Lion d'Angers place had thirty-one, all greys except three. The essential point is that horse breeding continues to be bolstered by the government-backed stud farms and the mares bred on the ten such farms in 1977 numbered 2,377.

There are other breeds of French horses but the Percheron, said one of the French breeders proudly, "is the only breed to have foreign stud books." Canada and the United States, after gaining large Percheron populations of their own, almost ceased to be importers. But France, since 1951, has exported Percherons in modest numbers to Argentina, the United Kingdom, Chile, Poland, Spain, Germany, South Africa, Mexico, Ireland, Yugoslavia, Holland and Japan, with the latter being the biggest customer of them all.[4] At the same time, the biggest overseas concentration of Percherons was to be found in the United States and Canada.

VANGUARD OF THE BREED IN THE UNITED STATES AND CANADA

Horses sent from France to the colony on the St. Lawrence River in 1665 were the first of the domesticated race to set foot on what was to become Canadian soil. They had, no doubt, more admirers than a visiting prince. They were the predominantly black horses that gave rise to the intensely hard, all-purpose Canadien or French-Canadien breed. Nobody could have questioned fairly the versatility and usefulness of the strain. The animals may have been related to the French stock from which the Percheron breed came, but they had no claim at that early period to the Percheron name. The real Percherons from the Province of La Perche would come later.

How much later is a matter of some speculation. The American authority on Percheron history, Alvin Howard Sanders, displayed interest in a French stallion, a dapple grey described only as a Norman horse, brought to Lower Canada in 1816. Known as the McNitt horse, he was recognized as of the type favored in France at the time, obviously of the diligence type. His weight was twelve hundred pounds, his height between 15.2 and 15.3 hands, and he could trot with the best of them. But after speculating with the idea of the grey stud being the first Percheron on this side of the Atlantic, the author practically dispelled the thought, noting that the French government, at the time, was only beginning to pursue the goal of heavier horses in the region of La Perche.

The McNitt horse was taken from Canada to New York State where he and his progeny became popular, although still without the benefit of the Percheron name.[5] Not until 1839 were the first Percherons of proven identity—four head—brought to the United States. Sad to say, only one mare survived the troubled journey but instead of abandoning the purpose, the importer, Edward Harris of Moorestown, New Jersey, returned overseas to buy two Percheron stallions and two mares. His luck was somewhat better this time, but horsemen are never fully shielded from reverses. One mare died soon after arrival and one stallion vanished into obscurity. The other stallion, Diligence by name, proved to be an overwhelming breeding success. He lived to the age of twenty years and was reported to have left 400 offspring bearing the marks of his quality and worth.

Still more lasting was the contribution of two stallions imported from France to Dr. Marcus Brown of Ohio in 1851. One of these, Louis Napoleon, was taken to Illinois, and the other, Normandy—better known as Old Pleasant Valley Bill—spent his years in Ohio which was to become a leading state in Percheron breeding. Of Old Bill, it was told that he left an average of sixty foals per year for eighteen years and his offspring sold at premiums from "$50 to $125 over the common stock of the country."[6]

Louis Napoleon was not well received. He, too, was a grey but heavier—about sixteen hundred pounds in weight—and being blocky in shape, he was criticized by some horsemen who said he was bound to be clumsy. One of the critics reasoned that if he wanted an ox, he'd get one with horns. Hence, Louis Napoleon's use in his first years in the country was limited, but his popularity improved after his first foals appeared. Three years after his arrival in the district of Columbus, Ohio, this horse that cost his importer $350 in France, changed hands for $1500 and was bought in 1858 by the rising Percheron breeders, the Dillons of Normal, Illinois. The stud died at twenty-three years of age. But with practically no mares of pure breeding in the country, it was impossible for a stallion, regardless of his breeding powers, to make more than a slight impact upon a breed's future. And like all the early French horses in the United States and Canada, Old Bill and Louis Napoleon were still known as Normans, regardless of what part of France they came from. Some people argued with success that they should be called French Draft. The National Association of Importers and Breeders of Norman Horses was organized at Chicago in

1876 and two years later the name was changed to Percheron and Norman Horses.

Even before an organization meeting, J. H. Saunders, who took one of the first French stallions to the State of Iowa eight years before, set himself the task of gathering pedigree records in anticipation of a stud book. He saw them used for the preparation of the first stud book for draft horses on either side of the Atlantic, and the second book for horses of any breed. The world's first was the *General Stud Book of England* published for Thoroughbreds. Saunders' book carried the breed name Percheron-Norman.

The truce between the Percheron and Norman factions did not last long. Those who supported the Norman name—including the Dillons—went along with the *National Registry of Norman Horses* while the Percheron group proceeded to publish the *Percheron Stud Book*. After more debate a reorganization produced the Percheron Horse Society of America and in 1934, the Percheron Horse Association of America.

Importations from France to the United States became more numerous. Thirty-one Percheron stallions were imported in 1868. E. Dillon and Co. were importing by this time and William Singmaster of Iowa, another who was to become widely known, began in 1874. But it was the entry of M. W. Dunham of Oaklawn Farm, Wayne, Illinois, into the dual business of importing and breeding in 1868 that made the year one of singular importance in North American Percheron history. It was estimated that half of the horses imported to the United States in the seventies came to the orders of Mark W. Dunham.

W. L. Ellwood added his name to the list of early importers and breeders in 1881 and distinguished himself by placing greater emphasis upon size as shown by height and weight of horses. But the main feature of the period was to be found in 1881 when Leonard Johnson of Minnesota imported the black stallion Brilliant and Mark Dunham imported the four-year-old black stud, a second named Brilliant, sire and son respectively. Both horses had been in service in France. The arrival of these two horses was of great significance to the breed in the United States and Canada, as nothing like it had happened before and it is doubtful if anything like it has happened since. So impressed was Mark Dunham by the first foal crop from these stallions that he bought thirty young horses sired by the two Brilliants in France, probably the best Percherons in the world at that time.

The most important advances in American Percheron breeding came with the two Brilliants, father and son, and then Dunham's purchase of Brilliant 3rd, considered the greatest Percheron in France when he was bought in 1889. The benefit was felt in Canada about as much as in the United States.

It was a wonder that the French horsemen allowed the two older Brilliants to leave the country, especially after they had proven themselves as breeders of rare distinction in the stud of Ernest Perriot. The younger Brilliant was retained in Mark Dunham's Oaklawn stud in Illinois for the balance of his long life and came to be recognized as the greatest sire of the breed. The older Brilliant, weighing nineteen hundred pounds and standing slightly more than sixteen hands, might have been an equal if he had the opportunity to head a band of mares with the individuality of those at Oaklawn.

The best return from the imported Brilliants was not realized until later when the progeny of the two stallions were line-bred to produce a surprisingly large percentage of the showring and breeding leaders in Percheron history. Even in France, most of the outstanding Percherons of the last two decades of the nineteenth century traced to one or both of the two Brilliants that had been allowed to leave the country in 1881. The three stallions, Brilliant 3rd, Seducteur, and Marathon, all grandsons of the younger Brilliant and pronounced the best showhorses in France in their earlier years, were from mares sired by the older Brilliant.

In the United States and later in Canada, one of the leading lines of descent was through Brilliant 3rd, the grandson of the younger Brilliant, foaled in France in 1884 and somewhat handicapped in later years by what appeared to be founder. The famous Calypso, chosen in 1936 to portray the ideal type in Percheron stallions, was another great grandson of Brilliant 3rd. The celebrated Carnot was a fifth generation offspring of Brilliant 3rd; Job and Monarch of Canadian fame were fifth and sixth generations respectively.

The Brilliant impact was no less evident in other lines. Seducteur was a grandson of the younger Brilliant from whose line came Laet, Rolaet, Cy Laet, Monarch's Sir Laet, Drake Farm's Laet, Drake Farm's Leonet, Sir Laet, Lo Lynd Douglas, Chief Laet, Colonsay Prince, Morden Chief, Don Laet, Donald Laet, Drake Farms Chief, Maverick, and La Don's Koncarnona Hector.

Carnot's line shows Jehovah, Dean, Captivator, Don Degas, and Lynnwood Don; and Calypso's line, Koncarcalyps, Enchanter,

Kadella U. A., Koncarhope, Riverbend Monkoncarlaet, Justamere Showtime, Justamere Par Excellent, and Ricinus Koncarlaet.

These and many more well known names from Percheron history in Canada and the United States give weight to the sense of respect displayed for the two Brilliants imported in 1881.

There were other lines of breeding, to be sure, especially in France, but it has been said that all North American Percherons of the present time can be found to trace in one ancestral line or another to the elder Brilliant and many of them could boast a direct sire line to one of the Brilliants if not all three of the famous breed builders. Hence, the Canadian Percheron heritage is so interwoven with that of the United States, it would be extremely difficult to draw lines of separation. A good Percheron pedigree to American breeders is a good pedigree to their Canadian counterparts and vice versa. Canadian and American breeders meet in international competitions and admit proudly that their type ideals and traditions are co-equals. They will readily cross the border in their search for sires and breeding stock and still guard their fierce independence and the independence of their respective organizations. Canada had its own pioneers with Percherons and Canadians will tell their own story about struggles, problems, and triumphs. It is entirely laudable that there be two overlapping breed histories which neighboring horsemen can study and enjoy together.

The Percheron breed was later in starting and slower in maturing in Canada than in the neighboring country. British settlers to Canada brought their own breed preferences with them, often very rigid ones, and the first Clydesdales were well ahead of the first Percherons in point of time. They remained ahead in popularity and numbers for some decades.

A few of Canada's foundation Percherons were imported directly from France but most by far were stallions and mares imported to or raised in the United States before being sold into Canada. And the name encountered most often in any study of pioneer Percheron transactions is that of Mark Dunham, the man to whom Canadians as well as Americans have a big debt for the quality and numbers of good breeding stock he distributed across the continent. More than that, Dunham was a kindly and admirable personality of whom horsemen could be proud. Alvin Sanders who knew him well, said he

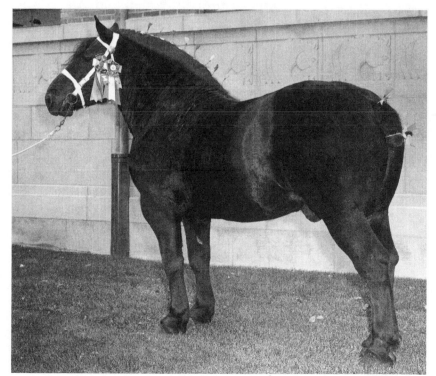

Colonsay Prince, three times grand champion stallion at the Royal Winter Fair, 1968, '69, and '70, for Patrick J. Hendrick. His lineage can be traced through Seducteur, one of the best showhorses in France at the end of the nineteenth century, directly to the younger Brilliant.

was "first of all a good farmer," presiding over "the greatest triumph ever known in draft horse breeding."[7]

J. and A. W. Pringle of Ayr, Ontario, bought the imported French stallion Dauntless from M. W. Dunham in 1878 and had the courage to take him to the staunchly Clydesdale-biased home district. The horse was a grey and three years old at the time of purchase and, sad to say, not much more is now known about him. Nor is there much more that can be reported about another grey, the imported stallion Arthur, foaled in 1880 and bought from Dunham along with a grey mare, Peerless, by Ballachey Brothers of Brantford in 1881. It is known that the mare in the Ballachey deal produced a filly foal in 1882 and another in '83 that was sold to the Ontario firm of Brickman and Baker, who showed determination by going at once to buy a highly regarded stallion, Producteur, from Dunham.

But what of direct importations from France to Canada? Such a procedure was not as simple as crossing the border to Wayne, Illinois, and buying from Mark Dunham, but Canadians were trying it. The McGarvin Brothers of Chatham, who were ultimately breeding Percherons in a fairly substantial way, may have made their start with the imported stallion Mouton and four imported mares: Lissette, Silphide, Castelle, and Blanchette, all immigrants of 1884.

Another direct importation made about the same time held special interest for students of Percheron pedigrees. It saw P. Whelihan of St. Mary's, Ontario, bringing in the mare Maud and stallion Prince of Normandy, the latter a black three-year-old sired by none other than the incomparable younger Brilliant. Unfortunately, in coming to Canada he lost the chance to mate with more than a small number of purebred mares and his full potential was not realized. But horsemen travelled great distances to see him and argue and admire. In a rural Ontario community where a new horse was always an attraction, he would be enough to leave Shakespearean scholars—if there were any—muttering:

> So did this horse excell a common one,
> In shape, in courage, color, pace and bone, . . .
>
> Look, what a horse should have, he did not lack,
> Save a proud rider on as proud a back.

A grey daughter from Maud and Prince of Normandy, Rose, was foaled in 1887 but, as might have been feared, she was quickly snatched up by an American buyer.

The Percheron stallion Dean, grand champion at the Royal in 1930 and 1931, for C. M. Rear of Regina. Dean's credentials come through Carnot, a fifth generation offspring of Brilliant 3rd. *Photograph by Live Stock Photo Co.; courtesy* The Western Producer.

Another Brilliant was brought from France to Nova Scotia in 1888, this one registered as Brilliant 22nd, the new property of F. H. Black of Amherst. Actually, there were dozens of stallions being given the Brilliant name in France and confusion resulted. In some cases the horses so named had no blood relationship to the two famous stallions that made the name popular and breeders were warned of possible misrepresentations. Still another famous French name came to Canada in 1889 with the imported stallion Bayard that was brought by way of the United States to the School of Agriculture at La Trappe, Quebec.

As might have been expected, the first purebred Percherons to make appearance in the new West of Canada were later than in the East. George Lane, about whom more is related on another page, was the distinguished western pioneer whose influence was national as much as regional. Robert Reid of Forrest was one of the first Percheron breeders in Manitoba; R. P. Stanley of Moosomin may have been the first with purebreds in the Northwest Territories, and J. Roper Hull, widely known rancher and "meat king," appears to have been responsible for the first purebred Percherons in British Columbia.

The financial depression that struck Canada and the United States in the nineties and gave all businesses, including horse breeding and importing, a setback, had almost vanished by the beginning of the century and Percheron fortunes improved greatly. The Canadian Percheron Horse Association was formed in 1907 and many new faces appeared in the ranks of Percheron importers, dealers, and breeders. Prominent among the importers and dealers were E. J. Wigle of Kingsville,

Roch Marien of Montreal, Hamilton and Hawthorne of Simcoe, J. B. Hogate of Toronto and Brandon, W. W. Hunter of Olds, B. Beaulieu of St. Jerome, W. B. Thorne of Aldersyde, Colquhoun and Beattie of Brandon, Vanstone and Rogers of Wawanesa, J. C. Drewry of Cowley, W. E. and R. C. Upper of North Portal, W. H. Devine of Calgary, E. A. Davenport of Acme, and R. W. Bradshaw of Magrath, Alberta.

It would be wrong to pass the name of R. W. Bradshaw without recognizing him for his part in bringing one of the greatest Percherons on the continent to Alberta, the stallion Pink. Foaled in France in 1900, he was imported to the United States by Dunham, Fletcher, and Coleman when two years of age. The best possible tribute to the stud's worth was the fact that he was retained for breeding at Oaklawn, the Dunham farm in Illinois, for eight years. Exhibited in those years, he was grand champion at the International show at Chicago in 1903 and 1904, a handsome black standing seventeen hands and weighing twenty-one hundred pounds. At the end of his years at Oaklawn, he was sold to R. W. Bradshaw and created quite a stir in Alberta, as he had every right to do.

One service performed by Pink in Canada was in demonstrating a changing Percheron image. Draft horses should have draft conformation; in other words, they should be big with appropriate frame and bone. Increased size came to the breed from bigger sires. The pioneer stallion Diligence would have no more size and weight than are now demanded in general purpose horses. But the two Brilliants weighed almost a ton each and Pink, sixty years after Diligence, would scale twenty-one hundred pounds and stand seventeen hands with refinement of bone that was scarcely known in the time of Diligence. It is not uncommon in modern showrings to see Percheron stallions weighing twenty-four hundred pounds and mares weighing twenty-three hundred. Perhaps that amount of weight will not be needed or wanted, but breeders will be able to tell convincingly that their Percherons have it if it is needed and have it without loss of quality.

George Lane

George Lane was the Canadian counterpart of Mark Dunham. Both were men of enterprise, imagination, and kindness, and both exerted immeasurable influence upon their chosen breed. Alvin Sanders, who knew both men and said of Dunham that he had "the courage of a lion and the heart of a child," might have said the same about the man who guided the affairs of the Bar U Ranch for forty years and became the best known member of the Canadian ranching fraternity. From 1912 until his death in 1925 he was the acknowledged leader of Alberta's Big Four cattlemen. If there had been a Big Four among horsemen, he'd have been a part of it also.

Born in Iowa in 1856, George Lane accompanied his parents westward and when he was old enough to be on his own and his principal skill was in riding, he served as a scout with the United States Cavalry when it was engrossed in Indian conflicts. He then took to cowboying and worked for some of Montana's biggest and best ranches. He was twenty-eight years old and a tested ranch hand when the North West Cattle Company, owned by Sir Hugh Allen of the Allen Steamship Company, needed a foreman. An order was placed with the Sun River Stock Association in Montana for the best cattleman that could be hired for $35 per month. Lane qualified and rode north to join the roundup in the Fort Macleod district in the spring of 1884.

Being an enterprising fellow, the new man very soon had cattle and horses of his own. He then acquired a ranch, the Flying E, on Willow Creek in the foothills, and then another, the YT, east of Stavely. In 1902, the new company, George Lane, Gordon, Ironside and Fares, bought the big Bar U from the Allens.

Lane had faith in the future of horses, especially if the horses were Percherons. In 1898 he visited the Mauldin Horse Ranch at Dillon, Montana, and bought the entire band of purebred Percherons—thirty-five head in all—and prepared to drive them along with twelve hundred grade Percherons bought at the same time, to Alberta. Most of the young purebreds had been sired by the stallion Americo, that James Mauldin had selected in France, and the general quality was high.

A short time later in the same year, Lane was back in the United States, this time to enlarge his foundation of pedigreed horses with selections from the Riverside Ranch in North Dakota. Thus was started a stud of Percherons that was to become one of the biggest and best in the world.

Lane's next move was to visit the Dunham establishment at Wayne, Illinois, hoping to find a stallion that would measure up to his ideals. He selected the black horse Presbourg, foaled in 1900 and imported from France by the Dunham firm. The choice was a good one and Lane, many years later, recalled him as one of the best sires he had used. At the same time, he bought an old stallion from the Dunham firm, the American-bred black, Paris, foaled in 1889. He, too, bred well at the Bar U Ranch.

Adding to the interest in these two early sires is the fact that they appear with registration numbers [1] and [2] respectively in volume I of the *Canadian Percheron Stud Book*, published in 1912. Moreover, the stud book entry that shows George Lane as Presbourg's third owner, shows another well-known pioneer farmer and rancher, Charles G. McKinnon, Bassano, Alberta, as the fourth owner.

Having made a first class beginning with purebred horses and seen them multiplying on his range, Lane turned his gaze to the home of the breed and made the first of a series of visits in 1907. The resulting importation to Canada in 1909 contained seventy-two mares and three stallions. The average cost in France was reported to be "about $1,000."

Still more notable was the big importation of 1910, declared to be "the largest and best importation of purebred horses ever made to Canada."[8]

In this shipment were twenty-five stallions and fifty mares and Mr. Lane was present for all the transactions which took place at the Percheron Horse Society Show at Nogent le Rotrou. The horses purchased were being delivered in two shipments with Mr. Lane accompanying the first one and M. Louis Aveline, son of the president of the Percheron Horse Society of France, travelling with the second.

The newspaper story took note of a display of anxiety by French horsemen who said it was regrettable that so much of the country's best breeding stock was being removed. Nevertheless, the French horsemen were glad to get George Lane's Canadian money and seemed ready to congratulate him on his hope "of establishing in Canada a band of Percherons of the very best class, such as has never hitherto existed on the continent of America."

George Lane's Percherons made more history in the autumn of 1918 when they became part of the first shipment of pedigreed horses of the breed to cross the Atlantic eastward from North America. Twenty-six mares and the stallion Newport, by Halifax, were consigned to England. And a bigger shipment consisting of fifty-three head was made in the following year and sold well. The breed had been introduced at an earlier date to England with horses from France, but the George Lane shipment did much to broaden the breed base in that stronghold of the Shire and Suffolk.

When the aforementioned Louis Aveline from La Perche was in Canada and visiting the Bar U Ranch and recognizing many horses he had seen before, he pronounced the Lane Percherons he saw to be as good as the best in France.

The Bar U Percherons at the time of George Lane's death numbered 700 head, making it easy for outsiders to accept the claim that here was the biggest aggregation of purebred and registered Percheron stock in the world at the time.

ORGANIZATION, STUD BOOK, AND ANGER

Breeders had another distinct debt to George Lane and his friend and neighbor W. B. Thorne of Aldersyde, for their invaluable part in bringing the Canadian Percheron Horse

Association into existence in 1907 and guiding it through its infant years.

The American organization, known as the National Association of Importers and Breeders of Norman Horses, began in 1876 and the similar body with record-keeping purposes had its birth in France seven years later. Canadian breeders of Percherons had to wait almost twenty-five years for their own organization and still longer for their own stud book facilities. In the meantime, they registered their Percherons in the United States books.

Lane and Thorne discussed the need for an organization repeatedly and Thorne wrote letters. They studied the Canadian Live Stock Pedigree Act and decided to call an organization meeting. It would have been convenient to hold it at Calgary, but to avoid possible criticism of parochialism, they named Regina as a meeting place and there, in an office of the Saskatchewan Department of Agriculture on August 3, 1907, a group of six western horsemen and a representative of the Dominion Live Stock Commissioner, exercising a minimum of formality, organized the Canadian Percheron Horse Breeders' Association and elected provisional officers. W. B. Thorne was president, R. P. Stanley, Moosomin, was vice-president, and F. R. Pike, High River, was secretary-treasurer. George Lane, who tried always to escape conspicuous roles for himself, agreed to be a director. A proposed constitution was approved and Thorne promised that an early start would be made in the preparation of a stud book. In a shorter time and with fewer speeches than such a thing had ever been done before, six Percheron breeders and one guest created a national organization.

One year later, in 1908, the association held its first annual meeting in the administration building of the Calgary Exhibition and confirmed the officers who had been given provisional status at the Regina meeting. The president promised to have a report on the stud book for the next annual event and was able to announce at the 1909 meeting that preparation of the book was going forward satisfactorily, adding: "We will print 500 copies."

The *Canadian Percheron Stud Book*, volume 1, edited by the Canadian National Live Stock Records, Ottawa, and published by the Canadian Percheron Horse Breeders' Association, appeared proudly in 1912. Here was the official register, showing registered names, birth dates, colors, breeders, sires, dams, owners, and registration numbers for 2,193 stallions and 2,111 fillies and mares. Where an animal was previously registered in one or two other countries—perhaps the United States and France—its registered name would be followed by three registration numbers with the source of each number being identified by brackets or the absence of brackets. A Canadian number was to be written with square brackets, a French number with round brackets, and a United States number without brackets. In recent years there emerged the practice by Canadians of writing their numbers without brackets, just like the Americans. Considerable confusion resulted.

The distinction of having number [1] for stallions in the Canadian Percheron book went, as noted, to the distinguished Presbourg, brought to Canada by George Lane and used on the Bar U mares for many years. The corresponding distinction among Canadian mares of the breed was for Nancy Lee, a black foaled on June 13, 1899, in North Dakota. Her second owner was George Lane, her third George Lane and Gordon, Ironside and Fares, Pekisko.

The new book was enlightening in various ways. It showed the West as the Percheron stronghold of Canada in 1912. Of twelve life members listed at that time, eleven of them had mailing addresses in Saskatchewan and Alberta. And George Lane's overwhelming involvement in Percherons could be judged by a count showing his name appearing as the sole breeder or owner, or as a member of the firm of George Lane, Gordon, Ironside and Fares, a total of 307 times in the section for mares and 124 times for stallions. It made a total of 431 entries, roughly 10 percent of the total entries in the stud book.

W. B. Thorne, with unquestioned dedication to the breed, was president of the association from 1907 to 1911, during which time he joined the ranks of breeders with imported French stallions, having brought over the horse Illico, sired by Etudiant. Lane did accept the presidency in each of two years, but he preferred to be a director where he could speak his views without restraint. His advice was good and his influence steadying. Pike remained as secretary-treasurer for eight years.

Then came a series of years in which the association officers and directors were greatly exercised about the continuing preferential treatment being extended to the Clydesdale breed by public workers. Following executive instructions, the secretary wrote angry letters to exhibition managers, ministers of agriculture, professors of animal husbandry and deans of agriculture. As the minutes of annual meetings show, most letters of protest about scarcity of classes at fairs and exhibitions, disproportionately low prize money in competitions, absence of Percherons in agricultural college stables and so on, brought polite replies without being very helpful. Association officers believed they were making headway in winning farm friends but making no impression in official circles.

One of the leading offenders, as the association officers saw it, was the College of Agriculture at the University of Saskatchewan, where Dean W. J. Rutherford was known to have an honest feeling of affection for the Scottish breed. The horses occupying the handsome new barn at the university and those used for student instruction were said to be exclusively Clydesdales. The Percheron devotees were losing patience and members attending the annual meeting in 1919 saw copies of letters sent to certain

The two-year-old stallion Romulus, bred by the University of Saskatchewan and shown to the reserve grand championship at the Canadian Royal in 1931. *Photograph by Hillyard; courtesy* The Western Producer.

public figures on their behalf. Some of the letters were less than diplomatic but they reflected the resentment of people whose horses were not getting the recognition they believed was deserved. The letter to the premier of Saskatchewan was passed to the minister of Agriculture, Hon. Charles Dunning, for reply. The latter had some harsh words about the tone of the letter, which, of course, did nothing to improve the injured feelings:

"I must say frankly at the outset," said Dunning, "that the tone and language of your letter is not calculated to produce a very friendly feeling in the mind of the recipient, but in any event it shall be answered with the proper courtesy."[9]

The letter addressed to the dean of Agriculture was still awaiting an answer after several months. The following part of the original letter, however, leaves little doubt about the bitterness that was being allowed to inflate:

Dean W. J. Rutherford
University of Saskatchewan, Saskatoon

Dear Sir—
    At a recent meeting of this association the authorities in your Province came in for some very scathing criticism for their attitude on the breeding of draft horses in Saskatchewan. Some of the representatives from your Province presented views at the meeting which would seem to indicate that the entire emphasis placed upon the breeding of draft horses by your officials who have to do with instruction and inspection work is based upon so-called quality, to the exclusion of those other prime essentials, substance, weight and constitutional vigor. After a very general and spirited discussion the accompanying resolution was unanimously adopted and forwarded to your Minister of Agriculture. The reply which I have just received from his office places the entire blame for this very serious condition of affairs as affecting the draft horse breeding interests in Western Canada . . . upon your Department of the University of Saskatchewan.
    If these charges as represented to us at our meeting are founded upon facts as we believe they are, and if the responsibility for this condition rests upon you as indicated by your Minister, you are undoubtedly open to much severe criticism from many of your ratepayers since we have upwards of one thousand owners of Percherons in your Province as indicated by the records of your stallion enrollment and our membership roll, a number which is rapidly increasing . . . [10]

The Percheron association protests were directed at public institutions right across the Dominion. The responses were mixed but generally positive. They were thought to be better in Alberta than in most areas. The George Lane presence in the province was probably helpful and the provincial government could not fail to be conscious of the political strength of the thousands of American settlers who had come to Alberta to stay and brought their preferences for Percheron and Belgian horses. In any case, when the Canadian Percheron Horse Breeders were assembled in annual meeting in 1919, the Government of Alberta was taking steps to purchase the best Clydesdale stallion available in Scotland and the best Percheron stallion procurable in the United States and appropriating the same sum of money for each.

The Clydesdale Craigie Masterpiece was bought for about $10,000 and those who saw him after his delivery pronounced him the best stallion of the breed ever brought to Canada. Later in the same year the Percheron purchasing committee bought the reserve grand champion Percheron stallion at the International show at Chicago for $8,000.

When the twenty-four-hundred-pound stallion with superb quality was delivered in Alberta, connoisseurs were ready to describe him as "the best stallion of the breed ever brought to Canada." Members and officers of the Canadian Percheron Horse Breeders Association were pleased.

JOB AND LAET

Just as the celebrated Clydesdale stallion Bonnie Buchlyvie almost came to Canada following the Seaham Harbour sale in Scotland in 1915, so the similarly great Laet, bred by E. B. White of Virginia and foaled his property in 1916, was also a candidate for Canadian ownership. In 1919 the Province of Alberta was hoping to advance the cause of draft horse improvement by buying and importing two of the best stallions available, one Clydesdale and one Percheron.

Alberta legislators voted what was considered sufficient funds and early in the next year, Hon. Duncan Marshall, minister of agriculture, reported the purchase in Scotland of the seven-year-old, twenty-one-hundred-pound Craigie Masterpiece at a cost of £2,500 or about $9,825 in Canadian money.

Negotiations for the selection and purchase of "the best Percheron stallion money will buy" began in the early part of 1920 when the minister announced that the search would be carried out by a well-qualified committee. One member would be nominated by the Canadian Percheron Horse Breeders Association and one by the minister. The veteran Percheron breeder and first president of the Canadian Percheron association, W. B. Thorne of Aldersyde, was the choice of the organization and S. G. Carlyle,

recently appointed live stock commissioner for Alberta, was named by the minister.

To save time and also to help the members of the selection committee, the Canadian association's secretary, W. H. Willison, was instructed to open correspondence with Ellis McFarland, secretary of the Percheron Association of America. It was hoped that the selection committee would thus ascertain the identity and particulars of the most outstanding, eligible stallions on the continent and others inviting further consideration.

According to Bruce Roy, former secretary of the Canadian Percheron association and a leading authority on Percheron breed history, one of the most helpful responses was from Senator E. B. White who could speak as an active breeder of superior horses and also as president of the Percheron Association of America. White suggested several outstanding stallions, including two that he pronounced "two of the best two-year-old stallions I have ever seen." He then added: "I am trying to get W. H. Butler, Sandusky, Ohio, to price Laet, grand champion stallion at last Ohio Fair."[11] The horse, one of White's own breeding, had been sold to Butler, but as "a rising star," the horse's real worth was not yet fully recognized.

Either of the exceptional two-year-old stallions to which White referred—both sired by the imported Dragon—could be bought at $10,000. One of the animals, Doughboy, was his own property but White promised his full cooperation and that of the American secretary, Ellis McFarland, to ensure that the Canadian horsemen could see and study the very best stallions American breeders could offer.

In the meantime, Wirth Dunham of the renowned Oaklawn stud in Illinois, replied by telegram to say that he could offer three of what he regarded as the best stallions in the country. In that trio was the big French-bred grey that had never been exhibited but was being fitted for showing at the time. The reference was to Job, half-brother to Jasmine, grand champion at the Chicago International in the previous year and "generally conceded to be the best Percheron stallion in America today."[12]

"If you decided to buy one of these," Dunham added, "we will try to meet your price as we realize the value of advertising this sale carries."

The Alberta committee was on tour in the autumn of 1920 and inspected all the most likely stallions. The great Laet, however, was not among those offered. He, said Bruce Roy, could not be bought. "W. H. Butler of Sandusky refused to price him although the Canadians bargained hard."

The touring horsemen continued on to the International at Chicago where the twenty-four-hundred-pound grey Job won his class and then the reserve grand championship for stallions. During the course of the show the decision was made to buy and Job became the property of the government of Alberta at a cost of $8,000. The big eleven-year-old stud was shipped out with Alberta livestock returning home after the show.

Some Percheron breeders believed that Job was too big for the popular demand. However that might be, he was magnificent in form and action; he possessed the quality in feet and legs that Canadians wanted and an enthusiastic welcome awaited him in Alberta. Already a proven sire of large, superior offspring, Job lived up to his reputation, but Alberta at that time could not furnish as many high class Percheron mares as, for example, the state of Illinois from which he came. For that reason it is easy to speculate that a stallion like either Job or the incomparable Laet would have had less opportunity to transmit to the full extent of his potential in Alberta than in older communities with a greater Percheron population. Laet's purchase by the government of Alberta might have wrought wonders for Canadian horsemen while failing to contribute the greatest good for the breed as a whole. As it was, Laet stock became very popular in Canada and extremely influential in breed improvement.

Moreover, both Job and his Clydesdale counterpart, Craigie Masterpiece, experienced some Alberta indignities as well as fortunes. The two stallions won lasting admiration but Albertans, going to the polls in a provincial election in 1921, elected a new government with the usual deflated respect for the policies of its predecessor. Horsemen were shocked at the official announcement of an auction sale in the spring of 1922:

AUCTION SALE OF FAMOUS
ALBERTA GOVERNMENT STALLIONS

The celebrated Percheron stallion, Job, and the Clydesdale Craigie Masterpiece, owned by Alberta Department of Agriculture will be offered for sale by
Public Auction
Thursday, April 15th
At 2 P.M. at Exhibition Grounds, Edmonton, Alberta, During Annual Spring Horse Shows. These are two of the largest, best and most valuable stallions that have ever come to Canada, and both are sure and satisfactory breeders. Foals by both horses were winners at last year's shows, one filly by Job winning 1st prize at Chicago International.

Job was reserve Grand Champion at Chicago in 1920 and is a half-brother to the famous champion stallion, Jasmine.

No such horses have been offered under the hammer in recent years. Further particulars on application to Alberta Department of Agriculture, Edmonton, Alberta.[13]

To many readers, the announcement was incomprehensible. It was still less than three years since the two stallions were bought at prices totaling close to $20,000, and there was no satisfactory explanation for the sudden reversal of policy. Most breeders of Percheron and Clydesdale horses were angry; all were puzzled. Nevertheless, horsemen wanted to be present at the sale and an overflow crowd assembled. The Percheron stallion was the first to be led into the sale ring. But bidding was slow and finally stalled at $1,150, well short of the reserve bid of $2,000 determined by officials in the Department of Agriculture.

Bidding went to $2,000 with Craigie Masterpiece in the ring but with the government's reserve bid at $5,000, there was once again no sale. Hence, the auction ended without a sale, but not without more debate and some humiliation. Neither the upset prices of $2,000 and $5,000 nor the bidding that fell far short of these reserve figures was in any way flattering to the horses or the policy makers. The two highest bids, totaling $3,150, were for stallions that cost six times that much in government cash and very much more if all related costs were included.

But after the embarrassing auction and other rebukes, government officials agreed that the two stallions would remain in public ownership and under the supervision of S. G. Carlyle, live stock commissioner for the province. They would be placed for service where they could be expected to accomplish the most good for the heavy horse industry.[14] And, happily, both stallions lived to strengthen their claims to superiority as heavy horse sires.

THE ARNOLDS

George Lane of Bar U Ranch fame had the distinction of owning the biggest band of pedigreed Percheron horses in the world. Of Gilbert E. Arnold, another giant in Canadian Percheron history, it could be said that he registered more Percherons in the Canadian stud book than any other breeder or importer, dead or alive.

Nor did any other family name in Canadian heavy horse history become more widely known. For more than a hundred years, Arnold horses were being raised on and sold from the family farms on the north side of the Ottawa River, not far west of Lachute, where the founding father, Thomas Arnold, carved out the first Arnoldwold fields from Lower Canada's hardwood bush. His grandson, J. E. Arnold, registered three stallions, Cladius (imp), Veilleur (imp) and Roscoe, born in Nova Scotia in 1891, all listed in volume I of the *Canadian Percheron Stud Book*. Incidently, the Canadian-bred Roscoe was bred by Frank H. Black of Amherst who imported the mother, Agatha, in 1887 and the father, Brilliant 22nd, in 1888, both from France.

In volume VIII of the stud book, published in 1933, 10 Percherons were registered in the joint names of J. E. Arnold and Son, Grenville, Quebec, and 130 other registrations carried the sole name of the son, Gilbert E. Arnold, of the same address.

In addition to being Percheron horse pioneers, the Arnolds soon rated among Canada's biggest operators in the business. And with horse breeding becoming an important activity on the same farm for five generations, the family established the best of claims to persistence and durability.

The scale on which Gilbert E. Arnold operated may be judged by the advertising space he bought. In April, 1947, for example, he was offering 3,000 horses, including both purebreds and grades for use on farms and in forests. These were to be found on Arnoldwold farms "comprising 70 units on which all field work is being performed by horses."

The scale of horse-related activities would bring other surprises. At one point, the Arnold holdings were said to include 5,000 breeding mares. Buyers discovered that regardless of their particular needs, they could be sure of finding what they wanted at Arnold's. By 1950, the advertising was being conducted over the names of Gilbert E. Arnold, president, and Gilbert E. Arnold, Jr., vice-president.[15] Gilbert E. Arnold, Jr., in this instance represented the fifth generation of the horse-breeding family on the home farm.

Friends of the Percheron breed will, quite reasonably, insist that their breed was Gilbert Arnold's specialty and first love, but he could wax enthusiastic about a good horse of any breed and became an exhibitor and promoter of Belgians as well as Percherons. Volume I of the *Canadian Belgian Draft Horse Stud Book* that contained the registrations collected up to 1920, carried the names of two stallions, Patron and Duc, owned by J. E. Arnold, the latter having been imported in 1911. And J. E. Arnold and Son had three other Belgians recorded in the same book, all bred in the United States.

By 1950, Gilbert E. Arnold was inviting buyers to inspect his Percherons, Belgians, Clydesdales, Shires, Hackneys, Thoroughbreds, Standardbreds and French Coach.

Among the thousands of Percherons and others that he either brought to Canada or raised in Canada, were many that distinguished themselves as show horses and breeders. Seven times Arnold entries won the grand championship honors for Percheron stallions at the Canadian Royal and once for Percheron mares. The mare in this instance was Sunray Betty, by Jason, winner in 1956. Five of the stallion championship awards were won by the great show and breeding stallion, Rex Mondraghope, sired by Koncarhope. Once, the grand championship went to Jason, a stallion which was for many years at the head of the Arnoldwold Percheron stud; and once it went to Ricinus Koncarlaet. Arnold entries won the grand championship at the Canadian Royal six times for Belgian stallions and twice for Belgian mares.

Gilbert Arnold assisted the National Breweries in carrying out their policy of buying superior black Percheron stallions and making them available, at modest breeding fees, in farming communities in the Province of Quebec. His involvement meant that Arnold could take almost as much satisfaction as the owners in seeing the brewery-owned Percherons winning championship ribbons and improving the horse stock of the province.

The same busy horseman gave valuable leadership to and through the Canadian Percheron Horse Breeders Association, especially after the troubled years in the early forties. He was elected president of the Canadian association on December 7, 1940 and was re-elected to remain in the position through five consecutive years, after which he was named honorary president. It was one of the best tributes to his tested leadership that after a lapse of time, he was called back to become the national president of the association again. Those horsemen who remember Gilbert E. Arnold in office said he was tough but fair and he was the principal means of rescuing the organization from its years of adversity.

A Boost from Beer

Brewing interests long ago recognized the peculiar advertising benefits to be derived from the use of large, good-looking horses hitched in two-, four-, and six-horse tandem units. Whether the horses were Percherons, Belgians, Clydesdales, Shires, or Suffolks, a six-horse hitch of big, well-mannered horses pulling a heavy duty beer wagon or other vehicle was sure to capture public attention and bring pride to owner and driver. For horsemen breeding high class draft-type stock, the brewery market offered a limited but attractive incentive.

Policy-makers at Dawes Black Horse Brewery in Montreal, afterwards part of National Breweries Limited, fixed upon the idea of publicizing the black horse label while, at the same time, helping Quebec farmers to improve their horse power. They achieved this by purchasing the best black Percheron stallions obtainable and placing them for breeding purposes at little more than token fees in rural Quebec. It proved to be a popular and useful program, one that well deserves a place of prominence in the breed's history in Canada.

The idea may have had its birth in the fertile mind of Gilbert A. Arnold of Grenville.

Clearly, he had good counselling for the brewers and he bought many of the black stallions that ultimately made their homes at the National Brewery stables in Montreal.

Among the first stallions obtained for the project were four blacks imported from France in the name of "Kenneth T. Dawes for National Breweries" in Montreal. The oldest of the stallions, Clairay, was a six-year-old and the youngest, Garant, a two-year-old. All were of splendid type and quality and drew instant admiration.

Thereafter, most of the selected stallions were from the United States, with registration certificates showing Gilbert E. Arnold as second owner and National Breweries as third. Most were royally bred, like Gerard Laet, grandson of Laet, the stallion bred by Michigan State College, and also one whose papers showed him to be a grandson of Treviso. A few were Canadian bred such as Lakeside Kalarama, grandson of Koncarcalyps and raised by Albert J. Berner of Breslau, Ontario. There was also Macdonald Laet, sired by Mel Laet 3rd and bred by Macdonald College.

The all-black Percheron stallions had to possess a showring degree of quality and substance to be acceptable to the Dawes purpose, but two of them were outstanding—Captivator and Crescent Laet. The former, rated as one of the best on the continent, was sired by Carvictor and foaled in 1924. The sire changed hands once at $9,000 and some horsemen considered Captivator a better horse. On Gilbert Arnold's long record, it should not have brought surprise that it was he who stumbled upon him, recognized his potential, and bought him. That was in 1927 and upon arrival in Canada, Captivator was bought by R. G. Chester, Hespler, Ontario.

But Arnold reminded his friends in Montreal that if they had acted promptly, they would have had the best stallion in Canada. He advised them to buy the horse, even though they would have to pay more to get him. After just a short stay at Hespler, Captivator moved to Montreal where, according to one Montrealer's telling, the great horse developed a taste for Black Horse beer.

From that time forward, Captivator was often in the showring and frequently qualifying for championship awards. Three times he was reserve champion at the Royal Winter Fair for National Breweries and in 1933 he was the grand champion. He continued to be the foremost showpiece in the National Breweries' barn full of show horses until 1943 when he was nineteen years old and was allowed the relaxation that goes with retirement. It was part of his record that he won more championships and left more colts than any other stallion in the Montreal barn.

There was probably no horse in Canadian history whose likeness was displayed as widely. It was a photograph of Captivator that provided the material for the black horse cut seen on the label of Black Horse beer and on the maker's stationery. And the metal statue that has rested on the author's desk for the past forty years was created in the image of the great National Breweries horse.

The other National Breweries' Percheron to gain special fame, Crescent Laet sired by Cy Laet, won the Percheron stallion grand championship at the Canadian Royal in each of three years, 1947, '48, and '49. To the time of writing in 1986, only six other Percheron stallions in Canadian history have surpassed or equalled that record; they were Cy Laet, Monarch, Rex Mondraghope, Justamere Par Excellent, Colonsay Prince, and Lo Lynd Douglas.

A National Breweries news release made to coincide with the opening of a new stallion stable in Montreal in June, 1950, told that in the first nineteen years of the horse improvement program, the foals left by the Black Horse stallions numbered more than 19,000, an average of 1,000 per year.

While inviting the public to visit the new stallion quarters, Norman Dawes, speaking for the company, said: "Our horses have always won public affection wherever they have appeared. Now, with the facilities provided for viewing them, we hope they will become still more attractive for visitors."

THE PERCHERON TRIPLE TRIUMPH OF 1983

Rarely, if ever, have horsemen won more international attention than in July, 1983, when the organized breeders and friends of Percherons planned and presented the World Percheron Congress, the World Percheron Horse Show, and the World Percheron Horse Pulling contests. Both federal and provincial departments of agriculture and the Calgary Exhibition and Stampede contributed to the enormous success of the event.

It was a triple triumph coinciding with the hundredth anniversary of the birth of stud book recording in the homeland of the breed and the echoes of praise sounded around the world. It was also the first time the congress had been conducted in North America and the week-long events made the host city appear suspiciously like a community bidding to become the Percheron Horse Capital of the World. It was a tribute to a few dedicated workers who spent two years dreaming, planning, and organizing prior to the show. Committee members who deserve to be honored and remembered include Chairman Don Jess, Bruce and Adair Roy, Jack and Carol Bellamy, Glyn and Marion Furber, Earl, Cathy, and Ron James, Bill Lucas, Don Swanston, Donald Strandquist, and Audrey Turner.

The idea took shape when Bill Lucas of Lucasia Ranch, Claresholm, attended a World Percheron Congress in France and extended an invitation to schedule the 1983 event at Calgary. The proposal was accepted and the July dates, seventh to thirteenth, were approved.

The internationally known Calgary street parade that marked the beginning of the Exhibition and Stampede, did exactly the same for the Percheron program. At times it looked like a Percheron parade as the big black and grey horses seemed to be catching the spotlight much of the way. Leading the parade was the celebrated eight-horse team of black Percherons from Disney World, Florida, inadvertently setting the stage for Percheron week.

The sparkling congress entry that became the winner of a special parade award included Percherons hitched in sixes, four abreast, pairs, and singles. They all complemented the handsome float designed by a member of the Percheron fraternity, Carol Bellamy of Cremona, Alberta. The float carried Congress Queen Marlane Valentine and Princess Laurie Allen in regal elegance. If estimates are accepted, close to a million spectators along the parade route had every reason to be impressed by the big horses and their friends.

Reporting to the press, Bruce Roy wrote of the Percherons in the parade that they "received a thunderous ovation the total distance of the parade route. However, no reception was as moving or as emotional as when the Disney World hitch, the World Congress section and the many other Percherons drawing an assortment of vehicles and floats passed the stands reserved for the French, British, Australian, American and Canadian breed enthusiasts in attendance."[16]

The Percherons on parade were excellent but what of the highlights of the week? One visitor remarked that everything he saw and heard was a highlight—congress formalities, receptions, speeches, reports, and showring classes. But for the majority of visitors and delegates interest would reach a climax in the big and inspiring breeding classes, some of them the biggest spectators could recall—eighteen filly foals, twenty-six yearling fillies, twenty-four two-year-old fillies, thirteen brood mares, twenty yeld mares, and so on.

The numbers and the widespread regions from which the entries came brought Bruce Roy to declare: "No exhibition has drawn horses from such an expanse of geography, the Royal Agricultural Winter Fair, Chicago's International Livestock Exposition and Denver's National Western Livestock Show included."[17]

And as might have been expected, every winner seemed to have something of romantic interest about it. The winning filly foal, Fantasy Princess, bred and exhibited by Mrs. R. L. Robinson, Jr., of Michigan, was a daughter of South Valley Did It and thus a granddaughter of the regionally revered Justamere Showtime. If more were needed to generate interest, the knowledge that the filly was a full sister of eminents such as Confetti, Blizzard, and D.I.D., would ensure it.

In the amazingly big class of yearling fillies, it was Blackhome D. Gloria, bred and

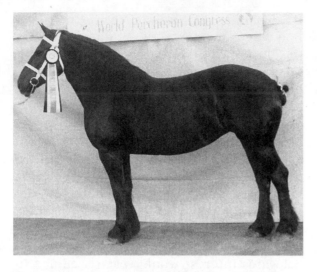

Blackhome Connie Lyn by Lo Lynd Douglas, winner in the yeld mare class and also world champion Percheron mare at the World Percheron Congress in Calgary, 1983. Shown by Reg M. Black and Sons, Blackhome Farms, Moorefield, Ontario. *Photograph by Browarny.*

shown by Reg M. Black and Sons, Moorefield, Ontario, that went to the top. Another entry from the Blacks won the class for two-year-old fillies, this one Blackhome Dayna Lyn, a daughter of Highview Dragano. In the three-year-olds, the winner was Rena of Glynlea, bred and exhibited by Glyn and Marion Furber, Bowden, Alberta.

Judging-ring interest may have reached its peak in the classes for yeld and brood mares, the classes that ultimately furnished the world championship and reserve world championship respectively for Percheron females. It was Blackhome Connie Lyn, an increasingly familiar showring figure to Canadians, sired by Lo Lynd Douglas and shown by her breeders, Reg M. Black and Sons, that was awarded the highest place in the memorable yeld mare class. She also won the world championship. The same mare had been grand champion at the Canadian Royal Winter Fair the previous year. Placing next to her when the world championships were awarded was the winner in the brood mare class, Carin Koncarlaet, shown by Jon and Bobbie Bast from Cocalalla, Idaho.

Stallion classes were well filled but not quite as big as those for mares and fillies. Another Bast entry from Idaho, Conqueror Koncarlaet, was the winning stallion foal; and Lucasia Jo, sired by Lucasia Sir William and shown by Lucasia Ranch, Claresholm, Alberta, became the first prize yearling stallion. With thirteen two-year-old stallions in the ring, the winner was Glynlea Black Hawk by Foremark Forest Pride, exhibited by Glyn and Marion Furber from Bowden. He later qualified for the reserve world championship for stallions.

The class for three-year-old studs was smaller than most. The popular winning grey Confetti—son of South Valley Did It—won the class and then the world championship for his owner, Ironwood Farms, Renfrew, Ontario. Confetti, it should be noted, became a many-times champion in Canada, including grand champion at the Canadian Royal in 1982 and 1984.

There remained only the nine entries making up the class for mature stallions. It was a striking sight. Creating some surprise and considerable approval, the red ribbon award went to a newcomer to the showring, a black stranger to most onlookers, Exe Colonel's Duke, shown by Mike Sabina, Hilliard, Alberta.

Serious students find get-of-sire and progeny-of-dam classes to offer the best opportunities for study. For westerners with sentiment for the great breeding stallion Justamere Showtime, these classes at the congress were doubly rewarding. Bred by Jonathan Fox, Jr., the black Showtime was owned for some years by Allen Bexson of Lloydminster and then by Gordon Young, Cayley, in whose hands the horse grew steadily in fame.

With sixteen entries in the get-of-sire class—indicating a total of forty-eight animals before the judge—the winning lot was sired by Highview Dragano by Justamere Showtime and presented by Reg M. Black and Sons. But the most striking feature about the class was that more than half of all the horses in the ring carried Justamere Showtime blood; the famous sire was either sire, grandsire, or great grandsire of six of the nine top-placing lots, a singular record.

The progeny-of-dam class with its twenty-three entries, meaning forty-six animals in the line, was the biggest competition anybody could remember. The winning entry consisted of a pair from the mare College Lynda, mother of Blackhome Connie Lyn who was already carrying the world championship for mares at the congress. An entry from Reg M. Black and Sons, it was from the same stable that furnished the winning get-of-sire and various other notable winners. As for College Lynda by College Major, by Morden Chief, she had already come to be recognized as one of the greatest breeding mares of the breed.

There was a class for stallion and three mares, property of the exhibitor, won by Glyn and Marion Furber, also a class for three mares which was taken by Reg Black and Sons.

That was not all; there were still the gelding classes and the hitches, big classes and magnificent. Everybody, including the judge, loved the members of the winning team in the class for pedigreed mares; they were none other than Blackhome Connie Lyn and Blackhome Carrie Doll, world champion mare and second prize brood mare respectively.

The heavy draft team of two geldings from Lippitt and Smith, Wisconsin, won its class and was judged the world champion Percheron team, while a pair of greys from

Donald Swanston, High River, gained the highest award in the class for light draft teams.

The great and versatile Blackhome Connie Lyn returned to the ring to win the ladies' cart class and High River's Donald Swanston delighted spectators with his winning two-horse tandem outfit.

Patrons viewing the nine four-horse teams in the ring and the eight six-horse teams must have muttered "magnificent!" Harold Schumacher from Minnesota won both classes.

The World Percheron Pull was a show in itself with team entries divided into three weight classes: lightweights between thirty-two and thirty-five hundred pounds for the pair, middleweights from thirty-five to thirty-eight hundred pounds, and heavyweights above the latter figure.

And so the world congress program ended, the ring crowded with dignitaries, visiting delegates, champion Percherons, a band, the congress float, and a lot of emotional farewells. Canadian Percheron breeders knew they had made history and were proud.

Confetti, grand champion stallion at the Royal of 1982 and at the World Percheron Congress, Calgary, 1983, for Ironwood Farms, Renfrew, Ontario. He was grand champion again at the 1984 Royal for Mrs. R. L. Robinson of Michigan. *Photograph by J. E. McNeil.*

PERCHERON SIRES OF WINNERS AT THE CANADIAN ROYAL WINTER FAIR

In identifying the leading sires of winners in Percherons at the Royal Winter Fair—first for the prewar years, 1922 to 1938, and then, by a separate study, the postwar years, 1946 to 1985—the methods employed were exactly the same as those described in the Clydesdale chapter under "Leading Sires of Clydesdale Winners."

In compiling the list of leading Percheron sires in the recent forty-year period, 249 Percheron stallions were listed as sires of Royal show entries winning first, second, or third prizes in the breeding classes. From these, the 15 sires with the best scores were listed and presented in the following table. The two tables show first, the 10 leading Percheron sires of winners in the early period and second, the top 15 in the later, longer period.

FIGURE 1

PERCHERON SIRES OF WINNERS IN ORDER OF SCORES, ROYAL WINTER FAIRS, 1922 TO 1938[18]

1	Monarch [10386]	by	Gray Wonder
2	Laet [12306]	by	Seducteur
3	Carinn [10359]	by	Carnot
4	Rolaet [13277]	by	Laet
5	Rival [12393]	by	Klientor
6	Madagascar [9589]	by	Farnay ex Lucas
7	Perlaet [12309]	by	Laet
8	Ames Jalap [12511]	by	Jalap
9	Keota Jalap [7610]	by	Jalap
10	Erik of Lakeview [12309]	by	Perlaet

PERCHERON SIRES OF WINNERS IN ORDER OF SCORES, ROYAL WINTER FAIRS, 1946 TO 1985

1	Riverbend Monkoncarlaet [18432]	by	Rockwood Grandeur
2	Drake Farms Chief [19311]	by	Morden Chief
3	South Valley Did It [20128]	by	Justamere Showtime
4	Koncarhope [19037]	by	Koncarcalyps
5	Justamere Showtime [19450]	by	Riverbend Monkoncarlaet
6	La Don's Koncarnona [19756]	by	La Don's Chief
7	Lo Lynd Douglas [20137]	by	Lincoln View Douglas
8	Wilkie [237507]	by	Lancelot
9	Morden Chief [18942]	by	Chief Laet
10	Topper's Baryton [19501]	by	Topper
11	Ann's Silver [19841]	by	Silver Dawn Koncarno
12	Highview Dragano [20240]	by	Justamere Showtime
13	College Major [19494]	by	Morden Chief
14	Rex Mondraghope [19274]	by	Koncarhope
15	Ricinus Koncarlaet [19296]	by	Koncarhope

FIGURE 2

Grand Champion Percheron Stallions, Canadian Royal Winter Fair

Year	Name of Winner	Sire of Winner	Exhibitor
1922	Count Vimy	Koimao	J. E. Fraser
1923	Carbonn	Carnot	Maryvale Farms, Ohio
1924	Conqueror	Premier	J. H. Crowe
1925	Marathon Acme	Marathon	Davenport and Greenway
1926	Monarch	Gray Wonder	Carl Roberts
1927	Monarch	Gray Wonder	Carl Roberts
1928	Cadeau	Romand	Charles Rear
1929	Monarch	Gray Wonder	Carl Roberts
1930	Dean	Rockaway	Charles Rear
1931	Dean	Rockaway	Charles Rear
1932	Monarch's Laet	Rolaet	Carl Roberts
1933	Captivator	Carvictor	National Breweries Ltd.
1934	Chief Laet	Sir Laet	Dominion Experimental Farms
1935	Kable	Etalon	Holmes Foundry Co.
1936	Cy Laet	Laet	National Breweries Ltd.
1937	Corlaet	Sir Lact	W. B. Murray, Ohio
1938	Paramount Carlaet	Erik of Lakeview	National Breweries Ltd.
1939	to 1945, no Royal Winter Fairs owing to World War II		
1946	Jason	Corlaet	Gilbert E. Arnold
1947	Crescent Laet	Cy Laet	National Breweries Ltd.
1948	Crescent Laet	Cy Laet	National Breweries Ltd.
1949	Crescent Laet	Cy Laet	National Breweries Ltd.
1950	Silver Dawn Kontact	Silver Dawn Ace	John W. Sanders
1951	Silver Dawn Kontact	Silver Dawn Ace	John W. Sanders
1952	Morden Chief	Chief Laet	Director, Experimental Farms
1953	Rex Mondraghope	Koncarhope	W. K. Russell
1954	Konot	Koncarhope	Carl J. Hanson
1955	Ricinus Koncarlaet	Koncarhope	Gilbert Arnold
1956	Konviso	Koncarhope	Hardy Salter
1957	Ann's Silver	Silver Dawn Koncarno	Robt. E. Jones
1958	Rex Mondraghope	Koncarhope	Gilbert Arnold
1959	Rex Mondraghope	Koncarhope	Gilbert Arnold
1960	Rex Mondraghope	Koncarhope	Gilbert Arnold
1961	Rex Mondraghope	Koncarhope	Gilbert Arnold
1962	Rex Mondraghope	Koncarhope	Gilbert Arnold
1963	Duke Ricinus	Ricinus Koncarlaet	Patrick J. Hendrick
1964	Justamere Par Excellent	Riverbend Monkoncarlaet	Michalyshen Bros.
1965	Easter Fury	Don's Valentine Rex	W. E. Harrison
1966	Justamere Par Excellent	Riverbend Monkoncarlaet	Michalyshen Bros.
1967	Justamere Par Excellent	Riverbend Monkoncarlaet	Michalyshen Bros.

Year	Name of Winner	Sire of Winner	Exhibitor
1968	Colonsay Prince	Cremona Chief 2nd	Patrick J. Hendrick
1969	Colonsay Prince	Cremona Chief 2nd	Patrick J. Hendrick
1970	Colonsay Prince	Cremona Chief 2nd	Patrick J. Hendrick
1971	College Chief	College Major	V. E. Cookson
1972	Lo Lynd Douglas	Lincoln View Douglas	Wilfred J. Habel
1973	Lo Lynd Douglas	Lincoln View Douglas	Wilfred J. Habel
1974	Maverick	Drake Farms Chief	Art Bast and Family
1975	Maverick	Drake Farms Chief	Art Bast and Family
1976	Lucasia Big John	Justamere Showtime	Lucasia Ranches
1977	Golden Ridge Shiner	La Don's Koncarnona Hector	Fred Hampson
1978	Lo Lynd Douglas	Lincoln View Douglas	Wilfred J. Habel
1979	Blizzard	South Valley Did It	Joseph Michalyshen
1980	Blizzard	South Valley Did It	Joseph Michalyshen
1981	McGee	D.I.D.	Art Bast and Family
1982	Confetti	South Valley Did It	Ironwood Farms
1983	Lucasia Mr. Black	Lucasia Big John	Irvan Chamberlain
1984	Confetti	South Valley Did It	Mrs. R. L. Robinson
1985	Blackhome Duke	Blackhome Donnet Lyn	Reg Black and Sons

FIGURE 3

GRAND CHAMPION PERCHERON MARES, CANADIAN ROYAL WINTER FAIR

Year	Name of Winner	Sire of Winner	Exhibitor
1922	Carnona V	Carnot	Maryvale Farms
1923	Carnona V	Carnot	Maryvale Farms
1924	The Marne	Madagascar	Bater Bros.
1925	Turquoise of Acme	Marathon	Davenport and Greenway
1926	Monarch's Rose	Monarch	Carl Roberts
1927	Monarch's Rose	Monarch	Mrs. E. Wood
1928	Laet's Magic Queen	Laet	Frank B. Foster
1929	Susanna	Sir William	Frank B. Foster
1930	Blanche Kesako	Kesako Larue	Charles Rear
1931	Blanche Kesako	Kesako Larue	Charles Rear
1932	Monarch's Ruby	Monarch	Carl Roberts
1933	Monet	Rolaet	Carl Roberts
1934	Monet	Rolaet	Carl Roberts
1935	Ollie	Oak Forest Synod	Dominion Experimental Farms, Lethbridge
1936	Crocadon Katisha	Dean	George T. Fraser
1937	Monet	Rolaet	Carl Roberts
1938	Monet	Rolaet	Carl Roberts

Year	Name of Winner	Sire of Winner	Exhibitor
1939	to 1945, no Royal Winter Fairs owing to World War II		
1946	Lynnwood Kondora	Don Again	Lynnwood Farm
1947	Leona Ann	Hesitation Leona	J. M. Sanders
1948	Starlight Koncarness	Koncar	Hardy Salter
1949	Tallulah D.	Count Vimy 2nd	S. E. Bennett
1950	Tallulah D.	Count Vimy 2nd	S. E. Bennett
1951	Jane Laet	Acme Carlaet	John Kogut and Sons
1952	Starlight Koncarness	Koncar	Hardy Salter
1953	Silver Belle	Silver Dawn Kontact	Stittsville Lumber Co.
1954	Decorator's Dinah UA	Justamere Decorator	University of Alberta
1955	Decorator's Carolina UA	Justamere Decorator	Hardy Salter
1956	Sunray Betty	Jason	Gilbert Arnold
1957	June Laet	Therma Jud	Gar E. Robinson
1958	Justamere Stylish Stella	Riverbend Monkoncarlaet	Victor E. Cookson
1959	Justamere Stylish Stella	Riverbend Monkoncarlaet	Victor E. Cookson
1960	Justamere Stylish Stella	Riverbend Monkoncarlaet	Victor E. Cookson
1961	Justamere Stylish Stella	Riverbend Monkoncarlaet	Victor E. Cookson
1962	Justamere Stylish Stella	Riverbend Monkoncarlaet	Victor E. Cookson
1963	Justamere Stylish Stella	Riverbend Monkoncarlaet	Victor E. Cookson
1964	Justamere Stylish Stella	Riverbend Monkoncarlaet	Victor E. Cookson
1965	Top Girl	Drake Farms Chief	Hughes Bros.
1966	Justamere Stylish Stella	Riverbend Monkoncarlaet	Victor E. Cookson
1967	Justamere Stylish Stella	Riverbend Monkoncarlaet	Victor E. Cookson
1968	La Roxie	La Rock	Walter Sparks
1969	La Roxie	La Rock	Walter Sparks
1970	South Valley Lady Grey	Justamere Showtime	Wm. Gordon Young
1971	South Valley Lady Grey	Justamere Showtime	Wm. Gordon Young
1972	South Valley Lady Grey	Justamere Showtime	Wm. Gordon Young
1973	Candelichte Doreen	Starlight Calypso	Brown Bros.
1974	Mitzy Jane	Drake Farms Chief	Joseph Michalyshen
1975	Mitzy Jane	Drake Farms Chief	Joseph Michalyshen
1976	South Valley Showtime	Justamere Showtime	Wm. Gordon Young
1977	College Lynda	College Major	Reg M. Black and Sons
1978	Valentine	South Valley Did It	Mrs. Robt. L. Robinson
1979	Jodi of Glynlea	Lo Lynd Joe Laet	Kirby Bros.
1980	Princess Grace	South Valley Did It	Mrs. Robt. L. Robinson
1981	Jodi of Glynlea	Lo Lynd Joe Laet	Kirby Bros.
1982	Blackhome Connie Lyn	Lo Lynd Douglas	Reg M. Black and Sons
1983	C-Jewel	Donald Laet	Irvan Chamberlain
1984	Blackhome Dayna Lyn	Highview Dragano	Reg Black and Sons
1985	Summertime Rena of Glynlea	Foremark Forest Pride	Glyn and Marion Furber

First prize heavy draft team, Royal Winter Fair, 1979. Shown by Don Robertson, Lindsay, Ontario.

RIVERBEND MONKONCARLAET

If horses were granted citizenship, Riverbend Monkoncarlaet would have qualified as a good Canadian; from a Canadian-born mother and an immigrant father, he was born in Manitoba, moved to Saskatchewan, and then to Alberta, and in point of influence he reached all parts of Canada.

The year of 1942 was not a propitious time for a young stallion to be making his entry upon the Canadian scene. The prevailing opinion was that the big need in the country was to get rid of a burdensome surplus rather than to acquire more horses. But a few stub-born breeders were saying, as they have always said, that "tractors or no tractors, there'll be an unending need for good farm horses."

Carl Roberts, one of the sons from the pioneer firm of C. D. Roberts and Sons, Osborne, Manitoba, breeders and importers of Percheron and Belgian horses, was among the horsemen who refused to surrender to popular whims. His program of herd improvement was practically uninterrupted. Moving away from the family partnership to farm independently nearby, he took with him a first class breeding foundation consisting of a few purebred mares and the stallion of mounting fame, Monarch. He met with success from the outset, notwithstanding the low estate of the horse business.

With Monarch's Rose, Roberts won the grand championship for mares at the Canadian Royal in 1926. He won again with Monarch's Ruby in 1932 and with Monet, he won it four times between 1933 and 1938. With Monarch, the leading sire of winners in the years before 1938, Roberts took the grand championship for stallions in 1926, '27, and '29. Then with Monarch's Laet, he took another of the same awards in 1934.

By 1942, when Riverbend Monkoncarlaet was foaled, Roberts was on the new farm at St. Adolphe and gaining fame. Monarch's Ruby became the mother of Monarch's Laet, the stallion that became the Royal grand champion in 1932. She was also the mother of Monet, many times champion at the national Winter Fair. Monet, to the service of Rookwood Grandeur, gave birth to the matchless Riverbend Monkoncarlaet, which may have been Carl Roberts' finest achievement of all. Credit for the stallion's fame, however, would have to be shared with George Fraser, Jonathan Fox, Jr., and others.

George Fraser, born in Nebraska in 1887, was a homesteader with a sod shack and stable soon after the provinces of Saskatchewan and Alberta were created. These meagre beginnings set the stage for fifty years of enterprising Percheron breeding. In 1917, he purchased his first purebreds, an imported French stallion, Koimao, and several mares including one better than the others and registered as Jersey. The grey Count Vimy, the first of Fraser's home-grown champions, was sired by Koimao and mothered by Jersey.

There were difficult years, like 1932 when Fraser, with more luck than cash, was able to buy one of the leading sires of the depression period, Erik of Lakeview, for $150.

By 1946 Fraser needed another stallion and fancied the big colt Riverbend Monkoncarlaet, seen at Roberts' farm, and bought him with borrowed money. But the debt was quickly liquidated with the returns from the significant sale of the grey stallion Paramount Monarch's Laet in England in 1946. Then, still rejoicing over Riverbend Monkoncarlaet, he fitted him and took him to the Royal in the fall of '47 and was rewarded with the reserve grand championship.

It was there at the Toronto show that the big stallion—twenty-two hundred pounds—caught the enthusiastic interest of Jonathan Fox, Jr., second generation breeder of Percherons at Lloydminster. Horsemen hadn't forgotten how to barter when cash was scarce and a deal was made by which Fox got

Blanche Kesako, reserve grand champion mare at the Royal, 1929, and grand champion in each of the next two years for C. M. Rear of Saskatchewan. *Photograph by Live Stock Photo Co.; courtesy* The Western Producer.

Jodi of Glynlea, grand champion mare at the Canadian Royal in 1979 and 1981. *Courtesy Canadian Percheron Association.*

the horse and Fraser got another stallion, the American-bred Dragano, and some cash.

It was after this that Monkoncarlaet sired his most famous offspring, among them Justamere Stylish Stella that ended her notable show career with nine grand championships at the Royal; Justamere Showtime, fifth on the sires of winners list, the wonder horse that reached the pinnacle of his breeding success when owned by Gordon Young of Cayley, Alberta; Justamere Par Excellent, three times grand champion at the Royal for Michalyshen Brothers; and Justamere Handsome Harry, full brother to Justamere Showtime, and retained by Fox for breeding at home until sold to Roy Ferren of Cavan, Ontario.

From Justamere, Riverbend Monkoncarlaet was sold to the Canadian Department of Agriculture for $2,000 to follow Koncarhope at the experimental station at Lacombe. At his new home, the great sire was available to more owners of purebred mares, and Jonathan Fox was among those who continued to use him.

DRAKE FARMS CHIEF

With Riverbend Monkoncarlaet and Drake Farms Chief ranking first and second among the Percheron sires of winners at the Canadian Royal in recent decades, it should be noted that one was bred and raised in the West and the other was just as completely a product of the East. The two horses of eminence were separated in age by eleven years and were never within a thousand miles of each other.

Drake Farms Chief, bred by Drake Farm at St. Mary's, Ontario, was foaled in 1953. His

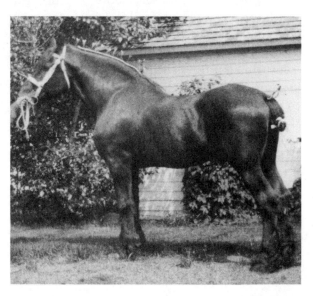

Justamere Showtime by Riverbend Monkoncarlaet. Bred by Jonathan Fox, he ended his years of distinction at the head of the stud of William Gordon Young, Cayley, Alberta.

THE PERCHERON

breeding was of the best. His sire was Morden Chief, by Chief Laet, by Sir Laet, by Laet, and his dam was Lynnwood most of the way. She was Lynnwood Dixiana 2nd, by Lynnwood Don, by Don Again, by Don Degas.

As a show horse at the Royal, however, Drake Farms Chief was not a notable success. He had size and muscle and good action in his favor and even his pictures show the excellence of his feet and hoofheads. The same pictures also show a straightness in his hind legs that would draw criticism. The critics might add, too, that he was often difficult to handle.

He was not shown as a foal but after being sold as a lean yearling to Sherman Read of Michigan, he was a regular entrant at the Royal for half of his years. In his yearling form, he stood sixth in a class of seven and passed unnoticed by most horsemen. Back at the Royal as a two-year-old, he did no better and placed fifth in a class of six. As a three-year-old, he made a slightly better showing, winning third prize in a class of seven.

Older horsemen were quick to say that Sherman Read was a good horseman with a pronounced dislike for overfitting; they reasoned that because of this objection to excessive fat, he was probably satisfied to show his own young horses with the handicap of being underfitted. Anyway, the Chief's fortunes at the Royal Winter Fair were not improving and in 1965, appearing in the ring as a twelve-year-old, he placed seventh in a class of seven. But more important, his progeny was now coming to the forefront in the get-of-sire classes and the race for championships.

The Chief's march of progress quickened

Monarch, three times grand champion stallion at the Royal Winter Fair and the highest scoring sire of winners at the Royal between 1922 and 1938. Owned and shown by Carl Roberts, St. Adolphe, Manitoba. *Photograph by Cook and Gormley.*

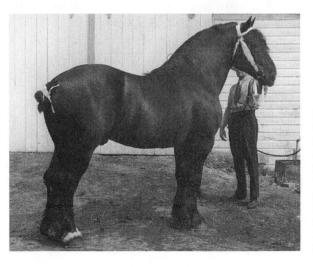

Riverbend Monkoncarlaet, the leading sire of winners at the Canadian Royal between 1946 and 1985, and one of the greatest breeding Percherons in Canadian history. *Courtesy* The Western Producer.

Jonathan Fox of Justamere Farm, Lloydminster, a long-time breeder of high class Percherons, Polled Herefords, and other breeds. He has been the recipient of numerous honors including admittance to the National Agricultural Hall of Fame

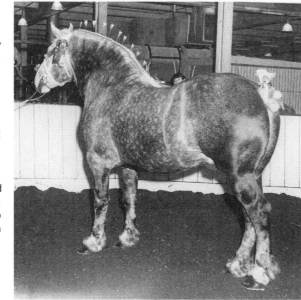

Justamere Par Excellent, by Riverbend Monkoncarlaet, three times grand champion at the Canadian Royal Winter Fair—1964, '66, and '67. Both Justamere Par Excellent and Riverbend Monkoncarlaet trace back through Calypso to the famous imported French stallion Brilliant 3rd, whose line was so influential in Percheron breeding on this continent. Shown by Michalyshen Brothers, Brandon. *Photograph by Lensmen Photo.*

spectacularly in 1961 when La Don's Chief by the old sire won his class and was awarded the reserve grand championship for owner Merril Johnson. By 1964, the winnings by sons and daughters of Drake Farms Chief were looking like a record. The filly Papoose, shown by Sherman Read, was a class winner for yearlings; Charmony, shown by Hughes Brothers, was the winning brood mare; Top Girl, another Hughes Brothers entry, was the second prize yeld mare; La Don's Chief was third prize mature stallion for Merril Johnson; both first and second prizes were taken in the get-of-sire class, and Top Girl came back to collect the reserve grand championship ribbon. These were all sons and daughters of Drake Farms Chief. Top Girl returned the next year, 1965, to win the grand championship.

In the few years following, the mare Mitzy Jane, shown by Joe Michalyshen of Brandon, and the stallion Maverick, belonging to Art Bast and Family, Hartford, Wisconsin, both sired by the Chief, were the leading subjects for conversation in the Percheron community. Both won reserve grand championships at the Royal in 1973 and both won grand championships in 1974 and '75.

Clearly, the impact of the Ontario-bred Percheron that lived to the age of nineteen years was felt on both sides of the international border. A writer in a leading draft horse magazine offered the timely summary: "A strong case can be made that Drake Farms Chief has been the biggest single influence on the contemporary Percheron breed in America . . . His offspring are setting the trend for the modern day Percheron . . . Not only was he siring a lot of colts for that period, they were in the right hands to gain public attention and make breed history . . . And as some will argue, [he] changed the direction of the breed in this country toward the more upstanding, hitchy type horse that is currently in vogue."[19]

PERCHERON MARES OF EXCELLENCE

Much has been written about prepotent sires and sires of winners in livestock breeding. The average stallion will leave many more offspring than the mare and will win more attention, but that parent contributing nourishment and protection as well as an equal complement of genetic determiners is in no way less important. It is only right that representatives with proven distinction on the mother's side should be presented for recognition.

DUCHESS AND LYNDA

College Duchess, bred and raised by the Ontario Agricultural College and owned later by Ontario breeders Fred Hampson and then Ananius Bauman, had all the qualifying characteristics for a great brood mare, unless a showring record peppered with championships were considered necessary. Her daughter, College Lynda, that came to Reginald Black at Moorefield, Ontario, before she was two years old, however, seemed to have everything, including the showring record with championships. Between them, the performance record was one to be enshrined in breed history.

College Duchess, foaled in 1960, was sired by Morden Chief and from College Flora by Buddy Surprise on the dam's side. She was constantly on view at the college but otherwise too busy raising foals to have time for the showring. This big black mare—eighteen hands—produced eleven foals from seven different sires, eight of which were exhibited at the Canadian Royal out of which four were awarded championships. One son, College Chief, was bought to be a herd header for Victor Cookson and was grand champion at the Royal in 1971. Another, Rolling Acres Morden Chief, was sold to a United States buyer and ultimately brought back to Canada by Reginald Black.

The Duchess lived to enter her twenty-third year and her eleventh and last foal was born when she was twenty-one years old in 1981.

If any single member of her family was to surpass the old mare's record, it had to be College Lynda, the daughter that became the corner stone of the distinguished stud of Percherons owned by Reginald Black and Sons, Moorefield, Ontario. The Blacks showed Lynda to win the brood mare class and then the grand championship at the Royal in 1977 and the same high award at the Canadian National Exhibition on three occasions.

Reg Black bought his first registered Percheron, Leanna Laet, in 1946, and gained his first major championship at the C.N.E. in 1959. He was president of the Canadian Percheron Association from 1974 to 1979. After his success with Lynda he and his family began to wonder if they might some day achieve the distinction of winning a Royal grand championship with a Percheron of their own breeding. It happened when Lynda's daughter, Blackhome Connie Lyn that had been reserve champion at the Royal in 1981, was made grand champion in 1982. Then, as if to pay a bonus, Connie Lyn was named the world grand champion mare at the World Percheron Congress at Calgary in 1983. There was more to come: another daughter of the cornerstone mare, this one Blackhome Dayna Lyn, was reserve grand champion at the Royal in 1983 and grand champion in 1984.

"Now," wrote Mr. Black, "College Lynda has had nine foals in as many years and is due to foal again in May, [1986]."[20]

STYLISH STELLA

Justamere Stylish Stella was a show mare more than a brood mare but proved that she could be both. Her total of nine grand championships at the Royal Winter Fair was enough to make her distinctive in any company and qualify her for a prominent

Chief Laet, grandson of Laet, was foaled in 1932 and brought to Canada by the Department of Agriculture. He was grand champion at the Royal in 1934 and will be remembered as one of the greatest sires of the breed. Unfortunately his offspring became most prominent in the years when there was no Royal Winter Fair. *Courtesy* The Western Producer.

was twenty-two years old.[21] The mare was sired by Jason, grand champion stallion at the Toronto Royal in 1946 for Gilbert E. Arnold, from whom Brault bought most of his herd sires, including Arnoldwold Jasaclo, which was the best known.

Carin Jason's owner, a breeder of purebred Percherons for sixty years and among the foremost in eastern Canada, liked to exhibit his horses at the local fair at St. Alexandre d'Iberville and other Quebec shows. He never made entry at the Royal. But Carin Jason's offspring were frequent winners wherever shown and might have been strong contenders in the best national competitions.

place in breed history. Foaled in 1952, she was sired by Riverbend Monkoncarlaet, bred by Jonathan Fox, Jr., and owned for most of her life by Victor Cookson of Bowmanville.

Stella won her first grand championship at the Royal, showing as a yeld mare, in 1958, and made her last appearance at the show eleven years later, showing as a brood mare and demonstrating her versatility by winning second prize in a big class of the matrons. Her breeder, Jonathan Fox, could say with pride in 1986: "I have a full sister at home, now eighteen years old."

CARIN JASON

Foaled and raised by Arthur Brault of St. Alexandre d'Iberville, Quebec, Carin Jason came to be seen as one of the most prolific mares of the breed. She is known to have produced seventeen purebred Percheron foals, the last of which was born when she

SOUTH VALLEY LADY GREY

A daughter of the immortal Justamere Showtime, the grey mare South Valley Lady Grey was bred and owned by William Gordon Young, Cayley, Alberta, and foaled in 1965. Three times she was grand champion mare at the Royal—1970, '71, and '72. In 1975 she was back to win the brood mare class. She was a big mare with a showtime weight exceeding twenty-two hundred and fifty pounds and much admired for her refinement of feet and legs and exceptional brood mare character.

JUSTAMERE PERFECTION

Any mare that could claim two of the greatest stallions of the breed in Canada deserves a place of honor. The mare was Justamere Perfection, a member of the crop of 1946, sired by Dragano and bred and owned by Jonathan Fox, Jr., Lloydminster.

The older of the two sons was Justamere Handsome Harry, foaled in 1953 and sired by Riverbend Monkoncarlaet. When Mr. Fox sold the latter to the federal Department of Agriculture, he selected Handsome Harry to follow as head sire in the Justamere breeding program. After some years, Handsome Harry was sold to Roy Ferren in eastern Canada where his successes continued. Many sons and daughters won prizes at the Royal. It was a serious loss to the breed when this great mare died from sleeping sickness at the age of six years.

The second of the two famous sons of Justamere Perfection was the very distinguished Justamere Showtime, foaled in 1956 and a full brother of Handsome Harry. He was sold from Justamere to Allen Bexson, Lloydminster, and later to William Gordon Young. In the list of sires of winners at the Canadian Royal for the years 1946 to 1985, there are only four stallions placed above this great son of Justamere Perfection.

Princess

The black mare Princess, owned by Mrs. R. L. Robinson, Jr., Richland, Michigan, could not be called a Canadian, but she had so many Canadian admirers, so many famous offspring from a Canadian-bred sire, and made such a big impact upon the Percheron competition at the Royal and elsewhere on the continent, that it would be a mistake to ignore her unmatched influence.

Princess was born in 1968, sired by La Rex. On the dam's side, she was a granddaughter of the great Canadian-bred Drake Farms Chief. She won prizes and a few championships at American shows in her early years and then settled down to producing foals as a full time occupation. At the time of writing these pages, she had given birth to at least thirteen foals. The first two did not excite much attention but it was at this point that a new stallion came into her life; the Robinsons bought South Valley Did It, a son of Justamere Showtime, from William Gordon Young of Alberta. He was a stallion that seemed to bring magic with him. In the next eleven years, Princess produced eleven foals sired by South Valley Did It and the result was enough to bring fame to both parents. Most of the progeny became champions, some of them notable. Most of them appeared at the Royal Winter Fair and some became grand champions there. Six of the family, full brothers and sisters, appeared at the World Percheron Congress at Calgary in 1983. One of them won first in the filly foal class; one placed third in the brood mare

Justamere Stylish Stella won nine grand championships at the Royal Winter Fair—a breed record. *Photograph by McNaught.*

South Valley Lady Grey, by Justamere Showtime, grand champion at the Royal in 1970, '71, and '72, for William Gordon Young, Cayley, Alberta.

class; and the grey three-year-old stallion Confetti won first and grand championship for his owner, Ironwood Farms, Renfrew, Ontario.

The sons and daughters of Princess have won numerous prizes and championships at the Royal Winter Fair. The mare Valentine was grand champion in 1978 and D.I.D. was reserve grand champion stallion in the same year. Princess Grace, later sold to Joe Michalyshen of Brandon, was grand champion female in 1980. The stallion Blizzard appeared at the Royal again and again. He won as a foal in 1977 and as a yearling in 1978. He then became the property of Joseph Michalyshen of Manitoba, for whom he won first prize in each of three years at the Royal and the grand championship in 1979 and '80. And the stallion Confetti, mentioned previously, won the Royal grand championship for Ironwood Farms in 1982 and for his breeder and original owner, Mrs. R. L. Robinson, in 1984. And that is not all. What a brood mare record! On her performance in both Canada and the United States, Princess must be seen as the brood mare of her generation.

Blizzard, by South Valley Did It. A well-known son of Princess, he won the Royal grand championship twice for Joseph Michalyshen, Brandon, Manitoba. *Photograph by J. E. McNeil.*

The Belgian

A Powerhouse in a Horsehide

To the pride of the people of Belgium shown in their progressive little country—about two-thirds the size of Nova Scotia—can be added their wartime resilience, peacetime enterprise, staunch independence, and national breed of heavy horse, the now internationally known Belgian.

What is today Belgium, plus parts of Holland and France, seems to have been the home of the biggest horses in Europe and probably in the world even two thousand years ago. When his armies were invading Gaul—meaning western Europe—Caesar was so impressed by the big and powerful horses that he took some representatives of the native strain to Rome for breeding purposes.

Nobody can positively identify the horses Caesar saw and pre-empted except to say that they must have belonged to one of the native strains in that homeland of the big Flemish stock. They were either the locally popular Brabancon, the Ardennese that took its name from the mountain range in which Belgium and France had similar interest, or the Belgian breed that was to win attention from draft horse users around the world. It is possible that all three were entitled to be classified as Belgians.

The Ardennese breed, whose strength and stamina came to Napoleon's notice when he was conducting his campaign against Russia in 1812, was requisitioned for use in transporting artillery and was later very popular in Sweden. Perhaps it would not be unfair to regard the Ardennese and the Brabancon as sub-breeds of the Belgian. Doubtless the three lines with similarities in scale and conformation had equal similarities in ancestry and origin, all resting squarely on the same Flemish foundation that had been sought by breed builders of Shires in England, Clydesdales in Scotland, and Percherons in France, to infuse added size.

After returning from the Third Crusade to the Holy Land in the twelfth century, Richard the Lion Heart introduced representatives of the Flemish stock to England and thereby influenced the destiny of draft horse breeds in England and Scotland.

All the heavy breeds and strains of old

Previous page: Paragon Fan by Paragon Major, many times a champion, including grand champion at the Royal in 1935 for Robert Thomas, Grandora, Saskatchewan. *Photograph by Hillyard.*

The modern Belgian in harness. The first prize unicorn hitch of Belgians shown by Leduc's Lynnwood Ranch, Aldersyde, Alberta, at the 1984 Calgary Exhibition and Stampede. *Photograph by Bruce Pickering; courtesy Leduc family.*

THE BELGIAN

Flanders gained high favor when knighthood was in flower and aristocratic horsemen went to war clothed from head to foot in wrought iron overwear weighing as much or more than the warriors. It was warfare at a slow pace—about plowing speed—but that didn't matter as long as the cavalryman's body was snugly sealed in a lance-proof metallic uniform. If the total weight of the horseman and his iron-ware protection exceeded 450 or 500 pounds, nothing less than a big and powerful horse was suitable to carry it for hours at a time. The same circumstances brought the English Shires to favor and fame, leaving the Belgians and Shires to share the distinction of being the biggest horses in the world.

The people of Belgium chose to believe that the best knights and the best horses for war were raised in the valley of the Meuse River, in some ways the cradle of the Belgian breed. A legendary Belgian stallion, Bayard by name, was credited with carrying four knights in full metal uniforms for a distance of ten leagues, about thirty miles, without evident indication of fatigue. Such a horse would have been a perfect teammate for the fabled Paul Bunyan's big blue ox that hauled a string of bunkhouses from one lumber camp to another every time the need occurred. There is nothing to suggest that the big ox left any descendants, but in the case of the stallion Bayard, there are still horses of the breed carrying his name and, allegedly, his blood.

Prof. J. Leyder, writing for the magazine *Le Cheval Belge*, published in Brussels in 1905, gave support to the view of consanguinity of Belgian, Brabancon, and Ardennese. One extract carried by volume I of the *Canadian Belgian Horse Stud Book*, stated: "By awarding to the Belgian Ardennese horse, Spirou, the championship for stallions of French draft breeds, to Caline II the championship for mares of foreign draft breeds and to the Brabancon stallion, Reve d'Or the world championship for draft breeds of any origin, the International Jury of the Paris fair has proclaimed the Belgian horse the leading draft horse of the world." As Prof. Leyder saw the winners, they were all Belgians and so they might as well be accepted.[1]

The discovery of gunpowder and adoption of firearms in warfare left the heavy horses with little other immediate purpose than that of moving the country's freight wagons over primitive roads. Policy-makers reasoned that lighter and more active horses would prove more useful. They knew that knights from the region taking part in the crusades and enjoying the biggest horses and the heaviest armor, had been impressed by horsemen from North Africa riding horses with Oriental breeding—Turk, Barb, and Arabian. They returned with new ideas about improvement by breeding the heavy native mares to imported eastern stallions. They were willing to trade Belgian scale for a measure of Arabian refinement.

The idea was well received by everybody except the farm breeders who were not ready to sacrifice the rare quality of size in their horses. Time proved the horsemen to be right and by resisting the advice to crossbreed, the Belgian changed only slightly and survived as a first class farm horse with weight, muscle, and the good disposition needed for farm service. Again the Belgian was wanted for export and again the demand became so heavy that government policy was shaped to ensure against the best breeding stock being bought for shipment out of the country.

Paying tribute to the Belgian breeders, Prof. J. Leyder said: "After all, the Belgian farmer was the only one who seemed to have had an intuition of what was going to happen, when, faithful to popular traditions, deaf to all learned arguments praising the advantages of the crossbred horse, he stood firm in his refusal to allow his big mares to be crossed by Thoroughbred stallions and when, later on, the supply of heavy horses fell far below the demand, he was in a position to benefit greatly by the situation. It must be admitted, however, that the Belgian breed was for a time stopped in its development and threatened with a condition of fatal stagnation. Unshackled, relieved from pressure and left to himself, the Belgian breeder has followed his own dictates in the pursuit of his industry and the whole world knows what success he has attained."[2]

The showring and the subsidy system played important parts in Belgian breed improvement in the recent century and a half. Provincial shows were started about 150 years ago and all stallions standing for public service were expected to be entered for competition. Most horses were started at small, local fairs and moved to bigger ones as long as they were winning. Consistent winners would end up at Brussels where the first National Show was held in 1874. Brussels in 1913 reported an entry of a thousand horses.

Four years after the birth of the National Show at Brussels, the Belgian stallion Brilliant won the highest honors for draft stallions at the Paris Exposition. It was the first international victory for the breed but not the last. At another international show at Paris in 1889, Jules Hazard, who was gaining a world reputation, qualified for a special award after being named the winner of a grand championship over all breeds and open to the world—with one of his own Belgians, of course.

A showring triumph of no less significance came in 1900 when the famous stallion Rève d'Or was awarded the supreme championship over all heavy horse breeds, also at Paris.

The government of Belgium, over many years, assisted in horse improvement by offering generous subsidies to owners of outstanding animals and administering a rigid system of examinations. Subsidies might be added to top prize money for stallions of exceptional type and quality, free from all unsoundness and with proof of breed purity. With such bonuses, owners could not afford to sell them for export.

Again and again since the time of the Roman invasion the little country has become a battleground and both its peace-loving citizens and good horses have suffered. Caesar commended the people of Gallia Belgica for their valor, and Canadians have heard many times of the Belgian fibre and heroism displayed in the face of atrocities during World Wars I and II, and the courage and fortitude displayed in rebuilding the country.

Not so well known was the near disaster that threatened to annihilate the Belgian horses, except for pools of breeding stock in the United States and Canada, in the years of the first World War. As it was, Belgian agriculture was devastated; many of the good horses were lost; some were sent to Holland for safe keeping; others went to England. At the end of the war, horse numbers were seriously depleted, many of them having been consumed by hungry soldiers and civilians. Fortunately, some of the best survived in

Holland, England, and Belgium, to say nothing of the sizable pools of high quality horses from Belgians exported to the United States and Canada. Consideration was given to a draft of superior animals from North American studs for return to the homeland, but it wasn't necessary. The breeders in Belgium succeeded in recovering most of the animals sent out of the country and the breeding bands regained their formal excellence.

There was devastation again with some valuable breeding horses being lost to army rations as war swept over western Europe in 1940, but again the Belgian horses returned to normal numbers after the end of hostilities.

Even the briefest review of the breed in its homeland demands mention of some of the leading breed builders and their best horses. Jules Hazard of Fosteau in the province of Hainaut seemed to qualify as the foremost breeder of his time and one of the best of all time, bearing a place in breed history like that of Ernest Perriot in the Percheron breed.

There was much of the typical success story about Hazard's life with horses, like the poor boy who made good and died a millionaire. In Hazard's case, he had the faith and courage to buy a fourteen-year-old lame stallion, Orange 1st by name. But as Hazard suspected, the lameness was not hereditary and the horse possessed better breeding and more quality and type excellence than most people would recognize in an aging animal. In Jules Hazard's hands, the horse became one of the most successful sires in the breed and the owner's fame spread.

Orange 1st was followed at the head of the Hazard stud by Orange 2nd, then a grandson, Brin d'Or, each in turn leaving his mark of merit upon the Fosteau stud and the breed.

A few of the first Belgian horses to be brought to Canada were sired by Brin d'Or. His most notable distinction was as the sire of Hazard's greatest champion, Indigene du Fosteau.

Eight times Jules Hazard won the championship for stallions at Brussels and eight times he won it for mares. It was a unique record.

An honor roll list of "six of the most noted stallions in Belgium" was published in volume XI of the *National Registry of Belgian Draft Horses*, 1924, by the American Association of Importers and Breeders of Belgian Draft Horses. It appeared as a useful summary of leading sires in the homeland at that period and is presented here for what it can contribute to Belgian history:

1. Orange 1st was foaled in 1863 and sired by Fortin 1st; he became a national success when in the ownership of Jules Hazard and continued to head the Fosteau stud from the age of fourteen until his death at twenty-four years.
2. Brilliant was a son of Orange 1st, foaled in 1868. Described as a powerfully built horse with superior type and quality, he was a winner in many showrings, including those at Paris in 1878 and Brussels in 1880.
3. Jupiter was also sired by Orange 1st and foaled in 1880. Some students regarded him as the greatest sire of them all in the native land of the breed, although the weight of opinion would still rest with Indigene du Fosteau. Sons and grandsons won championship honors at Brussels nine times in the ten years beginning with 1894, and the old horse himself won the Brussels championship when nine years of age.
4. Rève d'Or was foaled in 1891, sired by Jupiter. He was champion at Brussels in 1898 but his most distinguished triumph

was in winning the championship against all breeds at Paris in 1900.

5. Indigene du Fosteau was regarded by most observers as the greatest stallion of the breed up to his time. Foaled in 1902 and sired by Brin d'Or, he was bred by Jules Hazard but had several owners in his life. He was champion at Brussels in four consecutive years, 1906, '07, '08, and '09. In 1912, '13, and '14, the same high award was won by sons of the famous horse. Some of his get gained fame in North American showrings, the most notable of which was Alfred de Bree Eyck.

6. Paul, another noted breeding horse in Belgium, was foaled in 1906 and won the championship at Brussels in 1911.

THE BELGIAN ON NORTH AMERICAN SOIL

Horses displaying Belgian colors, type, size, and muscle to one degree or another—often called Boulonnais, sometimes called Flemish—were pounding North American fields and trails before 1866 but it was only in that year that Dr. A. G. van Hoorebeke of Illinois introduced the first Belgian horses to be accepted as purebreds. That was still thirty-six years before the first of the breed eligible for registration were delivered in Canada.

The fact was, that in relation to other draft breeds, the Belgian was a late-comer to both Canada and the United States and, except in the Province of Quebec, far from being an instant success.

Breeders and users of Clydesdales and Percherons who were accustomed to horses with higher heads, longer strides, and more refinement in fetlocks, shanks, and hocks were inclined to sneer at the chunky or "porky" specimens. But the snickering did not last because farming people with more interest in utility than glamorous appearance were attracted to the Belgians and their popularity grew.

E. Lefebure of Fairfax, Iowa—himself a native son of Belgium—began importing from the homeland to the United States shortly after 1888 and won growing attention on both sides of the Atlantic. Many of his Belgians were sold to Canadians. But the imported strain was soon undergoing striking changes in form and quality. North American horsemen wanted more height at the withers, more stretch, more length of pasterns, and generally more quality of limbs without loss of thickness and muscling. In consequence, a new Belgian was being fashioned, bringing together the best of two ideals.

It was easy for producers to believe the emerging Belgian, still supremely muscled but more prepossessing than the orthodox representatives from the homeland, would win a growing share of public support. If the number of registrations entered annually with the National Live Stock Records is used as an indicator, they were right. The best regional support for the breed came in the states of Iowa, Indiana, and Ohio in the United States and in the Province of Quebec in Canada.

The search for the first Belgian horses in Canada calls for some explanation. Robert Thomas of Grandora, Saskatchewan, who, with help from the progeny of a son of the famous Farceur, became one of Canada's most successful horse breeders, remembers a bay Belgian stallion, registered in the

United States but never in Canada, that was brought to Manitoba in 1900 by Harry Galbraith of Hartney. The stud sired many excellent grade horses, among them a pair with which Thomas won a team class at Saskatoon Exhibition in 1912. This stallion may have been the first Belgian of pure breeding in Canada but missed appropriate recognition because his entry in the Canadian stud book was neglected. Hence, the honor of being a nation's first went to members of a shipment brought from Belgium for the Department of Agriculture in the Province of Quebec, in 1902.[3]

The foundation importations of that and succeeding years, authorized by the provincial government, deserved more recognition than was ever accorded. Quebec had its French Canadian or Canadien breed of relatively small, generally black, and always robust horses tracing to the earliest importations of horse stock from Normandy and Brittany in the seventeenth century. Tempered to toughness by the law of survival of the fittest, these all-purpose horses were probably more appropriate to the needs of the colony than most people realized. In any case, by the middle of the nineteenth century, local opinion about the real worth of these little black horses of iron, was divided. Some observers acknowledged the qualities of versatility and hardiness that gave them the distinction of suitability, but just as many viewers, no less vociferous, believed the Quebec farmers needed heavier draft animals.[4]

By 1901, the average size of farm in Quebec was 103 acres with about half of it cultivated. Oxen and small horses were the principal source of power. Simultaneously, however, there was a movement afoot to protect the identity of the provincial breed and make heavier horses available. The provincial government through its Department of Agriculture voiced support for farm horses with added weight and pulling power as a means of improved farm efficiency.

The British breeds of draft horses had never won much favor in Quebec and in weighing the merits of the alternative breeds, Department of Agriculture opinion favored the Belgian. It then became departmental policy to import Belgian stallions from their native land and sell them on credit terms to agricultural societies and stallion clubs.

The selection and purchase of stallions in Europe were left largely to agents of the government. Some of those were later engaged in importing and selling Belgians on their own account in various parts of Canada, among them Eugene Pootmans and Sons, Alphonse Haazen, Baron de L'Epine, and

"Doc," a four-year-old gelding Reserve Champion at Edmonton, standing 18.2 hands, owned by Leduc's Lynnwood Ranch, Aldersyde, Alberta.

Baron de Champlouis. Each of the first three conducted extensive advertising in agricultural magazines and rarely missed the opportunity of mentioning the earlier connection with the Department of Agriculture. Baron de Champlouis of Danville seems to have been the first to advertise his own Belgians and thereby share his enthusiasm. In his advertising space in the *Farmer's Advocate* in 1903 he was offering Belgians "imported last September" and owning any one of them would be like having "a Klondike in your stable." His mare, Amie d'Elcour, sired by one of the leading sires in the homeland, Brin d'Or, and imported in 1902, had to rank among the earliest mares of the breed in Canada.

Although the first volume of the *Canadian Belgian Draft Horse Stud Book* was not published until 1920, entries followed a degree of chronological order and registration number one honors a bay mare, Pierette De Chaussée, foaled in Belgium in

Greentop Don, by Naden's Bill, an eastern Canadian champion of recent years. He was grand champion stallion at the Fredericton Exhibition, 1983 and '84. *Courtesy John Sandwith.*

1899 and imported in 1902 by Baron de L'Epine of Quebec City for the government of the province. The mare was sold after delivery to Paul Tourigny, Victoriaville, Quebec.

Of the next ten entries, seven were stallions and three mares, all imported in 1902 or one of the next four years by Baron de L'Epine for the government of Quebec. The recorded third owners of these can be taken as an indication of the government's purpose and policy. All the stallions in the group were sold to agricultural societies with Lac St. Jean Agricultural Society being the principal buyer.

Alphonse Haazen, whose name became well known to western horsemen, appeared most prominently as a government purchasing agent in 1910, just a few months before he started a horse breeding farm near Regina and a Belgian sales stable in Regina.

For the first few years after its introduction the Belgian breed made spectacular gains in the Province of Quebec but not in other eastern provinces. The most active new importers in Quebec were Bruno Beaulieu of St. Jerome, who made annual purchasing visits to Belgium after 1907, H. E. Martinette of St. Hyacinthe, and Dr. J. C. Reid of Chateauguay.

Volume I of the stud book points to W. C. Kidd of Listowel as the first owner of purebred Belgians elsewhere in eastern Canada. He is shown as having in 1908 bought three imported stallions from the well known A. B. Holbert of Greeley, Iowa. Buying stallions in numbers seemed to mark this man as a dealer rather than a breeder, but in any case, he qualified as a Belgian pioneer who performed useful service in promotion.

In the Canadian West

The opening act in the dramatic introduction of the Belgian horse in Canada took place in Quebec. The second was in the West where the stage was set on the Belgian Horse Ranch, close to the Elbow River and about eighteen miles southwest of Calgary in 1903. The author of it all was Raoul Pirmez, recently from Belgium, who bought four sections of choice grassland made enchanting by borders of spruce forests and mountain scenery. His plan was to specialize in breeding French Coach and Belgian horses in this region where most people had never seen representatives of either breed.

His first Coach Horse was imported by the same Baron de L'Epine who brought many of the first Belgians to Quebec and arrived in time to show and win at the Calgary Spring Fair in 1904. But the more important maker of horse history was the three-year-old Belgian stallion, Pothin, by Voltaire. He was inspected by a representative of the *Farmer's Advocate* who reported in admiring terms that the stud was a winner in Belgium and would be a sure winner in the Territories.[5] Pothin won his class at Brussels as a foal, repeated as a yearling, and won at the Calgary spring show.

This prize-winning stallion must now be recognized as the first Belgian of either sex with full stud book qualifications in western Canada. Such distinction is enough to warrant a close examination of the stud book essentials:

Belgians have been bred extensively in Alberta since the Belgian Horse Ranch was established close to Calgary in 1903. Here is a modern pair, Tim and Ted, winning the light draft team at the 1984 Calgary Exhibition. Owned by Gus and Lil Leduc, the geldings are driven by Keith Hobdon of Lindsay, Ontario. *Photograph by Browarny; courtesy Leduc family.*

Pothin, (Imp.), male, black, hind feet white, bred by M. François Grandru, Belgium, imported in 1903 by Baron de L'Epine, Quebec; 3rd owner Raoul Pirmez, Calgary, 4th owner, A. A. Downey, Govan, Sask.

It was Raoul Pirmez's intention to build his herd of breeding mares to 100 head. That numerical goal was never attained but in breeding and quality of the imported mares, the achievement was a worthy one. The importation of 1907 included another stallion of note, Pompon, along with some of the best mares. At the Winnipeg Industrial Exhibition of 1910, Pompon was the only Belgian on the grounds but it was said that he was one of the most admired horses of any breed at the show. "Wide as a wagon with quality to spare," was the way one reporter described him.

The absence of competition was something that had to be expected in a new breed. At first Belgians, Shires, and Suffolks were shown in the same classes. By 1911, this was changing and Belgian entries at the Regina Winter Fair were big enough to more than justify their own classes; seven came out in the class for mature stallions, and eight in the class for three-year-old fillies. It marked a new day for the breed, for which the Belgian Horse Ranch could take much of the credit.

But it was in that same year, when the breed seemed "to be coming of age in the West," that the public heard of the sale of the Belgian Horse Ranch to an English syndicate at the surprisingly low price of $100,000 for everything. The report added, comfortingly, that the good horses would remain on the ranch and be a continuing part of the breeding project started by Mr. Pirmez. "The former owner will reside in this city of Calgary and the ranch will continue to breed fine Belgians," the report stated.

Raoul Pirmez became the Belgian Consul in Calgary and maintained his interest in the horses, but when on an extended visit to Brussels in 1920, he became suddenly ill and died. Horsemen of all breeds had reason to mourn.

From volume I of the *Canadian Belgian Draft Horse Stud Book* it is easy to conclude that the second purebred and registered Belgian in the West was the steel grey Champagne De Berthem, imported to the United States in 1905 and then taken to Brandon by Alex Galbraith and Son. He was resold to Henry Tennant and Sons of Coutts, Alberta.

With a distinctiveness not uncommon among horsemen, Henry Tennant was not an ordinary man and should not be passed over lightly. Born of British parents in Bombay, India, in 1837, he was clearly the kind of individual that gives horse history a fillip. He served as a drummer boy during the Crimean War and was an eyewitness of the historic Charge of the Light Brigade. Tennant saw Canada when as a British soldier his unit was sent to quell the Fenian Raids across the border. When his unit left Canada, Tennant remained, took to farming at Goodrich and later at Coutts, where he took his imported stallion and where the horseman died in 1913, age seventy-six years.[6]

Within a year after the delivery of the Tennant stallion, another imported and registered stallion of the breed—the third in the West—was being brought to the new Province of Alberta. This one was Major 2 de Tierne, imported by the Sainte Anne Ranch Trading Co. at Trochu, the business wing of the colorful settlement of French army and naval officers, "too old to fight and too young to quit." As settlement progressed, it appeared that "no person with lower rank than colonel need apply." The idea of a frontier settlement of French military aristocrats was born when Armand Trochu located land for himself northeast of Calgary in 1903. Within a year, he was joined by Count Paul de Beaudrap, a former member of the colony of French Counts at Whitewood in what is now south-eastern Saskatchewan. He located east of Trochu's homestead and called his place Jeanne d'Arc Ranch, to which he brought superior breeding stock of Percherons and at least one Belgian stallion. The stallion, before long, was sold to the recently established Belgian Horse Ranch where the said Major 2 de Tierne was used most successfully for some years.

THE POOTMANS

The year 1910 was especially important in Belgian history. The government of the Province of Quebec received one of its biggest importations from Belgium in that year and the incomparable stallion Farceur was foaled, signalling a new direction in Belgian breeding. And of special local impor-tance, the old family firm of Eugene Pootmans and Sons with headquarters in Antwerp and a branch in Quebec City, opened a sales stable at Regina and became the leading promotional force on the prairies. If more were needed to give the year a special significance, new breeders and exhibitors appeared. Notable among these was the Baxter Reed Ranching Co. of Olds which appeared at Calgary Exhibition to challenge the Belgian Horse Ranch and win the highest praise with the Belgian mare Fanette. She had earlier won the grand championship at the World's Fair at St. Louis.

The senior member of the Pootmans firm had been a leading exporter from Belgium for twenty-five years, with most shipments going to breeders and dealers in the United States. He remained in Belgium to keep the supply of horses coming forward and in 1910, two sons, Gaston and George, took up residence at Regina. The Pootmans business became worldwide and as some indication of the magnitude of operations, it was reported that Belgian horses exported from Belgium in 1911—mostly stallions—numbered 500. Regina was to become the most important overseas branch. Speaking through one of the farm papers in June, 1911, the brothers in Regina reported four import shipments from Belgium in that spring from which they had sold seventy-seven stallions. Shortly thereafter, they were complaining about the problem of obtaining sufficient ocean space for their shipments.

The Pootmans brothers were faithful exhibitors, often timing their importations to coincide with winter fairs or exhibitions at Regina or Brandon, then announcing that the new horses would be in the competitions and on display for the benefit of prospective buyers.

In conjunction with their sales stable at the corner of Ninth Avenue and Cameron Street, the firm operated a breeding farm outside the city, something that proved espe-cially useful during the years of World War I when most trans-Atlantic trade was sus-pended. The Pootmans' response was to expand the local breeding program and announce a hope of supplying most needs.

The Pootmans, at first, enjoyed a sort of prairie monopoly but before long Alphonse Haazen, who had been importing for the Quebec Department of Agriculture, moved in during 1911, opened a sales stable in Regina, and started a breeding farm outside the city. It looked like a duplicate of the Pootmans and Sons enterprise. But there was more than enough business for both. Before long the western Canadian horsemen who were to become widely known as Vanstone and Rogers of Wawanesa, Manitoba, entered the import business and by remaining longer in the trade, may have handled more Belgian horses than any other dealer.

THE DRAMATIC YEARS OF GEORGE RUPP

Every breed needed somebody with the courage and imagination of a George Lane as he conducted himself with Percherons, a Scotty Bryce with Clydesdales, or a George Rupp with Belgians.

The famous Farceur, for which C. G. Good of Iowa paid $47,500 in 1917, the highest price ever paid for a draft animal on the North American continent at that time.

Rupp was an Iowa man, medium tall, lean, dynamic, and forceful like a pile driver. He was part of a big movement of land seekers who flocked into western Canada in the first decade of the present century. He came to Saskatchewan in 1907 and settled on land (N. W. of 23–4–6–West of 2) southeast of the village of Lampman. He built modestly at first but as noted by one who wrote in *Poets' Corner*—a history of the Lampman district— Rupp constructed the horse stable with each stall "too large for one horse and too small for a team," obviously with single stalls for "broad-beamed" Belgians in mind.[7]

Rupp's boyhood dream was of owning and raising Belgian horses but it wasn't until 1914 that he had the capital with which to buy a stallion and two mares. He bought good ones conforming to his type ideals. The horses he wanted were very different from the first ones imported from Belgium. That first stallion on Pioneer Farm, Cesar de Naz, weighed twenty-two hundred pounds and possessed first class underpinning. He became the sire of Pioneer Masterpiece of which more will be said, and even if he had never left any other offspring, he would have earned applause.

In the next year, Rupp was in Iowa buying a carload of purebred mares with which to broaden his stud foundation. It was then that he saw the stallion Farceur, and was overwhelmed. "He is one of the most beautiful specimens of horseflesh I have ever cast my eyes over," he said. He resolved to have a Farceur son to head his band of purebreds. The result was the purchase in the next year of Paramount Wolver by Farceur, after he won second prize at the state fairs in both Iowa and Minnesota. By that time, George Rupp was claiming the distinction of owning the biggest stud of purebred Belgians in Canada.

In the next year, 1917, Paramount Wolver started his Canadian show career by winning the Belgian grand championship at Brandon Winter Fair. For the balance of that year and through 1918, Paramount Wolver and Dr. Charles Head's Fox de Roosbeke were battling for the championship awards at most shows. Fox de Roosbeke may have won most of them in 1918 but not in 1919 when Rupp was showing another son of Farceur, certainly the crowning joy of Rupp's life with horses. He was Paramount Flashwood, one of the greatest stallions in Belgian history in Canada.

Rupp was a leading supporter of the new North American type. Writing for the *Farmer's Advocate*, he admitted that "there are two distinct types of Belgian horses," and then went on to explain: "One is what we call the old type Flemish horse. He is low down, short necked, coarse headed, steep in feet and pasterns, round in bone and steep crouped, and matures at from 1600 to 1800 pounds.

"The modern type Belgian horse has a lot more stretch. He stands from 16½ to 18 hands high, has sloping shoulders, a longer neck, is cut cleanly about the head and throat-latch, has good feet and sloping pasterns, has lots of hard bone and a level croup, and is one of the largest drafters living. The progressive Belgian breeders are steering as clear of the former type as a ship does of an iceberg . . . What the Belgian breeders have done to improve their horses in the last 10 or 15 years is well known

Rupp's confidence in the West's enduring commitment to breed excellence is demonstrated in this outstanding six-horse hitch, winner of its class in the Calgary Stampede Parade of 1984. The outfit is owned by Leduc's Lynnwood Ranch, Aldersyde, Alberta. *Photograph by Browarny; courtesy Leduc family.*

to every student of draft horse breeding . . . The American breeder is producing a draft horse of superior merit . . ."[8] If a reader of his paragraphs had asked Rupp to further describe his ideal Belgian, quite likely he would have pointed at Paramount Flashwood, as if nothing more needed to be said. And he would not have been alone in seeing the big son of Farceur as the greatest Belgian of his time. Paramount Flashwood was bought from his breeder who was then the owner of Farceur— William Crownover of Iowa. In buying Flashwood in 1918, Rupp had two sons of Farceur for the next two years, until he sold Paramount Wolver to go back to Iowa, at the reported price of $11,400.

It spoke well for Rupp's judgment when he selected and bought Flashwood. It might have been expected that scores of other breeders on the continent at that time would have been watching this son of Farceur, full brother of the famous show mare Lista, who had championships at the International show at Chicago to her credit.

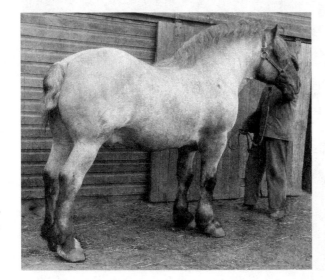

The Belgian stallion Monseur, bred by William Crownover and foaled in 1916, a son of the noted American stallion Farceur, and an influential sire in Canada. Owned by Robert Thomas, Grandora, Saskatchewan.

Paramount Flashwood had been a class winner and then junior and reserve champion stallion at Chicago in 1918, but the supreme achievement for this horse, entered from an inconspicuous community in Saskatchewan, came with the grand championship at the national Belgian Show at Waterloo, Iowa, in 1919. For Canadians, it was a championship to rank with the international championship for fat steers won by the twenty-four-hundred-pound Ontario entry, Clarence of Kirklevington in 1884, and the world championship for wheat won for Canada for the first time by Seager Wheeler of Saskatchewan in 1911.

After the win of 1919 Rupp had no hesitation about flattering his own and wrote: "It is said by many that he is even a greater horse than his illustrious sire," to which the editor added more wisely: "That stallion will make Belgian history in this country if he gets the mares."[9]

Following his triumph at the National Belgian Show, Paramount Flashwood was retired from showing to be used more extensively for breeding. He would be available for selected mares at a breeding fee of $100. But there were breakers ahead; the great Paramount Flashwood died on December 13, 1922, at the age of six and a half years. For the owner it was a severe blow as his note to the press indicated: "I feel the loss very keenly as Flashwood was not only a horse but a part of the family. The loss is partly offset by a $25,000 insurance policy carried by the Hartford Insurance Company."

But there was still a truly great horse at Pioneer Farm, Pioneer Masterpiece, sired by Cesar de Naz, and winner of many grand championships at Canadian exhibitions. So highly was he regarded that C. G. Good and Sons of Ogden, Iowa, borrowed him for their own use. In 1920 he was reportedly sold to a breeder at Drinkwater, Saskatchewan, for $10,000, but records show the horse back in Rupp's ownership in 1923 and being syndicated to the Willow Bunch Belgian Horse Club for the second year. The Willow Bunch breeders by this time had a substantial number of purebred mares, including some sired by Paramount Flashwood. They believed that if they could retain the use of Pioneer Masterpiece for a few more years, theirs would become the foremost Belgian horse district of Canada.

Pioneer Masterpiece would, indeed, be an excellent rock on which to build a breeding enterprise. Rupp called him a "duplicate of Paramount Flashwood," and as another star in Rupp's crown, Isaac Beattie of the pioneer firm of Colquhoun and Beattie and one of the best judges in Canada, pronounced Pioneer Masterpiece "The best Belgian horse I have ever seen."

In addition to leaving a vivid imprint upon the breed, Rupp left the Canadian Belgian association with something more with which to remember him. He believed the Canadian Belgian Draft Horse Breeders' Association was being dominated unjustly by eastern members and if nobody else would do something about it, he would act. He was angry that the East had four directors while the West had only one. Attending the annual meeting at Montreal in 1921, Rupp was carrying signed proxies from a large number of western members of the association. After making a speech about democracy, he insisted that members in far parts of Canada should have a chance to express themselves.

Until there was a better way, he demanded permission to vote on behalf of western absentees whose proxies he carried.

The secretary and some others opposed the unauthorized manner of voting and walked out of the meeting. The meeting was adjourned. When directors and members met the next day, a new and more representative board was elected with three directors, including Rupp, from the West. A promise was also given that the next annual meeting would be in a western city.[10]

A special general meeting was held in February, 1922, at which the constitution was amended to ensure that annual meetings would be held in the East and West in alternate years. In addition, the board of directors would henceforth comprise nine people, two from Quebec, two from Ontario, one from Manitoba, two from Saskatchewan, and two from Alberta.[11]

Again George Rupp was elected a director but it was the last time. Following the death of Paramount Flashwood, he lost his former zest and liquidated his stock of horses, moving

The Belgian stallion Paragon Major, grand champion of his breed at the Royal on three occasions, 1923, '24, and '26. *Photograph by Hildebrand.*

those that remained to the village livery stable. Nothing was the same and then, about midway through 1923, he and his family moved back to the United States. The unforgettable George Rupp died in 1952 and Mrs. Rupp in 1957, leaving Canadian horsemen of his generation with many rich memories.

THE FARCEUR FAMILY IN CANADA

What Baron's Pride meant to the Clydesdale breed and the younger Brilliant to the Percherons, Farceur was to the Belgians. Breeders in both Canada and the United States would agree. He was a handsome roan, foaled in Belgium in 1910 and imported to the United States by William Crownover of Hudson, Iowa, in 1912. In the importer's possession, the horse established a fine show-yard record that included the grand championship at the International show at Chicago in 1913.

Farceur's breeding worth was soon recognized and at the Crownover dispersion in 1917, the stallion was bought at the widely reported price of $47,500 by C. G. Good and Sons, Ogden, Iowa, with whom he remained until his death in 1921.

The price paid for this seven-year-old horse was the highest ever paid for a draft type animal on the North American continent to that time. Whether by coincidence or not, it matched the price that William Dunlop paid for the Clydesdale stallion, Baron of Buchlyvie, in Scotland, six years earlier.

Nobody could appreciate more fully the unusual prepotency of Farceur than the person who, like the writer, had the privilege of strolling through the barns and fields of the Good's Oakdale Farm where sons and daughters of the great sire were still to be seen in numbers. Before leaving the farm, every visitor was shown the small barn in which Farceur lived during his years at Oakdale. Following a custom in the native land of the Belgians, the horse, at death, was buried below his stall and the bar dedicated to his memory.

Farceur's closest rival during his years was the stallion Alfred de Bree Eyck, by the great stallion of the native land, Indigene du Fosteau. Both stallions were imported from Belgium in the same year—1912. Alfred de Bree Eyck's importer, Henry Lefebure, sold him to Charles Irvine of Ankeny, Iowa, who showed him to the grand championship at the Chicago International in 1916 and then to the same distinction at the National Belgian Show at Waterloo in 1920. Irvine could tell of refusing an offer of $60,000 for the stallion in 1919, just at the time George Rupp was turning down an offer of $30,000 for Paramount Flashwood.

The two famous stallions had much in common but as far as Canada was concerned, the Farceur influence far exceeded that of Alfred de Bree Eyck.

Beginning with George Rupp's purchase of Paramount Wolver in 1916 and Paramount Flashwood in 1918, Canadian breeders demonstrated that they wanted Farceur breeding. It didn't escape the bold and ambitious thoughts of Rupp, after winning the highest award at the National Belgian Show in 1919, that Farceur would be a tremendous hit in Canada. Rupp felt he should consider the possibility of buying him and bringing him to Saskatchewan. The stallion was then almost ten years old and might be available at a price within Rupp's range. Such, apparently, was George Rupp's dream.

Monseur, because of his many years of service in the Robert Thomas stud in Saskatchewan, may have been Farceur's most influential son in Canada. Bred by William Crownover and foaled in 1916, Monseur was brought to Manitoba by C. D. Roberts and Sons in 1918 and, after the spring show at Brandon in 1919, where the three-year-old roan won the grand championship for Belgian stallions, he became the property of Robert Thomas, in whose Grandora Saskatchewan stud he remained for the rest of his life.

Bob Thomas was an Ontario farm boy born north of Kingston. He lived there until 1892 when the family moved to a farm in Manitoba. Bob's young heart was set on horses and neither schooling, sports, nor girls could excite as much enthusiasm. Moreover, the horses of his early choice were Belgians and as soon as he had enough money, he bought two purebred mares and a young stallion. But fate seemed to be putting the lad to the test and before two years had passed, his stallion died. Searching for a replacement, he travelled to Iowa, saw some of the best Belgians on the continent, and selected a yearling. But misfortune was hounding him and the colt developed something like shipping fever and died before reaching what would have been his Canadian home.

It would have seemed like a good time to change his pursuit but the dedicated young fellow was determined. He tried again in the spring of 1919, visiting the Brandon Winter Fair where C. D. Roberts and Sons were exhibiting some recently imported stallions, among them the three-year-old Monseur by Farceur. Thomas was instantly convinced; he had to own this one.

The progeny from Monseur carried the Farceur stamp, exactly as Thomas had hoped.

As new crops matured, he was able to boast that every colt or filly when two years old was taller than its mother. Monseur's best son was Paragon Major that was three times grand champion at the Royal—1923, '24, and '26—and in each of four years—1928, '29, '30, and '31—his offspring won the get-of-sire class at the Royal. Adding to these distinctions was a daughter of Major, Paragon Fan, one of the noted show mares of her time and also a grand championship winner at the Royal.

Echo Dale Farceur by Farceur was, like Paramount Wolver, a Canadian stallion for a time but was not allowed to remain. He was ultimately rated as one of the leading sires of the breed on the continent. C. D. Roberts and Sons brought him to their Manitoba farm in 1921 along with other aristocrats from Iowa carrying their sire's name. Among them were King Farceur, Farceur Special, and Queen Farceur. It was an important shipment, and the two-year-old Echo Dale Farceur was the jewel of the package. The Roberts men exhibited him at the western fairs and exhibitions and Chicago. He was then bought to return to the Good stud in Iowa, the best compliment that could be paid to any stallion at that time.

One of his sons, Carmen Dale, foaled in 1923, was bought and brought to Canada by Charles Rear and sold to Haas Brothers of Paris, Ontario. There, at the head of the stud of Belgians, he crowned himself with glory. For four consecutive years—1929 to 1932 inclusive—this grandson of Farceur was the grand champion Belgian stallion at the Royal Winter Fair for Haas Brothers. And in 1932, sons and daughters of Carmen Dale won the get-of-sire class at the Royal.

Another grandson of Farceur, Balcan de Farceur by Major Farceur, bred in Ohio, came to Canada and made an outstanding breeding record for his owner, Arthur Lombaert, Mariapolis, Manitoba. His offspring won the get-of-sire class at the Royal Winter Fair in three consecutive years, 1933, '34, and '35. And as a sire of Royal Winter Fair Belgian winners over the first seventeen years of that show, as calculated on a point basis, Balcan de Farceur was the distinguished winner.

The top ten stallions emerging from that search for the leading sires of Royal winners are listed in paragraphs following; and it should be noted here that five of the first six sires on the list were sons or grandsons of the famous Farceur.

How Big Is a Big Belgian?

Large size and heavy muscling were always Belgian trademarks. If the breed had a rival in size, it was the English Shire, but there was never much mingling of the two breeds in Canada. Mature Belgian stallions were expected to stand between 16½ and 17½ hands

The Belgian stallion Samson, a western winner in the 1930s, owned by C.M. Rear of Saskatoon, SK.

and weigh nineteen hundred pounds or more. Mares commonly measured 16 to 17 hands and weighed seventeen hundred pounds or more.

But how much more? The great Farceur, with a height of 16¾ hands, weighed twenty-two hundred pounds for much of his mature years, while his most famous contemporary, Alfred de Bree Eyck, was weighed at twenty-five hundred and ten pounds. One of Farceur's best known Canadian sons, Monseur, weighed and measured about the same as his sire. Another son owned in Canada, the highly regarded Paramount Flashwood, is remembered as measuring 18 hands and weighing twenty-three hundred pounds when shown as a three-year-old to the grand championship at the National Belgian Show at Waterloo, Iowa, in 1919. Flashwood was undoubtedly one of the sires that set a new height ideal for the breed in Canada, making for more fashionable or "hitchy" harness horses.

Carmen Dale by Echo Dale Farceur and four times grand champion Belgian stallion at the Canadian Royal Winter Fair, was a seventeen-hands and twenty-two-hundred-pound horse.

But if all Belgians are big, how big is a big Belgian? Breeders in recent years have read about some astounding weight and height records. The great Penn State Conqueror, owned by Charles Orndorff, was reported to have weighed 2,765 pounds when five years old.

Brooklyn Supreme, a purebred Belgian stallion owned by C. G. Good and Son—the owners of Farceur at the time of his death—was pictured a few decades ago as the world's biggest horse, a claim that seemed entirely plausible. With Mr. Good standing beside the stallion, the animal looked very much the part of a giant. The alleged weight was thirty-two hundred pounds and the height, 19½ hands. It was reported that in harnessing the big fellow, a forty-inch collar was required. Anybody studying the picture of the giant would readily believe the figures.[12]

Another Belgian described as "the world's largest horse," Mighty Sampson by name, appeared in picture and print in a magazine advertisement in 1976. Described as "the magnificent giant" the animal was said to stand 20½ hands, "beautifully proportioned and extremely gentle . . . Priced at a low $25,000."[13]

If, as stated in the advertisement, Mighty Sampson was 20½ hands high, he might indeed have been the world's biggest known horse at that time—1976. His weight was not reported. The main purpose of the advertisement was to attract buyers who might be interested in potential circus or sideshow attractions. "The earning potential of a horse this large, placed on exhibition is unlimited," the ad noted. "Properly managed and presented, he could earn a million dollars over a period of years." Interested parties were invited to enquire at "Dan's Frontier Store and Harness Shop, Main Street, Woodbury, Connecticut."

In calculating records of animal performance, it is not enough to merely cite round figures or accept estimates. Anybody having a horse or cow or field of wheat likely to be a candidate for a size or performance record should obtain meticulously accurate evidence. Too often such care is neglected and claims to records lose validity.

Much interest was generated in 1983 in a nine-year-old Canadian Belgian gelding sired by Marquette Du Marais and known as Sid. In this case, all the proper steps were taken to make the report of the great height both official and convincing.

As reported by Mrs. Barbara Meyers, secretary-treasurer of the Canadian Belgian Horse Association: "I attended an official 'measuring party' for a nine-year-old Belgian gelding bred, owned and raised by Murray Grove of Stouffville, Ontario. Vic Wilson, a neighbor of the Groves, obtained the necessary forms and criteria for submitting the horse's measurements to the *Guinness Book of World Records* as a candidate for the 'tallest horse alive' [distinction]." The report then named the ten "enthusiastic witnesses to the measuring which came to the astounding height of 19 hands, 2½ inches." That, in other words, confirmed the horse as being slightly more than 6½ feet tall at the withers.[14]

BELGIAN SIRES OF WINNERS AT THE CANADIAN ROYAL WINTER FAIR

Showring results will not take the place of performance testing in livestock improvement programs but they will always have an importance, especially for draft horses. Dairy

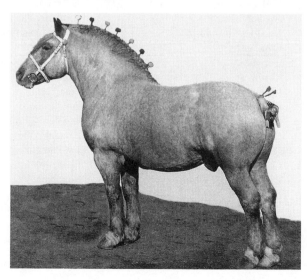

Paragon King by Paragon Goldie, grand champion at the 1938 Royal for Dr. H. E. Alexander of Saskatoon. The horse was later a senior sire for Gilbert Arnold, Grenville, Quebec. *Photograph by Strohmeyer and Carpenter.*

FIGURE I

Grand Champion Belgian Stallions, Canadian Royal Winter Fair

Year	Name of Winner	Sire of Winner	Exhibitor
1922	Bonnot de Hamal	Condor	C. W. Gurney
1923	Paragon Major	Monseur	Robert Thomas
1924	Paragon Major	Monseur	Robert Thomas
1925	Paragon Grant	Monseur	Robert Thomas
1926	Paragon Major	Monseur	Robert Thomas
1927	Sir Gaston	Master	Andrew Nolan
1928	Goliath	Labourer du Sartiau	C. M. Rear
1929	Carmen Dale	Echo Dale Farceur	Haas Brothers
1930	Carmen Dale	Echo Dale Farceur	Haas Brothers
1931	Carmen Dale	Echo Dale Farceur	Haas Brothers
1932	Carmen Dale	Echo Dale Farceur	Haas Brothers
1933	Dock	Pluton de Kleyem	Gilbert E. Arnold
1934	Dock	Pluton de Kleyem	Gilbert E. Arnold
1935	Dock	Pluton de Kleyem	Gilbert E. Arnold
1936	Baron D'Oultre	Triomphal de la Centrale	Jersey Health Farm
1937	Hector	Farceur's Crown	Sugar Grove Farm
1938	Paragon King	Paragon Goldie	Dr. H. E. Alexander
1939	to 1945, no Royal Winter Fairs owing to World War II		
1946	Echo Dale Filo Farceur	Filon D'Hondsocht	Nestor Lombaert
1947	Jan Farceur	Jay Farceur	Water Cress Farms
1948	Progress Farceur	Progress	Meadow Brook Farms
1949	Progress Farceur	Progress	Meadow Brook Farms
1950	Cadet Farceur	Jan Farceur	Water Cress Farms
1951	Cadet Farceur	Jan Farceur	Water Cress Farms
1952	Jay Farceur 2nd	Konfleur's Jay Farceur	C. O. House
1953	Dock Du Grand Air	Jay Du Grand Air	Gilbert E. Arnold
1954	Conquest	Conqueror	Meadow Brook Farms
1955	Conquest	Conqueror	Meadow Brook Farms
1956	Conquest	Conqueror	Meadow Brook Farms
1957	Congo	Conqueror	Meadow Brook Farms
1958	Ringmaster	Bandleader	Meadow Brook Farms
1959	Sunny Lane Don	Fairview's Rubis	Gilbert E. Arnold
1960	Commander House	Blondale's Progress	Douglas Palmer
1961	MacDonald Du Marais	Jan Farceur	Gilbert E. Arnold
1962	Commander House	Blondale's Progress	Douglas Palmer
1963	Contempo	Contact	Meadow Brook Farms
1964	Contempo	Contact	Meadow Brook Farms
1965	Dongordwal Ringo	Conqueror de Malmaison	Sheldon Walker and Sons
1966	Conceur	Conquest	Meadow Brook Farms
1967	Fairview Chief	Sunny Lane Jan	R. Freitag
1968	Contive	Conquest	Meadow Brook Farms

Year	Name of Winner	Sire of Winner	Exhibitor
1969	RKD Commander	RKD Captain	Ralph W. House
1970	Constable	Conquest	Mahogany Farms
1971	Congolaise	Conquest	Mahogany Farms
1972	Congolaise	Conquest	Mahogany Farms
1973	Rowdy D	Rowdy's Pride	J. McKeehan Farms
1974	Congressman	Conquest	Harold Clark
1975	Marquette's Dagger	Marquette Du Marais	Ira Leach
1976	RKD Bruce	RKD Commander	McKeehan Farms
1977	Marquette's Dagger	Marquette Du Marais	Ira Leach
1978	Remlap Spike	Constrico	Carlsberg
1979	Remlap Spike	Constrico	Carlsberg
1980	House's Ted Farceur	Farceur's Mona	Malvin House
1981	Master's Continue	Continental	Carlsberg
1982	Master's Continue	Continental	Carlsberg
1983	Imperial Lad of Greentop	Naden's Bill	Beattie Brothers
1984	Konrad K. Farceur	Colonel K. Farceur	Douglas Palmer
1985	Konrad K. Farceur	Colonel K. Farceur	Douglas Palmer

FIGURE 2

GRAND CHAMPION BELGIAN MARES, CANADIAN ROYAL WINTER FAIR

Year	Name of Winner	Sire of Winner	Exhibitor
1922	Acceptee de Roosbeke	Fox de Roosbeke	J. B. Coe
1923	Lady de Roosbeke	Fox de Roosbeke	Charles Head
1924	Rosalee	Buffalo	D. V. Runkle
1925	Hazel	What's Wanted	Tait and McClary
1926	Beauty of Deloraine	Emperor of Regina	Charles Andries
1927	Moss Rose	Alcali	Ontario Laundry, Ltd.
1928	Mary Jane de Naz	Cesar de Naz	R. J. Ferguson
1929	Peggy	Prince	Allan Cole
1930	Fanny de Thielt	Echappe de Quatrecht	Charles M. Rear
1931	Princess Astride	Elegant	Omer Lesy
1932	Mona	Bonnot de Hamal	Haas Brothers
1933	Brompton Dora	Midas de Ergot	Oka Agricultural College
1934	Queen Farceur	Balcan de Farceur	Arthur Lombaert
1935	Paragon Fan	Paragon Major	Robert Thomas
1936	Wyndot Rebecca	Balzac Debogaerdern	Gilbert E. Arnold
1937	Aida de Bierbeck	Mercure de Fosteau	Sugar Grove Farm
1938	Civette 2nd	Supreme Emblem	Sugar Grove Farm
1939	to 1945, no Royal Winter Fairs owing to World War II		
1946	Arnoldwold Docette	Dock	Gilbert E. Arnold

Year	Name of Winner	Sire of Winner	Exhibitor
1947	Paragon Kitty	Roy of Amisk	Robert Thomas
1948	Paragon Kitty	Roy of Amisk	Robert Thomas
1949	Paragon Kitty	Roy of Amisk	Robert Thomas
1950	Linda	Conqueror	Meadow Brook Farms
1951	Linda	Conqueror	Meadow Brook Farms
1952	Linda	Conqueror	Mrs. Matilda R. Wilson
1953	Sharon Kay	Jay Farceur 2nd	J. K. Pritchard
1954	May Farceur	Conqueror	Meadow Brook Farms
1955	Lady Ellen Farceur	Jan Farceur	Douglas Palmer
1956	Victory Farceur	Siehl's Kenny Farceur	Harkness Family
1957	Dot Farceur	Jay Du Grand Air	Menzie Dairy Farm
1958	Dorothy Farceur	Jay Du Grand Air	Menzie Dairy Farm
1959	Victory Farceur	Siehl's Kenny Farceur	George Harkness
1960	Brantview Susan Progress	Blondale's Progress	J. W. Howell
1961	Dorothy Farceur	Jay Du Grand Air	Douglas Palmer
1962	Becky Du Marais	Commander House	Douglas Palmer
1963	Consella	Conquest	Meadow Brook Farms
1964	Consella	Conquest	Meadow Brook Farms
1965	Orndorff's Martha	Penn State Conqueror	S. G. Nesbitt and Sons
1966	Miss Matilda	Conqueror	Meadow Brook Farms
1967	Henrietta Du Marais	Commander House	Douglas Palmer
1968	Condrita	Conquest	Meadow Brook Farms
1969	Henrietta Du Marais	Commander House	Douglas Palmer
1970	Consetta	Conquest	Mahogany Farms
1971	Consetta	Conquest	Mahogany Farms
1972	Princess Lou	Fairview Chief	Rudolf Freitag
1973	Conelrod Mary Lou	Conelrod	Carlsberg
1974	Contilda	Constable	Harold Clark
1975	Helga Du Marais	Marquette Du Marais	Carlsberg
1976	Master's Donna	Illini Masterpiece	McKeehan Farms
1977	Remlap Judy	Sunny Lane Don	Carlsberg
1978	Sunny Acres Condrea	Constrico	Carlsberg
1979	Sunny Acres Kate	Constrico	Carlsberg
1980	Remlap Vanella	Constell	Carlsberg
1981	Fashion Lady	Constrico	Carlsberg
1982	Nesbitt's Lady Jennifer	Marquette Du Marais	S. G. Nesbitt and Son
1983	Remlap Jewel	Congolaise	Carlsberg
1984	Mona Lisa	Constrico	Beattie Brothers
1985	Bonville Shirley Gwynne	Bonville Missy's Mike	Douglas Palmer

producers can weigh milk and butterfat and determine efficiency by relating production to feed intake. Breeders of Standardbred and Thoroughbred horses will rely mainly upon their stopwatches and the racecourse in determining values. Poultrymen will continue to count eggs. Breeders of draft horses, however, lack such obvious measuring sticks and

FIGURE 3

BELGIAN SIRES OF WINNERS IN ORDER OF SCORES, ROYAL WINTER FAIRS, 1922 TO 1938

1	Balcan de Farceur –4380–	by	Major Farceur
2	Paragon Major –3165–	by	Monseur
3	Bonnot de Hamal –2768–	by	Condor d'Ide
4	Monseur –1364–	by	Farceur
5	Carmen Dale –3503–	by	Echo Dale Farceur
6	Echo Dale Farceur –2964–	by	Farceur
7	Master –2052–	by	Inventeur du Fosteau
8	Fox de Roosbeke –1098–	by	Paul de Roosbeke
9	Elegant –3837–	by	Faro de la Lys
10	Pluton de Kleyem –3950–	by	Marquis de Kleyem

BELGIAN SIRES OF WINNERS IN ORDER OF SCORES, ROYAL WINTER FAIRS, 1946 TO 1985

1	Conqueror –27900–	by	Progress
2	Marquette Du Marais –12931–	by	Marcus Du Marais
3	Conquest –28729–	by	Conqueror
4	Constrico –29175–	by	Conquest
5	Jan Farceur –26607–	by	Jay Farceur
6	Siehl's Kenny Farceur –25473–	by	Master Farceur
7	Commander House –11662–	by	Blondale's Progress
8	Siehl's Tripsee Farceur –11149–	by	Lester Farceur
9	Progress –17224–	by	Douglas
10	Jay Du Grand Air –9647–	by	Jay Farceur
11	Contact –11401–	by	Conqueror
12	Constable –30618–	by	Conquest
13	Jay Farceur 2nd –10802–	by	Kenfleur's Jay Farceur
14	Penn State Conqueror –28833–	by	Conqueror 27900
15	Dock –4743–	by	Pluton de Kleyem

are thus more dependent upon the showring.

Canada became well furnished with fairs and exhibitions and was fortunate in having one big show with truly national character, the Royal Agricultural Winter Fair, offering services resembling those of the Highland Agricultural Show in Scotland, the English Royal in England, and the Royal Easter Show in Australia. Hence the choice of the Canadian Royal for this study.

The attempt to identify the leading Belgian sires of winners at the Canadian Royal followed along the same lines as those described for Clydesdales on another page—first for the seventeen prewar years ending in 1938 and then the forty postwar years, 1946 to 1985. The seven-year suspension of the show during World War II seemed to justify the decision to treat the prewar and postwar show results separately.

The technique adopted for the analysis was exactly the same for Belgian, Percheron, and Clydesdale breeds and can be seen for review in the Clydesdale section "Leading Sires of Clydesdale Winners at the Canadian Royal."

The ten high-scoring Belgian sires of winners from the seventeen-year prewar period, shown below and listed in order of their scores, are transcribed from a 1940 review made by the current author.[15] In preparing the longer list of top sires from the recent period it was found that 257 stallions fathered the first, second, and third prize winners compared with 248 listed in the study of the Clydesdales. From this number of contributing sires, the top fifteen will be listed.

CONQUEROR

It was positive evidence of the international character of the Canadian Royal Winter Fair when the stallion Conqueror, American-bred and American owned throughout his life, emerged as the foremost in the Belgian sires of winners analysis for the years between 1946 and 1985. The influence was bound to be favorable.

Moreover, there was a touch of romance in the fact that Conqueror, like his sire, Progress, almost passed unnoticed. The sorel Progress, foaled in 1931, had what would be considered a lowly background. But with striking, highheaded individuality, he caught the attention of some prominent breeders and after changing hands a few times, came as a still untested two-year-old to Mrs. Matilda R. Wilson of Meadow Brook Farms in Michigan. There he remained to become responsible for the Meadow Brook slogan, "Belgians of Progress."

But the stallion's surprising success was no guarantee that his sons and daughters would inherit his superiority. Conqueror's value was in doubt, even though he was from a well-bred dam, a daughter of Elegant du Marias. Foaled in 1944, Conqueror was not taken to the shows until he was two years old. It was then, 1946, that he made his debut at the first Canadian Royal to be held after World War II. There he won first in a small class but did not figure in the championships. His three-year-old fortune at the Royal was about the same, after which it dropped: his four-year-old appearance at the Royal was his last. Failing to impress the judge, he was placed fifth in a class of six mature stallions. If there was any consolation, it was in the fact that his Meadow Brook stablemate and half brother with the familiar name of Progress Farceur was the class winner.

It might have been seen as an inglorious end to a short show career, but there were more important reasons for his retirement from the tanbark. The reasons began to become clear when two of his offspring appeared at the Canadian Royal in 1949 and both won their classes. Next year, his sons and daughters won the get-of-sire class at the Royal, a most significant win, and continued to win it until they had a record of seven get-of-sire wins in eight consecutive years. After that, one of the Conqueror sons won the contest in each of two more years. That son was Conquest.

To make the Conqueror sire record still more impressive, it could be told that sons won the grand championship at the Royal on four occasions and Conquest by Conqueror was the sire of the grand champion stallion on six occasions. Five times a daughter of Conqueror was the grand champion mare at the Royal and five times a daughter of Conquest gained the honor. The Conqueror record was one not soon to be equalled.

MARQUETTE DU MARAIS

This American-bred stallion, Marquette Du Marais, that became a permanent resident of

Ontario, may have been the best bit of free trade fortune to befall the breed in Canada in a decade or more. With only one stallion ahead of him in the sires of winners at the Canadian Royal, it was bound to be argued that if Marquette Du Marais had had the opportunity to mate with as many of the best mares of the breed as Conqueror, the positions of the two stallions might have been reversed. Nobody can be sure.

Like the great Conqueror, Marquette Du Marais was a slow starter in his climb to fame. Neither was sensational as a show horse. The latter's mother was a mare that grew old without ever raising a foal and being one with a chronic grudge against harness and being hitched, she was finally marked for the slaughtering plant. But days before it would have been too late, Victoria Farceur's good breeding came to the attention of a knowledgeable horseman, E. R. Brass, who was ready to gamble with the hope of getting a foal or two from her, and he bought her at little more than meat price.

The old mare was bred to the well-known Marcus Du Marais by the revered Jan Farceur. It was late in the year but, sure enough, the mare was in foal and along in October, 1962, when most foals of the year were already weaned, Victoria Farceur dropped the chestnut colt that was to be registered as Marquette Du Marais.

At first the newcomer was just another colt, smaller than most because of his late birth. As a yearling he still looked small and was not taken to the shows in 1963. But at two years he was sold to an Iowa man who, soon thereafter, sold him again, this time to a Canadian, Jack Wood of Aurora, Ontario. By this time the stud was two years and six

months old and he was not used much until the following spring, 1966. The first of his descendants appeared at the Canadian Royal in '67, a yearling stallion that placed third in his class and two foals that won first and third prizes in their class for S. G. Nesbitt and Son and Douglas Palmer, respectively. The winning foal was Nesbitt's Centennial Lady from the great show and breeding mare, Conqueror's Silver Lady, sired by Penn State Conqueror and bought by S. G. Nesbitt from Charles Orndorff of Pennsylvania. While Silver lady was winning the brood mare class at the Royal that year, her baby daughter—one of the first of the Marquette Du Marais progeny to reach the Royal Winter Fair—was going on to win the junior and reserve grand championship for Belgian females, a rare triumph for a foal at any time.

The Nesbitt filly repeated her reserve grand championship in 1970 and another daughter of Marquette Du Marais, Dongordwal's Bonnie April, owned by Sheldon Walker and Son, was made reserve grand champion in 1973. Still another, Helga Du Marais from the

Remlap Jewel, sired by Congolaise, owned and shown by Douglas Palmer, Schomberg, Ontario. First prize four-year-old at Detroit in 1978. First prize yeld mare and reserve grand champion at the Royal in 1978. And grand champion Belgian mare at the 1983 Royal. *Photograph by Catherine Gillespie; courtesy Canadian Belgian Horse Association.*

stud of Douglas Palmer, did the same in 1974.

Marquette was getting into his stride and 1976 was to be his year of record-breaking success. A Marquette daughter won the brood mare class; two others placed first and second in the yeld mare class. Douglas Palmer's Helga Du Marais won the grand championship in mares and Walter Sparks' Marquette's Kelly Du Marais was reserve grand. In stallions, the grand championship went to Ira Leach on Marquette's Dagger, which meant that sons and daughters of Marquette Du Marais had taken three of the four major championships.

It was a notable year for one sire, by that time thirteen years old. And to prove that it was not an accident, 1975 was only a little less spectacular. The sons and daughters of the old horse did not do quite as well in championships, but the winnings included the two highest awards in the coveted get-of-sire class, and first prize in the big and excellent yeld mare class. In the brood mare class, instead of winning just one of the best ribbons, Marquette daughters won all three of the highest awards for three different owners. It hadn't happened before.

After coming to Canada, Marquette Du Marais became a sort of stay-at-home, but with his mounting reputation, there wasn't any reason for leaving; more and more good Belgian mares were being brought to him, some from great distances, and his impact upon the breed in Canada became ever clearer. Finally, to mark the end of a chapter, death came to the fifteen-year-old stallion that will be remembered as one of the foremost sires on the continent.

MARES OF DISTINCTION

Every breed has its great matrons that deserve to be recognized and honored in the same way that outstanding sires are accorded praise. There is no hope of identifying all the superior mares in the Belgian breed but a few can be named for symbolic acclaim while using the same notes as vehicles for timely references to the breeders and owners.

PEGGY

The gentle and much loved founding mare of the Freitags of Alameda greatly enriched the family story. The Canadian chapter began when Rudolph and Mary Freitag and three small children left their native Ukraine and came to Canada in 1927. Their journey ended near Estevan where Rudolph obtained a humble job as a farm hand. Wages were meager but in six years the frugal Freitags saved enough to permit a start on a rented farm at Alameda. Renting led to buying and then, in 1943, to the fulfillment of a dream to buy a purebred Belgian mare and build a herd.

Pure bred Belgian colts at a feed trough on Sugar Grove Farm, Illinois.

There was another immigrant family in Manitoba, the Lombaerts, who came from Belgium in 1906 and settled at Mariapolis where a son, Arthur, became a breeder of Belgian horses, good ones like his Queen Farceur by Balcan de Farceur that went to the Royal to win the grand championship for mares in 1934. Lombaert was already selling Belgians to the government of Quebec, the Trappist Fathers, and other individuals wanting foundation mares, like Charles De Pape at Bruxelles who founded well when he bought the mare Bella de Nil.

Arthur Lombaert's son-in-law, Remi De Pape, recalled Mr. Freitag coming unannounced to the Lombaert farm in 1943, his truck loaded with mixed livestock, grade horses and cattle, and not much money. He came to trade for a mare but didn't have enough resources to pay for a good young one; he had enough for a good old one and a deal was made for the seventeen-year-old Peggy, raised by Allan Cole of Brandon and shown by him to win the grand championship at the Royal in 1929.

Peggy was in foal but at her age it was doubtful if she would ever carry another foal. It was risky and the first disappointment came at the end of the long truck trip back to Alameda when the old mare lost her foal. But Peggy was of a durable breed and at nineteen years of age gave the Freitags a fine filly foal that took the name Cookie. At the age of twenty, Peggy repeated with the filly Betty Lou, and at twenty-one, still another filly, Bonnie Lou.

Peggy's three daughters became genuine show horses and served to introduce Rudolph Freitag to the small fairs, then the bigger ones, and finally the Royal—winning all the way. After winning in the West, Cookie and Betty Lou, in 1948, won the gold medal presented by the King of Belgium for the best pair of Canadian-bred Belgian mares at the Royal. In the next year, with the addition of Bonnie Lou, the Freitag mares won the class for the best group of three Canadian-breds at the same show.

At the age of twenty-three, with sixteen of her progeny registered in the Canadian stud book, Peggy seemed to see her purpose as completed and died quietly. The grateful Freitags saw to it that the gentle and lovable old lady was buried in a spot "on the west side of a nice poplar bluff, selected for its beauty."

The Freitag Belgians went on to win international honors. Son Edwin, after spending more than a decade working with the best Belgian horses on the continent, returned to further his reputation on the home farm, showing, counselling, judging, and serving as president of the Canadian Belgian Horse Association. And then there was a new generation of Freitags, grandchildren of Rudolph and Mary, taking their place in breed building.

A Famous Mother-Daughter Combination

Any search for the great and versatile mares of the breed should not miss the mother-daughter combination of Conqueror's Silver Lady and her daughter, Nesbitt's Centennial Lady.

It was a day of fortune for the breed in Canada when, in April, 1961, three two-year-old fillies, Conqueror's Silver Lady, Conqueror's Pervenche, and Conqueror's Roscoe Lady—all bred and owned by Charles

Orndorff and Son of Pennsylvania, all stylish sorrels and all sired by Penn State Conqueror—were bought for shipment to Ontario. S. G. Nesbitt of Carnarvon, Ontario, knew exactly what he wanted and made sure he got it.

Conqueror's Silver Lady proved to be the pick of the crop. She was the one that had everything and could do everything. She was shown in halter classes at the Royal from her first year in the country, 1961, when she placed second in the class for two-year-olds. She was frequently in harness and one way or another she was commonly at or near the top. Still, her best performance was in giving birth to Nesbitt's Centennial Lady in March, 1967, in which year mother and daughter did themselves proud at the Royal Winter Fair. The mare won in a big class of brood mares and the baby won in an equally big class of foals and carried on to be reserve champion female. It hadn't happened often.

In 1969 and '70, the aging Lady returned in the brood mare class; in the latter year there was only one mare placed above her. Her

Queen Farceur, grand champion in 1934 at the Canadian Royal for Arthur Lombaert, Mariapolis, Manitoba. *Photograph by Strohmeyer and Carpenter; courtesy Rémi De Pape.*

young son, Nesbitt's Bill, with a name that would become familiar in Belgian circles, was third. The latter won the grand championship at the Canadian National Exhibition in 1973 and some time later was sold to go to Alberta. At the age of seventeen years, the Silver Lady was back to place second in the brood mare class at the Royal. Her baby son, carrying the name Nesbitt's Misty River Marque and by Marquette Du Marais, was catching the eyes of breeders who are constantly searching for outstanding sire material.

In the meantime, horsemen saw Nesbitt's Centennial Lady coming annually to the Royal. She won the yeld mare class at the Royal in 1972 and the brood mare class and the senior championship at the C.N.E. in the next year—the year in which she produced Nesbitt's Lady Patricia. With other offspring like Nesbitt's Miss Haliburton, Nesbitt's Misty River Heddy, Nesbitt's Misty River Rowdy—winners all—and a growing habit of returning regularly to test the brood mare competition, she was matching her mother's record and combining with her mother to make an enviable record for Belgian motherhood.

HENRIETTA DU MARAIS

Her name appeared in every Royal show catalogue from 1964—the year of her birth—until 1976 when she was in her thirteenth year. In the course of those years, Henrietta Du Marais won prize ribbons of every color, including those symbolizing grand and reserve championships.

The many-times-a-winner Henrietta Du Marais was sired by Marquette Du Marais. She was bred and owned by Douglas Palmer of Schomberg, Ontario, and foaled in 1964.

Strangers were known to be confused by the names that surrounded her—Palmer, Carlsberg, and Remlap, but the explanation was quite simple. Douglas Palmer was the author of the big horse-breeding operation north of Toronto, an expression of the imagination and enterprise of the pioneer horseman. Carlsberg was the name of the Carling-O'Keefe brewery product for the promotion of which Mr. Palmer furnished and drove the magnificent big show teams of Belgian horses bearing the brewing company's name. And Remlap is simply the Palmer name spelled backward.

This man of many parts was a past-president of the Canadian National Exhibition, a long-time director of the Royal Winter Fair and one of the best known Canadians in international horse circles. His forefathers bred Clydesdales and he devoted many of his earlier years to Standardbreds, having bred them, trained them, and raced them. He will still react eagerly to any hint of a race. He has been showing Belgians at the Royal Winter Fair since 1946, the first year of operation after World War II. Breeding successes at the Schomberg farm led to a big demand for Remlap horses in the United States. And in 1975, Palmer became the first Canadian to ship a Belgian stallion to Japan.

Henrietta Du Marais was but one of hundreds of Belgians foaled on the Palmer farm, but she was rather special. In November of her foal year, 1964, she was taken to the Royal and won her class. She placed second as a yearling, first as a two-year-old, first as a three-year-old and then, second and reserve grand champion in her first year as a mature animal. When she appeared at the Royal in 1971 and each of the next three years, she was competing in the brood mare class and was never placed lower than second.

Still, Henrietta's greatest glory came, as a brood mare's should, through her offspring. Her greatest offspring was Helga Du Marais by Marquette Du Marais. Helga was foaled in 1972 and won the foal class while her mother placed second in brood mares. From then on she came close to being a constant winner—first as a yearling, first and reserve grand champion as a two-year-old, first and grand champion as a three-year-old, and first and reserve grand champion as a brood mare when four years of age. It was another mother-daughter record of excellence.

BELGIAN BREED ORGANIZATION AND REGISTRATION

Breed organization began in Belgium in 1886 when the Belgian Draft Horse Society was formed. The American Association of Importers and Breeders of Belgian Draft Horses had its beginning in the next year, 1887.

It was an indication of the breed's relatively late bid for acceptance in Canada that it wasn't until 1907 that the Canadian Belgian Draft Horse Breeders' Association was organized and incorporated under the Live Stock Pedigree Act. Volume I of the *Canadian Belgian Draft Horse Stud Book* was published in 1920 and other volumes followed at irregular intervals.

The association name was long and cumbersome and was eventually shortened to the Canadian Belgian Horse Association.

Canadian registrations entered in 1908—the year after incorporation—numbered only sixteen. Fourteen of these were from Quebec, one from Alberta, and one from the United States. And in the same year, just three memberships were taken. But in 1910, registrations leaped to 163 with 63 of them entered in the names of Quebec breeders and owners. Most of the others were for midwestern horses and horsemen.

The provinces of Quebec and Saskatchewan continued to make the largest numbers of stud book entries. By 1940, when new registrations had fallen sharply, Quebec was still a provincial leader with 103 new registrations, Saskatchewan was next with 80, then Alberta with 45, and Ontario with 21.

Twenty-five years later—1965—registration matters had not changed greatly. Quebec was still the leader in claiming new registrations and the eighty-one new Quebec entries in the Canadian stud book represented slightly more than half of the Canadian total for the year. Ontario's registrations increased sharply and Saskatchewan's fell just as dramatically.

The changes in numbers of memberships in the Canadian Belgian Horse Association told a slightly different story of ups and downs in breed fortunes. For 1935—at the middle of the depressed thirties when membership fees and grocery money were generally difficult to find—140 Canadian breeders and others interested in Belgians paid their dues. Fifty-three of them were from Quebec,

40 from Saskatchewan, 26 from Alberta, and 12 from Ontario. Thirty-six years later, in 1965, when the Canadian association had a total of 181 members, four-fifths of them had Quebec and Ontario addresses, Manitoba, Saskatchewan, and Alberta had only 10, 8, and 5 members respectively. Then, in the seventies, the Belgian encountered a boomtime enthusiasm right across the country; the supply of good horses was hopelessly inadequate for the demand and prices soared. Belgians experienced a particularly brisk demand and Ontario became the leading province in association memberships with Quebec in second place.

In 1984, when the breed association had 727 members—more than either of the other draft breeds—290 of them were from Ontario, 134 from Quebec, 122 from Alberta, 56 from Saskatchewan, 48 from Manitoba, 32 from British Columbia, 27 from New Brunswick, 9 from Nova Scotia, and 2 from Prince Edward Island. The remaining seven were from the United States.

In the same year, with the significant total of 1,023 new registrations for the Belgian stud book, Ontario was the biggest provincial contributor with 367 entries. Next was Quebec with 201, then Alberta with 186, Saskatchewan with 121, Manitoba with 75, British Columbia with 42, New Brunswick with 27, Prince Edward Island with 4, and none from Nova Scotia.

The 1,023 new registrations in 1984 brought the Belgian total from the beginning of stud book recordings to the end of 1984 to 21,360.

The Belgian association president in 1985 was Edwin Freitag, a second generation breeder at Alameda, Saskatchewan, and the secretary was Mrs. Barbara Meyers, Schomberg, Ontario.

Six-horse team of Belgians undefeated at Canadian shows, including the Royal, in 1982. They were also winners over all breeds at Detroit in the same year, for Beattie Brothers, Stayner, Ontario. Irvine and Ross Beattie are in the driver's seat. *Photograph by J. E. McNeil; courtesy Canadian Belgian Horse Association.*

The Shire

The Old English War Horse

The memory lingers, like that of the first viewing of Niagara Falls or Fort Prince of Wales. It was at the English Lancashire Royal Show at Preston in 1932 where the Shire breed of heavy horses was much at home. The halter class being called to the judging ring was for geldings four years of age and over.

The earth seemed to tremble as the equine leviathans entered, twenty-three in all, twenty-one of them weighing more than 2,100 pounds and carrying their weight like

Thoroughbreds. The lightest of the twenty-three contestants, it was told, weighed 1,925 pounds and the heaviest, 2,450 pounds. They were the old English war horses, the type once expected to carry an overfed knight with a heavy steel lance and a private fortification of iron plate, enough to shield both horse and rider. The total weight of 450 pounds or more demanded a big and powerful horse. For a rider wearing his fortified shelter like an overcoat, speed was relatively unimportant.

The Shire roots reach far into antiquity, probably to horse stock on the island of Britain before the Roman invasion in 55 B.C., at which time Caesar's soldiers were duly impressed by the horse-drawn chariots driven by the defenders. Those very early horses, not excessively big, would have to await the introduction of horses from Flanders before gaining the great size and weight noted in the Middle Ages. William the Conqueror brought heavy horses to England and from his warriors the English learned the art of combat from horseback.

During the reign of King John of Magna Carta fame—1199–1216—a hundred stallions of "large stature" were imported from the low countries of Europe. Doubtless, these imports were of Flemish stock and hence the infusion of this blood would give the Shire breed something in common with Belgian and Clydesdale horses. And while size and weight were important in war horses, the same characteristics were to be found valuable in horses for agricultural use as well as for hauling the heavily loaded freight wagons over the primitive English roads.

English sovereigns from the time of Henry VII offered guidance and encouragement to horse breeding. One of the acts made law by Henry VII was to prohibit the export of good horses, and Henry VIII went further by making laws that he believed would ensure improvement. He ruled, for example, that no stallion standing less than fourteen hands could be used for breeding in certain prescribed grazing areas.

"All owners and Fermers of parks and enclosed grounds of the extent of one mile in compass," he ordered, "shall keep [at least] two Mares, being not spayed, apt and able to bear foals of the altitude or height of thirteen handfuls at least, upon pain of 40/- . . . A penalty of 40/- is imposed on the Lords, Owners and Fermers of all parks and grounds enclosed as is above rehearsed, who shall willingly suffer any of the said Mares to be covered or kept with any stoned horse under the stature of fourteen handfuls."[1]

After 1541, by the king's order, the minimum height for stallions was fifteen hands and the decree made it very clear that "No person shall put in any forest, chase, moor, heath, common or waste—where mares and fillies are used to be kept—any stoned horse above the age of two years, not being 15 hands high, within the Shires and districts of . . ." What followed was a list of twenty-six English districts in which the king's instructions were to be followed. The regions named coincided closely with the parts in which the Shire breed was to develop.

Cromwell's soldiers wrought further change by adopting lighter horses for war purposes and it was then that the Great Horse was promoted to a larger role in agriculture without in any way inhibiting the forces of improvement. From the beginning of the seventeenth century the strain was looking more like a breed and successful breeders and notable sires were winning recognition. Size and weight were still wanted but improvement in quality and conformation was an obvious challenge. Too many horses, although supremely powerful, were coarse, round in bone, short and stubby in pasterns, contracted at the heels, and rough about the head and shoulders.

The earls of Huntingdon were among the earliest improvers, to be joined by Gallemore of Derbyshire and the celebrated Robert Bakewell. A stallion known as Packington Blind Horse, living between 1755 and 1770, seems to have been the first to gain immortal fame as a founder.

Horsemen and agricultural historians will find special interest in Robert Bakewell, (1726–1795) of Dishley, Leicestershire, partly for his work with Shires but largely because of his breeding methods that made him the foremost animal improver of his generation. His favorite breeds were Shire horses, Longhorn cattle, and Leicestershire sheep, but it was his discovery of closebreeding and inbreeding as instruments in improving and fixing the improved characteristics that made him famous. Church leaders frowned on the incestuous matings that were part of his technique and warned of damnation awaiting anybody who practiced closebreeding. But Bakewell persevered and shared his ideas with breeders across England and Scotland who beat paths to his door. The Shire breed was a direct beneficiary; most other British breeds gained benefit but only indirectly.

Students of the Shire horse have been ready to nominate Lincolnshire Lad, bred in Norfolk and foaled in 1865, as the greatest sire up to his time. He was big, standing 17½ hands, but his main claim to fame was from the breeding success of his son, Lincolnshire Lad 2nd, foaled in 1872, and the latter's son Harold, foaled in 1881. As a breed-building sire, Lincolnshire Lad 2nd may have surpassed his father, and Harold wasn't far behind. Harold was the champion stallion at London in 1887 and his grandson, Lockinge Forest King, foaled in 1899, was regarded as the most influential sire during the first years of the present century, bringing the most uncommon distinction to the Lincolnshire Lad line.

As breed characteristics became more clearly defined and more nearly fixed, the

The big and the small. A Shire stallion and a Shetland foal, pictured at Iowa State College in Ames. Not surprisingly, the two representatives of the same species view each other with disbelief.

Shire colors were seen as black, bay, brown and, occasionally, grey, with considerable white on the legs and some on the face. They were stylish color markings, bearing some resemblance to those of the Clydesdale. Mature horses were expected to stand 16½ to 17½ hands with individuals measuring up to 18 hands or six feet at the withers. Stallions could weigh up to twenty-four hundred pounds, geldings to twenty-four hundred and fifty and mares to twenty-one hundred. The only breed that seemed likely to equal or surpass the Shire in size and weight was the Belgian.

Whether or not it reflected the weighted wishes of the early breeders, the Shires had a conspicuously heavy growth of hair or feather on their legs. The early representatives had more than the later ones and many had a tuft of hair on each knee and sometimes the suggestion of a mustache on the lower lip. But there was no utility and not much beauty in such profusion of hair. The white markings could add a touch of class, especially to a trotting horse, but heavy white feather is difficult to keep clean and

Shire breeders must have concluded that they would be better served with less of it. They bred accordingly.

Over the years, the breed had more names or aliases than a criminal in flight, more surely than any other British breed. At one time or another it was the Great Horse, Giant Horse of Lincolnshire, War Horse, English Cart Horse, and Large Black English Horse.

The formation of breeders' societies served to curtail the birth and use of new names. The English Cart Horse Society, organized in 1878, was a good move and it was followed six years later by the formation of the Shire Horse Society of the United Kingdom of Great Britain and Ireland. After a few more years, in 1890, the first of the spring shows for Shires was conducted at the Royal Agricultural Hall at Islington where it became an annual event. The Royal Agricultural Show of England invited Shires to participate and found the breeders willing and ready.

The first volume of the English stud book was published in 1880 and the breed began to attract overseas buyers. At the beginning of the twentieth century, breeding animals were being exported to Germany, Russia, Australia, Canada, the United States, and Argentina, but the period of extensive exporting was brief.

THE SHIRE IN CANADA

The first Shire horses appeared in Canada before 1850 but information is sketchy. A stallion called Tamworth, described as a Shire, was brought from England to London, Ontario, by British troops in 1836. A grey stallion, Columbus, was imported to Massachusetts about 1844 and King Alfred, said to

A Shire stallion in England, Eaton Premier King, three times champion at the London Shire Show in the early years of the century.

have been a particularly good horse, was imported to Canada in 1847. From information available, it seems fair to conclude that Tamworth was the first Shire to set foot on the North American continent.

Importations to Canada were never extensive but they reached their highest point between 1875 and 1910. It was a notable triumph in interbreed rivalry when, in 1886, a Gardhouse entry from Highfield, Ontario, consisting of the imported Shire stallion King of the Castle and five of his offspring, won at Toronto and went on to Buffalo, New York, to win a similar victory in strong international competition.

The most extensive breeding and importing operation on the continent in its time was Truman's Pioneer Stud at Bushnell, Illinois, started in 1878 by J. G. Truman when he was then breeding Shire horses in England. The Trumans championed the breed for many years, exhibited at the International show in Chicago and sold stallions in the United States and Canada. For a few years after the beginning of the present century, the Trumans operated a sales stable at Brandon where there was good reason for the boast that more draft stallions changed hands annually than in any other town or city in the world. J. H. Truman was in charge of the Brandon branch of the family business. In 1903, the firm created a mild sensation at western Canadian fairs with two Shire stallions of exceptional size and quality, Prince Shapely and Gore's Best. The former was said to weigh more than twenty-four hundred pounds.

Eastern Canadian breeders and showmen of Shires were doing their best to capture more of the popularity that was going to the Clydesdales, but it wasn't easy. Two of the most successful were J. M. Gardhouse and the firm of Morris and Wellington of Fonthill, Ontario. The Fonthill breeders had the stallion Coronation, which won the championship at Toronto in 1903 and was regarded as the best specimen of the breed on the continent.

Aided by the family of which he was a part, the Gardhouse reputation was the more enduring. It is doubtful if any other Canadians have had as long an association with high class livestock as the Gardhouse family. The Canadian founding father, John Gardhouse from England's Cumberland County, settled in the York bush, not far from today's big city of Toronto, in 1837—the year of the Upper Canada Rebellion, led by William Lyon Mackenzie.

John Gardhouse brought with him a love for Shire horses and Shorthorn cattle. He began a dynasty of highly successful breeders—five successive generations, and more than a hundred years of progress in importing, breeding, exhibiting, and selling Shorthorns, and three full generations devoted in the same ways to Shires. The J. M. or Mart Gardhouse to whom reference was made in earlier paragraphs, was a grandson of the Gardhouse pioneer of 1837 and one whose enthusiasm for Shires never waned.

When the first volume of the *Shire Horse Stud Book* appeared in 1901 with 320 stallions registered and 155 mares, no fewer than six members of the Gardhouse clan had entries. While there may have been bigger importers of Shires such as Morris, Stone and Wellington of Fonthill, the Gardhouses must have been the most influential family of Shire breeders and supporters in the country.

That initial stud book showed W. E. Wellington of Toronto as the association president, J. M. Gardhouse of Highfield as vice-president and the faithful Henry Wade who had aided in the formation of a dozen new breed organizations in Canada, as secretary. And the author of the introduction to the book was none other than that eminent lover of good horses of all breeds, Alexander Galbraith, whose address then was given as Janesville, Wisconsin. Later it would be Brandon and still later, Edmonton.

Very few names of Shire breeders living in western Canada appeared in the 1901 volume. One of the earliest westerners to be recorded as an owner or breeder was Alexander Galbraith, giving his new address as Brandon, Manitoba, and appearing as the owner of the imported stallion Rockingham 2nd, foaled in 1895. Also with Brandon addresses, reinforcing that city's claim of being the center of heavy horse dealing on the continent, were

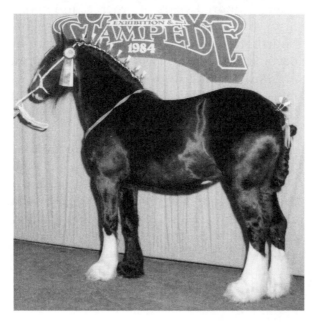

Fordon Sarah, a black Shire mare foaled in England in 1980. She was imported and owned by the Gentle Giant Ranch, property of Blake and Fran Anderson of Red Deer, Alberta. The mare won the championship at the Calgary Exhibition in 1984. *Photograph by Browarny; courtesy Canadian Shire Horse Association.*

J. S. Gibson, who had two purebred mares foaling in the nineties, and J. D. McGregor, who would later win international fame with his Aberdeen Angus cattle.

Farther west, A. P. Patrick, one of the country's most famous pioneer surveyors, was making news in 1901 by bringing in a Shire stallion, Southern Cross, for use on his ranch west of Calgary. "An exceptionally fine horse," said the editor—for whatever his opinion might be worth—"and should do a great deal for the horses of the neighborhood."[2]

But it was Thomas Rawlinson who homesteaded at Wimborne, Alberta, in 1909 and began importing Shires almost immediately, who drew the greatest attention to his chosen breed. Later president of the Shire Horse Association of Canada, he never waivered in his conviction about Shire superiority.

A small but historic shipment of English Shires came to Canada in 1923, two stallions and three mares, a gift from the Shire Horse Society of Great Britain to the government of Canada. The gesture, it was admitted, was actuated by the hope of demonstrating to farmers and others in Canada, that the Shire possessed a high potential for upgrading the country's heavy horses, especially for imparting weight and heavy bone. Included in the group of five was a stallion of exceptional size, type, and breeding, Marden Jupiter, by Champion's Goalkeeper, who was a winner at the Shire Horse Show at London in 1914 and was declared by many to be the most successful sire of his generation. That sire, Champion Goalkeeper, had sold at Lord Rothschild's sale for 4,100 guineas.

Marden Jupiter was a massive individual, brown in color. Taken to the Royal Winter Fair at Toronto and the Chicago International

Fat Stock Show in 1924, he was awarded the grand championship for his breed at both places. His stable mate, Essendon Jet, a daughter of Lochinge Forest King, won the grand award for mares. Marden Jupiter's weight at the time was 2,510 pounds.

The gift Shires were placed at the Dominion Experimental Station at Lacombe, Alberta, where, it was understood, they would be used for demonstration, exhibition, and breeding. Frank Reed, regarded as an outstanding horseman, was the superintendent at the Lacombe station at the time and was anxious to give the Shires a good home and a good chance. The new horses generated wide interest among stockmen and others, but for reasons never very clear, the animals were plagued with misfortune and did not survive for long.

As told in an anniversary report from the station: "The Shire mares lasted less than 18 months. They were in foal in late 1923 but only one foal was reared and she was the only female Shire entered on the year-end inventory of 1924."[3]

The stallions fared better but not a lot better. All the Clydesdale mares on the station farm were bred to the Shire stallions for the next few years and the senior sire, Marden Jupiter, served more than 200 outside mares brought to the station in the two breeding seasons before his death in 1925.

Following the death of this stallion, another outstanding Shire, Snelston Topper, was sent from England to Lacombe as a replacement and gift from Mrs. Stanton of Snelston Hall, Ashbourne, England. The new stallion weighed 2,310 pounds at four years of age and stood for public service until 1929. Superintendent Frank Reed said he was a horse of "excellent type and bred well, but the Shire breeding program did not last beyond Snelston Topper's years. The handsome horse died on March 9, 1930."[4]

The donors of the valuable horses hoped, of course, that the animals would stimulate an export trade with Canadian buyers. The Canadian horsemen were high in their praise for the massive Shires but trade revival did not materialize. If weight were the only or principal consideration, popularity would have soared. Canadians knew about the Shire stud imported by the Trumans in 1883 that weighed 2,830 pounds. They were impressed but not enough to change their preference for clean legs with not more than a moderate amount of hair on them. The excessive feathering on Shire legs could create practical problems when horses were required to work on heavy or gumbo soil. Moreover, Canadian horsemen had grown to admire quality of bone and leg refinement as much as they admired size. About the same reactions were reported from the United States and Argentina where Shires enjoyed early starts, but then lost the advantage to cleaner-legged horses.

When Shire prospects were bright in the early years, breed organizations were formed in both the United States and Canada. The American Shire Horse Association was formed in 1885 and the Canadian Shire Horse Association in 1888. The appearance of the first volume of the Canadian stud book in 1901 was an expression of optimism, but the number of registrations dropped rather than increased. Eventually they vanished. A total of three stud books were published—1901, 1909, and 1914. But by 1935 the new registrations for the year totalled only six, four of them from breeders in Saskatchewan and two from Alberta. The association could count only seven members and of ten officers and directors, three were members of the pioneer Gardhouse family who were not giving up.

In 1941, the Canadian Shire Horse Association ceased to exist and the Canadian National Live Stock Records assumed the responsibility of entering any new registrations in the *General Stud and Herd Book*, a repository for the pedigree records of breeds having no organizations. There was nothing in new applications for registrations in 1983, although the total Shire registrations in Canada from the time the Shire Horse Association was formed ninety-five years earlier was 3,434 individuals counting both sexes.

The statistical record suggested that the breed was extinct in Canada. But it was

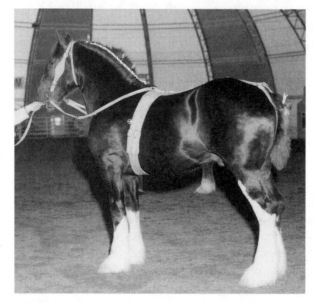

Upper Farm Charlie, foaled in England in 1982. Imported and owned by the Canadian Shire Centre, Fernand Barsalou, Bromont, Quebec. Winner of reserve grand championship for Shire stallions at the Calgary Exhibition in 1984. *Photograph by Browarny; courtesy Canadian Shire Horse Association.*

not; it was bracing itself for a comeback. At least two importations were made in 1981, one by Fernand Barsalou of Quebec and one by Blake and Fran Anderson of Alberta. And in the spring of 1982, an American-bred mare owned by Cliff Kelsey of Winterburn, Alberta, produced a purebred Shire foal, described as the first of its kind in the country in forty years. Interest was climbing and was reinforced when Fernand Barsalou's imported stallion, Rhyd-y-Groes Premier King, won the grand championship at the National Shire Horse Show in Oregon.

A few representatives of the breed appeared at the Calgary Exhibition in 1982 and a few more were entered to compete in the Clydesdale classes in 1983. In 1985, the Shire breeders had their own Shire classes and were encouraged.

The Shire seemed suddenly to have returned from the dead. Although the National Live Stock Records reported no new applications for registrations in 1983, there were eleven in 1984 and twenty-five in 1985. The numbers were still small but with the growing interest, breeders were meeting to discuss the rebirth of the Canadian Shire Horse Association.

Said one of the enthusiastic new owners exhibiting Shires at Calgary in 1985: "We have a first class foothold and Canadians will see and hear more of the old breed. And, believe me, they'll like the new Shire better than they did the old one."

The Suffolk

Handy, Hardy, and Good-natured

Alexander Galbraith, known to pioneer breeders as a one-man supreme court on questions pertaining to heavy horses, said he never met a horse user who didn't have something good to say about the Suffolk breed. He could not understand why it had not become more popular and numerous in Canada. The people who drove Suffolks and fed them pronounced them "easy keepers" and it happened significantly often that the lone member of the breed in a barn full of work horses was the one most likely to be dubbed—with apologies to Charles Dickens—"the fat boy."

It was easy to see how these horses with symmetrical shapes, good legs, and good nature were challenging Clydesdales, Percherons, and Belgians and surpassing Shires for a time in the contest for farm favor. But the reasons for the breed's fortunes being so brief were never very clear.

Called Suffolk or Suffolk Punch, the breed took its name from the County of Suffolk on England's eastern coast. There and in neighboring Norfolk and Essex, a breed-like strain of horses with plump bodies was recognized as early as the beginning of the sixteenth century. Suffolk, Norfolk, and Essex, all seacoast counties, made up a region from which London has drawn much of its food needs in dairy products, meats, and grains; also its entertainment inasmuch as Newmarket, famous over the centuries for horse racing, is in Suffolk. King James I of England thought so highly of racing that he built a house beside the race track at Newmarket so he would not miss any of the events.

It should be of interest that the northern part of the region claiming to be the birthplace of the Suffolk was the home territory of Queen Boadicea, queen of the Iceni tribe, who had the distinction of attacking and massacring a garrison of Roman invaders in 61 A.D. She took her own life when the enemy army, about a year later, reversed things by defeating the Boadicea tribesmen.

Scotland was unfailingly loyal to the Clydesdale and the English counties of Lincolnshire, Lancashire, Leicestershire, and others were loyal to the Shire. The agricultural people of Suffolk, Norfolk, and Essex never admitted that there was a better horse than the Suffolk—or one to equal it.

The seminative horses that constituted the foundation for the breed doubtlessly owed something to the Norman horses introduced by William the Conqueror. The debt for the distinctive chestnut color may have been due to Norwegian horses brought by Norse invaders of a still earlier date. This particular case will never be proven but the well-known British writer Robert Wallace subscribed to the theory. There were, most probably, other strains of English horses that left their mark upon the developing breed; one such horse seems to have carried the name Farmer, described as a Lincolnshire trotter and brought to the region in 1764. Another that qualified for a place in the stud book was Barber's Proctor that was said to have been from a Suffolk mother and a Thoroughbred or part Thoroughbred sire.

Every developing breed needs a cornerstone sire of outstanding worth, like Justin Morgan in the Morgan breed, Champion of England in the Scotch Shorthorns, and Anxiety 4th in the American Herefords. In the case of the Suffolks, the great one was Crisp's Horse of Ufford, influential enough to make 1768, the year of his birth, a landmark date in Suffolk history. The claim has been made that all modern Suffolk horses, at home and abroad, trace to Crisp's Horse. Apparently, he did not have the size to rival the Shires of his time; he was 15½ hands high but he had quality and exceptional action. So lively was his action that he was declared fit to produce horses "for either coach or wagon." He was a light chestnut in color.

Crisp's Horse's description would fit many modern Suffolk horses and best of all, he demonstrated an ability to transmit his popular characteristics to succeeding generations. His principal impact upon the breed was transmitted through three or four stallions that were to rank with the best. The one that many judges considered the best in a hundred years after Crisp's Horse was Garret's Cupbearer 3rd, foaled in 1874.

Arthur Young (1741–1820), a noted writer on agricultural subjects, made an extensive tour through the eastern counties of England in 1770. He drew attention to the new and stronger emphasis that horsemen in Suffolk were placing upon horse types wanted by farmers, rather than animals for the street or road market. Pulling competitions were being introduced and Suffolk horsemen were already boasting that their horses could and would outpull horses of similar weight from any other breed. Training and testing for pulling competitions were sometimes performed by hitching the horses to something immovable like a big tree. "A true Suffolk,"

Raveningham Mona, a Suffolk mare imported and owned in Canada by G. W. McLaughlin, Oshawa, Ontario, with foal at her side.

said an early writer, "will draw almost until he drops."

The modern Suffolk in England and abroad has great spring of rib and deep body, making the animal appear somewhat short in legs. But depth in the thorasic region and length of rib have their own merit. True, the average Suffolk is hardly as heavy as the average Belgian or Percheron, but the range of sixteen hundred to eighteen hundred pounds, with height of 16 to 16½ or 17 hands is likely to satisfy agricultural users. Occasional stallions have weighed up to twenty-two hundred pounds and mares to two thousand. A recent champion in England weighed 2,575 pounds.

The same average specimen is expected to live long and, in the case of mares, continue to produce foals until late in life. Breeders have reported mares continuing to produce foals until past the age of twenty-five years.

The breed was criticized in times past for reasons of small feet and short pasterns. Such conditions have been largely removed and the modern Suffolk will be seen with good feet and legs, comparatively free from unsoundnesses and free from long hair on the legs.

And the chestnut color, with a range of seven shades varying from light to dark, is a breed asset. Regardless of shades the chestnut color is always popular. Inasmuch as chestnut and sorrel colors are transmitted genetically as recessive factors, they can be perpetuated with confidence, meaning that a foal from a chestnut mated with a chestnut will always be a chestnut. It doesn't usually work that way with other horse colors.

The Suffolk Horse Society of England, organized at a meeting at Old Ipswich in 1879, served well. One of the aims was to trace the lines of descent as far back as possible for all animals presented for registration. Volume I of the stud book followed with 1,230 entries for stallions and 1,120 for mares. The society at the time had 174 members, something of a triumph in itself for a young breed.

Added testimony of Suffolk hardiness and adaptability came from men who watched horses performing in army roles during the years of World War I when, sad to say, they were obliged to do transport work and suffer the worst of all working and living conditions. The claim was that no other heavy horses withstood the rains and mud in the French war zone as well as the Suffolk.

A large percentage of English farmers would have expected nothing less from their Suffolks as loyalty to the breed was maintained. A report stated that of 730 stallions licensed for public service in England in 1947, Shires numbered 303 while Suffolks accounted for 148, Clydesdales for 141, and Percherons for 131. If Scotland had been included in the survey, the Scottish horsemen's traditional preference for the Clydesdale would have changed the result considerably, but the Suffolk would still be a favorite with a big segment of users in England and Wales.[1]

THE SUFFOLK IN CANADA

The first Suffolk horses of record in Canada were two or three imported from the breed's homeland by Frederick William Stone of Guelph in 1865. Stone, it should be remembered, was the merchant who took to farming and stock raising on his Moreton Lodge

Farm on the outskirts of Guelph and became a leading breeder of Shorthorns and Herefords as well as Suffolks. He bought his first Shorthorns in the United States and then turned to importing his new breeding stock from England. His first importation-to-be was lost at sea but stubborn Englishman that he was, he returned at once for another shipment, then another and another. He will be remembered, also, for his sale of part of the Guelph land which became the site of the Ontario Agricultural College which was to receive its first students in 1874.

The initial importation to Moreton Lodge was a mare, Canterbury Nun 2nd, and two years later he imported a two-year-old stallion, Butley Champion. Both captured much interest in Ontario. By 1886, Joseph Beck, Thorndale, Ontario, appeared as an importer and breeder and animals from his herd were being sold to Mossom Boyd of Bobcaygeon, Ontario, to start the breed at the latter's home farm and at Prince Albert, Saskatchewan. At both farms, the new horses would share premises with developing herds of Polled Hereford cattle for which Mossom Boyd was to win international recognition.

Ever on the forefront, Mossom Boyd was exhibiting Suffolk horses at the World's Fair at Chicago in 1893.

The first Suffolk horses in western Canada may have been a few head brought in by M. Steves of Steveston, British Columbia, about 1885, and those forwarded to the Mossom Boyd farm at Prince Albert in 1893 or '94.

The first with Suffolk horses in what is now Alberta were George and Archie Jaques, English immigrants who homesteaded in the Lamerton district east of Lacombe in 1899. Having brought capital from England, the brothers were in a position to import high class breeding stock and did. By 1910, the Suffolk Horse Ranch at Lamerton was exhibiting at Calgary and winning all the championships for the breed—which really wasn't difficult because they were still almost alone in the Suffolk showring. But the brothers were bringing their breed to public attention and making sales. What they were offering were: "Imported Suffolks from England's best studs and Alberta-bred Suffolks from imported stock. Females in foal to Rendlesham Matchem."

The biggest Suffolk news for lovers of the breed in Canada in 1911 was a report of the annual sale at Ipswich in Suffolk, under the auspices of the Suffolk Horse Society of Great Britain. Stallions, mares, and foals were offered; the feature of the big event was in the number of purchases "made by Mr. Mossom Boyd of Bobcaygeon and Prince Albert for shipment to Canada."[2]

The Boyd purchases included the first prize foal from the show, Smith's Battle, and eleven other sale lots of mares and fillies. Some of these bluebloods were marked for delivery at the Ontario farm, some at the Saskatchewan place.

The Canadian Suffolk Horse Society had its beginning in 1910 and the American Suffolk Horse Association in the next year. Members of the associations in both countries were optimistic. They had good horses—early maturing, plucky, friendly, hardy, and beautiful—and could see no reason why their breed could not attain as much popularity in Canada as it enjoyed in England. But Canadian progress was slow, very slow.

The Suffolk—or Suffolk Punch as many people continued to call the breed—gained some supporters in each of the provinces but failed to find backing comparable to what it had in England and did not find a stronghold anywhere in the Dominion. If what was written by a member of the Jaques family in the district history book, *Land of the Lakes*, is accurate, the Suffolk Horse Ranch in Alberta may have had as strong a claim as any to the title of Suffolk center of Canada. "For a few years," according to the writer, "Lamerton [looked like] the headquarters of the Suffolk Punch Association."[3]

The fact was that the rate of expansion in Canada left much to be desired. Volume I of the stud book did not have enough registration entries to warrant publication until 1939. When it did appear, it included only 307 stallions and 352 mares. An excellent stud of Suffolks was established by G. W. McLaughlin, Oshawa, but it was not enough to ensure a Canadian future. By 1935, the organization was failing seriously and the total number of registrations from the inception of the stud book to December 31 in that year was 607. In the twelve months of 1935, only eighteen new registrations were added and the association's list of active members had dwindled to four names.

By 1940 there were only thirteen new registrations, all of which originated in Ontario. For 1957 there were two new registrations and in 1958, none. Between 1980 and 1984, three more Suffolks were registered in the *General Stud and Herd Book of Canada*, bringing the all-time Canadian registrations for the breed to 776—just 119 more than at the end of 1939.

The great pioneer horsemen—Alexander Galbraith, F. W. Stone, Mossom Boyd, George and Archie Jaques, and other friends of the breed—would be surprised and disappointed. If they were still here to witness the changes in Suffolk fortunes, they would no doubt reason that the public's preferences for breeds can be fickle and unaccountable. They might say that it's too soon to dismiss the chance of a breed resurrection to Canadian favor like that which has existed in England for generations.

The Canadien

Little Horse of Iron

Of more than a hundred breeds of farm-related livestock in Canada, over 85 percent of them were introductions from other countries. Among the few exceptions developed and granted breed status right here were the Romnelet sheep, Lacombe pigs, Hays Converter cattle, Canadien cattle (Bovins Canadiens), and Canadien horses (Chevaux Canadiens). The oldest of these Canadian breed creations are the two developed in the Province of Quebec and known formerly as French Canadians.

New France probably received its first cattle in the breed-building operation earlier than its first horses, but almost a parallel development existed with these two breeds whose roots penetrate to the seventeenth-century soil of the St. Lawrence River valley. One of the similarities in the breed-making process can be seen in the simultaneous organization of the breed associations—the Société Des Eleveurs De Bovins Canadiens and Société Des Eleveurs De Chevaux Canadiens. Both were formed in 1895.

Previous page: Canadien horses on one of the provincial breeding farms in Quebec. Photograph by Strohmeyer and Carpenter.

A Canadien mare. Although black is their usual color, sorrels and chestnuts occasionally occur. The picture is of a sorrel mare of outstanding quality. *Photograph by Strohmeyer.*

Samuel de Champlain, the great colonizer of New France, settled hundreds of immigrants—more men than women—in the valley. But the shape of development left much to be desired until Louis XIV instructed his foreign minister, Jean Baptiste Colbert, to reorganize the colony. In consequence, Jean Talon was appointed intendant—a sort of general manager—and came to reside in New France in 1665. He recognized two great needs, French girls to become wives in the predominantly bachelor community, and French horses to serve all the settlers. Over a thousand of what became known as "the king's girls" were brought out and more is known about the girls than the horses.

It appears, however, that upon instructions from the king to his minister Colbert, twenty mares and two stallions were selected with care—some from the royal stables and some from the districts of Brittany and Normandy. The latter may have been related to the French horse stock from which the French Percheron sprang.

In selecting none but the best animals to be sent to the St. Lawrence, it is impossible to know if Colbert was thinking only of the immediate need for work stock. He may also have been dreaming of assembling and forwarding superior horses from which a breed might arise.

The ocean voyage was rough and eight of the good mares died en route. The remaining twelve mares and two stallions landed in good condition and may have been the first of their species in that area and the first domestic horses in what is now Canada.

They were not big but they possessed grit and stamina. They were the progenitors of the horses believed by their friends to be capable of generating "more power per hundred pounds of body weight than horses of any other breed." They were predominantly black in color and were to be called most aptly "the little horses of iron."

Be that as it may, the horses proved versatile and hardy and the colonists received them with gratitude, realizing, perchance, that their size, weight, and disposition would make them ideal as all-purpose workers.

More French horses followed, a stallion and two mares in 1667, eleven mares and one stallion in 1670, and so on. The horse population in the colony grew rapidly because the strain was naturally prolific. There were 145 horses in 1679; 1,875 head in 1706, and 5,275 in 1720.

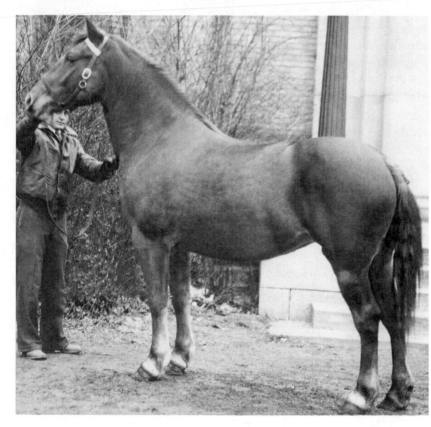

THE CANADIEN

At first the imported horses were allocated on lease terms to people of prominence and those who had given exceptional service to the colony. Thus, the horses remained initially in the ownership of the king. The rigid selection commonly followed in planned breed-building was probably absent, but a cold climate with poor roads and feed limitations would inevitably invoke the law of survival of the fittest. Horses of later generations may have been slightly smaller than the original breeding stock and they were not always handsome or glamorous, but they gained in hardiness and fleetness. They were not racehorses by design but they were both fast and sure-footed and were the candidates in scores of matched races on country roads over the years. It was not surprising that infusions of French Canadian horse blood was wanted by breed improvers working with Morgans and Standard Breds and some others.

For about 200 years there was but negligible effort to improve the Quebec horses and they became practically indigenous. Then, soon after the middle of the nineteenth century, they fell upon dangerous times and came close to complete loss of identity. With the coming of the new breeds of bigger horses, the seminative Quebec horses were discredited. The Quebec Board of Agriculture formed in 1852 was captivated by the big and imposing new breeds and its encouragement for the smaller and versatile breed was being withdrawn. Representatives of the Quebec breed were deprived of showring classes at many fairs and their former popularity was disappearing. The indigenous mares were being bred to stallions of other breeds and the impression was conveyed that the French Canadian breed was not worth preserving.

The drift might have gone all the way to oblivion had it not been for warnings sounded by one horseman in particular, E. A. Barnard, who argued the folly of allowing the breed qualities of hardiness and endurance to disappear. His message was heard and horsemen began to show interest in recovering the old strain before it became irretrievably lost.

Concerned horsemen at this point asked the provincial government to start a stud book and admit to it only those horses which conformed to the best type and quality found in the strain, to be confirmed by inspection. A stud book was opened in 1886 and inspectors were sent throughout the province to locate and examine every worthy candidate for admission.

It could be told that while Quebec in 1850 had about 150,000 horses, almost all of the same type and the same Quebec breeding, the province in the decade between 1895 and 1905 had not more than 2,000 with the qualifications for registration.

The French Canadian Horse Breeders' Association was formed in 1895, at which time the little black horse of iron was making a notable comeback. It was reinstated with classes at Quebec fairs and exhibitions and in due course had its own classification at the Royal Winter Fair.

Restored to public favor, the breed was embraced again by the Department of Agriculture and the experimental farms in the province. The Dominion Experimental Station at Cap Rouge became a leader in improvement and promotion. A bulletin written in 1927 by C. A. Langelier, superintendent of the station, reported the program.[1]

The experimental farm project began with a single mare, Helene, bought for the Cap Rouge station. Although she weighed only eleven hundred pounds, the superintendent reported, "she had lots of grit, a good gait and a conformation which gave her more strength than animals 200 pounds heavier. Many times she spent the full 10 hours on the corn binder with a mate weighing nearly 1500 pounds but never for a moment did her whiffletree get behind the other. Every teamster who worked with her said she always looked as lively after a hard day as she did in the morning, even when only a couple of weeks before foaling."

Mated to a black French Canadian stallion, Wilfrid, weighing about 1,200 pounds, the mare dropped a black stallion colt on May 31, 1913. The station superintendent called it a red-letter day for the breed of French Canadian horses. The black foal born that day and registered later as Albert de Cap Rouge was to become the most influential sire of the breed. He weighed 110 pounds at birth, 750 pounds at one year of age, and about 1,350 pounds at maturity. He possessed all the characteristics of a good general purpose farm horse and Quebec farmers applauded.

Speaking in 1925 about the first 100 foals sired by Albert de Cap Rouge, Mr. Langelier said: "Not one is balky and the percentage of unsound animals is remarkably small. This stallion is now admitted by all breeders of French Canadian horses to be the best in existence."

Extending the experimental station work with the breed, a bigger breeding program was undertaken at the St. Joachim Horse Breeding Station twenty-five miles east of Quebec City. Started in 1920, this station was under the supervision of the superintendent of the Cap Rouge station and had the support of both the federal and Quebec departments of agriculture. The station farm, consisting of 500 acres, had for some years more than 70 horses of breeding age, the biggest number in the Province of Quebec. Inasmuch as they were all Canadiens, it was the biggest stud of its kind in the world.

The Cap Rouge stud was maintained until 1940 when the pressures of war led the federal government to close out the operation. The good horses were sold widely in the province but a rather similar stud of selected Canadiens was established at La Gorgendière, under the supervision of the provincial Department of Agriculture and the improvement continued.

Notwithstanding widespread admiration for the Canadien breed, it remained almost entirely provincial in its distribution. A few representatives of the breed were bought for export to the United States and brought high

Canadien stallion Albert de Cap Rouge, used successfully in breed improvement in Quebec. *Photograph by Strohmeyer and Carpenter.*

praise, but horsemen in that country continued to favor the breeds with greater weight. A few members of the breed were used in western Canada and practical horsemen confirmed the reputed qualities of hardiness and tirelessness. Often they seemed to perform the impossible.

The author recalls from boyhood years a carload of eastern Canadian farm horses being shipped to Saskatchewan for sale. In it was one black French Canadian mare. The freight car was derailed close to the town and with the car lying on its side, there seemed no way by which the struggling horses could be removed. But an attendant who hoped to throw some hay to the imprisoned and frightened animals, climbed to the car's side that had become the top as it rested in the railroad ditch. He managed to get the only exposed door open, the one at the top. Inasmuch as freight cars were eight feet wide, the open door at the top would be eight feet above the level on which the trapped horses were standing. Nobody knew how it was done but as soon as the car door above the horses was opened, one horse scrambled madly—conceivably using the other horses as stepping stones—and jumped out, through the roof as it were. It was the French Canadian horse, to be sure, and the courageous and nigh miraculous performance left a lasting impression.

One chestnut Canadien stallion, Elegant De Yamachiche, was a resident at the University of Saskatchewan barn between 1942 and 1949 and became widely known to prairie horsemen. The purpose of his presence was to further a plan for the production of a strain of general purpose horses with the chestnut color, that might find a place of lasting importance as chore teams on farms that were otherwise totally mechanized.

The project was cut short but the tireless Canadien stallion won much admiration. This writer remembers very well how at the end of a thirty-mile ride from the east side of Saskatoon to Beaver Creek and back, he was tired and sore while his mount, "Frenchie" as he was known, seemed ready to start out again.

Like all breeds of heavy- or medium-weight work horses, the Canadien lost numbers as farm tractors became numerous. The breed in 1935 showed 80 new registrations—all from breeders in the Province of Quebec—just as all the officers and directors of the association had Province of Quebec mailing addresses. Forty-nine years later, in 1984, the new registrations for the breed totalled 115, all but four being from Quebec. The four exceptions were from applications submitted by Ontario horsemen. In maintaining the numbers of new registrations, the Canadiens were doing better than most breeds, especially the draft breeds. That total of 115 new registrations for the Canadien in 1984—practically all from one province—compared with 1,023 for Belgians, 582 for Percherons, and 293 for Clydesdales, Canada wide.

Purebred Canadiens registered with the National Live Stock Records since the stud book was opened until the end of 1984 totalled 4,866. What should have brought special satisfaction to friends of the breed, the Sociètè Des Eleveurs De Chevaux Canadiens could still count 276 members of all ranks. There were that many who had not lost their faith in the Canadien's resources of fibre, toughness, and longevity.

They were the people who liked to repeat a story that was first heard when the breed was young. It began with a farmer outside of Quebec who acquired a French Canadien gelding, not very big in size but big in some other respects. The little black horse was matched with a sixteen-hundred-pound Clydesdale, as the story was told, and together they did the cultivating, plowing, and long-distance hauling on the farm. The little horse never failed to keep an even whiffletree but, finally, the big horse died. When neighbors enquired about the cause of death, the owner replied: "That damned Canadien just worked him to death."

Elegant De Yamachiche, a chestnut Canadien stallion presented to the University of Saskatchewan by Quebec breeders. He was used at the university in a program aimed at producing a breed of general purpose horses. *Courtesy* The Western Producer.

Breed Rivalry in Harness

Politics and the private lives of country school teachers furnished dependable fuel for farm controversy over many years but nothing brought more debate and near violence than questions related to farm power.

The earliest arguments were between the horsemen and those intensely practical souls who believed in oxen because they alone could consume enough grass or hay to meet all daily needs, thereby living off the land. This advantage was enough, it was believed, to outweigh the typical bovine annoyances of slow motion and sulky dispositions. Those champions of the ox who went to the length of writing letters to the press conceded that horses would create a better public image and make more endearing working companions, but the oxen were more economical and practical sources of power.

Previous page:
The famous Shea
Brewery team of
Clydesdales from
Winnipeg.

But friends of the lowly ox were fighting a losing battle. Notwithstanding the common fare that sustained the "working bull critters," most homesteaders and farmers wanted horses and aimed to own them just as soon as the first cost and the cost of feed could be assured.

With a minimum of consideration for the feelings of the bovine slaves, most of the tired old oxen ended their days at a late autumn slaughtering when they were unceremoniously converted to supplies of tough winter beef. It was enough to make homesteaders understand what was meant by neighbors who reported sitting down at the dinner table hungry and getting up tired. But by the time the voices of the friends of oxen fell silent, the horsemen were facing the new challenge of steam power and then power generated by gasoline-burning internal combustion engines.

Before the horse-versus-tractor argument was resolved, new breeds of draft horses appeared and new lines of controversy were drawn. The friends of the Clydesdales, who accorded their favorites the kind of respect normally reserved for the names of Bonnie Prince Charlie and John Knox, saw the rival Shires and Suffolks being brought to the country and then the European mainland breeds, Percheron and Belgian. The majority of horse users, traditionally wedded to the Clydesdale, were at first unimpressed by the new types with bigger and more muscular

A six-horse team of Percherons owned by Armour and Co. of Chicago, 1908.
Photograph by Hildebrand and Smith.

bodies and less of the Scottish ideal in feet and legs which had come to be seen as a hallmark of quality. Backers of the new breeds believed that, on balance, they had the more serviceable horses and the controversy grew bitter. It might have been expected that the showring would settle the arguments. It didn't settle anything except the winning exhibitor. Most showyard judges were chosen from the ranks of the breeders and regardless of how conscientious those judges tried to be, they could not escape their type preferences. Judges who had no breed affiliations, such as livestock specialists from university staff ranks, tried seriously to approach this problem objectively, but the criticism was generally the same; if a gelding with Clydesdale characteristics was awarded the top prize in an interbreed class, the ringside whispers might be loud enough to be heard across the infield: "Another Clydesdale judge!" Or, when the top award settled on a Percheron, the comment often sounded like a conviction: "He's a Percheron man, damned if he isn't."

Not much was being achieved by such interbreed competition and as soon as exhibits and exhibitors were sufficiently numerous, the heavy breeds were given separate classes, except in the team competitions. Ultimately, interbreed classes were seen only in four-horse and six-horse teams, where much of the old rivalry was kept alive.

For additional years the stylish Clydesdales were winning a disproportionately large share of the contests for the big hitches. Even when such events were adjudicated by a committee of two, consisting of one person nominated by the organized Clydesdale breeders and one by the organized Percheron and Belgian interests, the two judges quite often disagreed, necessitating the appointment of a third or "independent" judge to fill the part of a referee. Even then, the third party, no matter how able and conscientious, knew how small was his chance of escaping the dub of being "a Clydesdale fancier" or a "Percheron and Belgian lover," depending upon the breed characteristics of the winning entry.

It was a problem for which there seemed to be no simple solution, and some horsemen felt wronged. But for spectators, viewing the big, magnificent horses wearing polished harness, Scotch topped collars, and generous displays of harness rings, these mixed breed classes reflecting patient training, skillful decorating and driving, had to be seen as one of the foremost attractions at any show. Exhibition patrons who might admit indifference toward breeding classes, left no doubt about the harness events being the crowning touch of the fair.

Harnessing and driving six-horse outfits in tandem pattern may have been an American idea before it became a Canadian showpiece. It could have been argued, quite properly, that six-horse teams hitched tandem had no practical place in recent farm practice, although frontier freighters and drivers of stage coaches on long and lonely trails did drive fours or sixes, tandem style, quite regularly, as notes in pioneer papers will show. The *Edmonton Bulletin* reported late in 1884, for example, that "Two four-horse and two six-horse teams belonging to Ad McPherson are expected to arrive shortly with loads of green apples, fresh oysters, whiskey and other Christmas groceries."[1] But when farmers drove more than four horses in field operations, they preferred to hitch them in tiers of four.

There were exceptions, of course, as when Slim Moorehouse was hauling grain over a twenty-two-mile trail from the farm in the Buffalo Hills to elevators at Vulcan, of which more is related elsewhere in this text. The immediate point is that farmers adopted big hitches for steady field work and then accepted the tandem six or four as an instrument in demonstrating the best in driving skill. There was no doubt: the six big horses driven tandem offered the best means of testing driving skills and a first class technique for public entertainment.

The first big tandem hitches of record were winning public attention about 1899. One of the first to gain North American prominence and certainly the most consistent supporter of six-horse teams was the Anheuser-Busch Breweries of St. Louis, Missouri. The company's first six-horse team of prominence consisted of Percherons, but a change to Clydesdales came shortly and the company became a powerful force in breeding and improvement within the breed. It also became a leading influence in the use of draft horses for business advertising.

Six-horse teams had classes at the International Fat Stock Show in Chicago from about 1906. An issue of the *Farm and Ranch Review* appearing shortly after that date reported: "The six-horse Clydesdale team sent over to Europe to advertise Morris and Co., meat packers of Chicago, is exciting unstinted admiration." Another item from the same pioneer farm magazine reported that "Armour and Co. are looking for material for a Percheron six hitch in France."[2]

The first Canadian six-horse hitch to appear repeatedly on city streets, in Hardy Salter's opinion, was George Lane's string of Percheron greys, selected and driven by one of the early masters of the driving art, Alex Fleming. He was an Ontario man who went West as a Mounted Police recruit in 1881 and obtained much of his driving experience while in a police uniform. In 1908 he hired with Lane and in the next year travelled to France in connection with the big importation of aristocratic Percherons—seventy-five head of the best available.[3]

Salter had lasting recollections of the perfectly matched greys with which Fleming campaigned and won championships. The outfit appeared at the Calgary Exhibition in 1912, which was before showring classes were offered for the big ones. Lane, with pride in his horses, wanted to share them with the public and with that thought in mind, he ordered a white show wagon and had his greys hitched to appear daily on city streets and twice daily in the showring.

Salter told also that "about 1923, Calgary offered classes and prizes for six-horse teams for the first time. Furnishing the competition were George Lane with Percherons, Union Milk with Clydesdales, Thorborn and Riddle of DeWinton with Clydes." The summer fair patrons loved it. "Before long, Union Milk changed to Percherons; Dunham Bros. of Fairlight, Sask., came out with Clydes and A. E. Theaker of Wilcox, Sask., brought out a lovely six of black Percherons." About this time, also, Shea's Brewery, Winnipeg, was starting to show.

Big teams with spectacular style and beauty became increasingly popular with brewing companies in both Canada and the United States. The purpose was advertising and the result must have been satisfactory because the companies continued to feature them, much to the delight of breeders of chosen breeds. Horsemen, especially those favoring Clydesdales, saved their best compliments for the Anheuser-Busch horses that held the brewery-team spotlight for more than fifty years and did much to enhance the draft horse image.

From 1857 when the young immigrant Adolphus Busch married Lilly Anheuser, thereby founding a brewing dynasty, an inherent fondness for big horses became apparent. The practical use of horses in working and advertising roles was revived about the time of the repeal of prohibition in the United States, more than fifty years ago, when eight geldings with harness were bought from the Union Stock Yards, Chicago. With the horses came one of the ablest horsemen of his time, Billie Wales. Almost immediately, there was the further purchase of ten geldings with harness and wagon from Wilson and Co., and still another in the acquisition of ten of the famous Shea Brewery horses taken from Winnipeg. In the latter deal, Canada lost one of its most distinguished team drivers, Scottish-born Andy Haxton, who followed his beloved Clydes to St. Louis. Then, in 1939, Walter Brady, another celebrated team driver, joined Anheuser-Busch to give the company some of the best teamster talent on the continent.

Then came the Budweiser Clydesdale Breeding Farm when August A. Busch, who was to become company president, called for an expanded program to include horse breeding. The dual purpose was to furnish replacement horses for the teams and, at the same time, encourage draft horse improvement across the country. As Berry Farrell, the able and popular manager of the breeding farm could tell, the company made repeated importations of the best Clydesdales available from Scotland and Canada, and entered breeding stock at the biggest shows on the continent, including the Canadian Royal Winter Fair. Furthermore, they won championships with, for example, the great show and breeding stallion Bardrill Glenord, with a record of five grand championships at the Canadian Royal.

Anheuser-Busch seemed to have done well from its boast that "THE BUDWEISER CLYDESDALE HITCH IS AMERICA'S LARGEST, LONGEST, HEAVIEST LIVING LEGEND."

Canadian horsemen would not forget the notable interbreed competitions that occurred when majestic six-horse teams of two or three breeds filled the showrings at Toronto, Brandon, or Vancouver and tortured judges searched for compromise solutions. And no less memorable were the men who trained and drove the teams, artisans of the highest order, some whose names have been mentioned and others, like Allan Leslie from Watrous, Saskatchewan, whose name should still be mentioned.

Lawrence Rye of Edmonton, who was himself among the best drivers of tandem teams, pronounced Alex Fleming and Allan Leslie as the best in his experience and then offered some personal recollections about the former: "I showed against him for six consecutive years after 1913. He always carried a long bullwhip and while holding all six lines in his left hand, he'd crack the whip over his horses without touching them and then collect the reins in both hands. It was sort of rough in those days and he'd make me mad when that whip would crack like a gunshot alongside my horses and just scare the daylights out of them. But, say, Fleming was a driver, the best I can recall."

Other horsemen were ready to pronounce Leslie as the greatest team driver in Canadian history. His driving career began, he explained, with oxen at the heart of the homestead country and ended under the bright lights of the Canadian Royal Winter Fair. Born near Brandon in 1887, he was on his way to occupy a homestead near Watrous, N.W.T., eighteen years later. The first part of that journey could be made by rail but after leaving the freight train at Strasbourg, he still had sixty-five trail miles ahead. For that part of the journey he was driving six oxen abreast, leading five horses at the back of the wagon, and carrying all other possessions like seed, plow, porridge pot, blankets, and colic cure on the wagon.

Four of the oxen were unbroken and the departure from Strasbourg was at such a gallop that plow, blankets, and cooking pots were strewn along the trail. But the young oxen became tired and settled down and ultimately broke the first land on the homestead.

Leslie's primary fondness for Clydesdales survived and at the first Watrous Summer Fair in 1912, he was competing with work horses. From there he entered horse classes at Saskatoon and Regina and, finally at the Royal Winter Fair. At various times his winnings included prizes for four-horse and six-horse teams. Even before the driving competitions were introduced at Toronto, J. G. Robertson, livestock commissioner for Saskatchewan, introduced Leslie as the best six-horse team driver in Canada.

What Leslie considered his best "big six" consisted of Johnny, Sandy, Tommy, Bruce, Prince, and Donald, all but Johnny having been sired by the Clydesdale Clan McNee, and raised on the Leslie farm. But it was his personal performance at the Royal that brought the highest honors. Nothing illustrated that success better than the record of having won the big team driving competition for six consecutive years after it was offered.

"When the Watrous farmer drove his six-horse team and wagon into the ring last night in competition with all the teams," a Toronto newspaper related, "the crowd forgot about the jumpers, saddle horses and ponies they had come to see and delivered round after round of thunderous applause. The big six circled the ring in perfect order, and drew up in line as a single horse. When the red ribbon was pinned on Tommy, one of the leaders, the noise was simply deafening."

Another Toronto reporter told that the coolheaded Leslie drove his well-matched Clydesdales to the most decisive win of the heavy horse show "and into the hearts of the public by his clever driving and giving the crowd an eyeful of masterful horsemanship."

A question from the Toronto bleachers was relayed to Leslie: "What strange power does this man have to make his horses respond to verbal signals that are almost lost in the distracting din of an exhibition?" The horseman replied with typical modesty: "We've worked together quite a while and we sort of understand each other."

As if to prove the point, he related an occasion when the circumstances might have produced disaster instead of another Royal Winter Fair championship. It was his sixth test in the annual six-horse driving event. His friend and neighbor, Smith Steen, helped him hitch for the class and a hurried glance seemed to indicate that everything was in order. With the customary dash, the heavy outfit entered the big arena the instant the door was raised. Ten thousand spectators roared with delight but, instantly upon entering, Leslie was shocked to discover that a rein buckle to one lead horse had become caught in a harness ring, practically ending all control of the leaders. To stop for the purpose of correcting the trouble with the judges' full gaze upon him would almost certainly rob him of a winning score. He wanted to protect his reputation as a driver. There was one hope, a dangerous one; he would attempt

completion of the complex drive virtually without control of the lead team. He knew there was a risk of accident; he knew also that he had reason for faith in his horses. He made the decision to leave everything to communication by whistle and the good judgment of his leaders.

The team galloped on as it had done on other occasions and Leslie made a pretense of driving and tried to appear relaxed and confident, even though his heart was beating madly. He whistled to tell the leaders when to "cut the figure of eight" and when to change paces and they received the messages. Finally the lead team answered the call to draw to the center of the ring to receive another red ribbon. The judges and spectators concluded it to be another near-

The winning six-horse hitch of Belgians at Calgary, 1984, owned by the Lynnwood Belgian Ranch, Aldersyde, Alberta. *Photograph by Browarny; courtesy Lynnwood Ranch.*

perfect performance; what they did not know was that the full credit should have gone to the members of the lead team.

Horsemen hoped that four-horse and six-horse teams as national traditions would never lose their fascination for Canadians, regardless of the breed involved and even though horses with the character-istics of one breed more than another appeared to go to the top of the class with annoying frequency. It is of uppermost importance that all the heavy breeds in Canadian history be kept alive and vigorous and that horse-users—be they farmers, breeders, fanciers, or brewers—will be in a position to make their own breed decisions.

The Pulling Contests

9

Horse pulling competitions were no respecters of breeds. Breed colors, conformation, or pedigree mattered not at all. Nothing counted except a contesting team's strength and will to move the near-impossible loads.

Horses would have had the best of reasons for hating the gruelling tests of strength and sometimes there was injury. But organized pulling became popular public entertainment. As a local pastime it wasn't new. Unscheduled barnyard pulling matches were probably as ancient as cockfights.

Hauling rocks from farm fields with stoneboats and teams offered useful training for competition. The work of picking and hauling stones was tedious, tiring, and uninspiring and needed something like an occasional on-the-spot test of horse strength with a bit of betting money to enliven it.

Every farmer had a stoneboat and most had field rocks, but if the stones were not available, it was never difficult to resort to bags of gravel or cement blocks. Still, the lack of a scale to measure the pulling force was a handicap, making it practically impossible to obtain a mathematical assessment of a performance to permit comparison with pulls in the next municipality or the next province. Supervisors, by requiring the use of the same stoneboats and as nearly as possible the same loads of stones, did well to minimize inequities. Without complete uniformity of pulling conditions,

Previous page:
Horse pulling contest
with dynamometer,
Regina Summer Fair,
1929. *Courtesy* The
Western Producer.

competitions could create as many disputes as they settled.

It could have been argued that horse breeds and breeding were not factors in determining a contest's outcome, but it was clear that the desire on the part of breeders to see representatives of their favorite breeds being called to the winner's circle at the pulling competition was fully as intense as at the conventional showring.

There were some exciting and spectacular private pulls before 1924 but it was not until that time that the awkward looking four-wheel vehicle—suggesting a hybrid offspring from a farm truck as one parent and an army tank as another—appeared to change the whole character of the contests. It was the heavy dynamometer of a kind first constructed at Iowa State College and then remade under the direction of Prof. A. E. Hardy of the University of Saskatchewan.

Horse pulling entered suddenly upon a new era of excitement, and for the next few years it would have been difficult to imagine either a horse race or a horse show holding more rural appeal than the western pulling events. One of the astonishing yet significant Saskatchewan headlines of 1925 announced: "Heavyweight Championship Of The World Goes To Lumsden." Nobody in the rural West at that time would confuse the editor's message with a prize fight.

All the big western exhibitions scheduled pulling competitions in 1924. It was a matter of yielding to public demand, although the fever of excitement didn't reach a climax until August of the next year when the two giant breeds and two proud prairie cities were locked in battle.

Saskatchewan could boast a million farm horses and every farmer had a breed preference. Brandon was still the horse capital of Canada—if not of the world—and might be expected to parade up to 200 draft stallions from the city's sales stables to mark the official opening of a winter fair. Heavy horses still ruled in Canadian farm fields and still ruled most human hearts and lives.

With the adoption of the dynamometer, competitions in pulling could be conducted with the same rules as those in use in the United States. Comparative pulling results astonished everybody. An American team had pulled 2,500 pounds on the dynamometer for the full regulation distance of 27½ feet to make what was considered a record. But at the Calgary Exhibition that summer, close to the beginning of the show season, a team of southern Alberta Clydesdales won with a registered pull of 2,615 pounds, accepted as a world record.

Edmonton was next on the exhibition circuit and there a Percheron team pulled 2,600 pounds. Then, in the next week it was Saskatoon's turn and previous pulling records tumbled when R. B. McLeod's big Percheron geldings, Dan and Tag, settled professionally into their twenty-eight-inch collars and brought shouts of glee when the dynamometer dial recorded a pull of 2,900 pounds, a new championship with pounds to spare.

This was but the beginning of the excitement. When the special midway train departed for Regina on Saturday night, the dynamometer was taken along to that community in which horsemen believed they had horses capable of outdoing the best pulling performances between Calgary and Saskatoon. Among the local horsemen who had been doing well in the stoneboat leagues were

Gibbs Brothers of Lumsden whose massive Belgian geldings, Jumbo and Barney, had shown a team weight of 3,790 pounds. The Regina people became so inspired that they were almost ready to expropriate the Belgians and annex the town of Lumsden.

As that last of the scheduled pulling contests of the 1924 season turned out, the Gibbs team was a decisive winner, having pulled thirty-one hundred pounds for the full distance. It was another world record, the third to have been made by Canadian horses in four weeks. Saskatoon horsemen were loath to surrender their supremacy of only a few days and to yield to a Regina contestant would be humiliating. They wished the two great city teams could be brought together for a showdown match.

There was still one day left in the Regina Exhibition program and Manager Dan Elderkin, never one to miss an opportunity to fill his grandstand, had an idea. He placed a telephone call to his poker-playing friend, Sid Johns, manager of the Saskatoon Exhibition, urging him to act at once to have Bob McLeod load his pair of Percheron geldings on the midnight express bound for Regina, to participate in a pulling battle of champions in front of the grandstand next day.

No doubt Sid Johns gasped and remarked that it would be costly to ship two tons of Percherons to Regina at the express rate. But Dan replied that the investment would be returned with dividends and, besides, his board of directors would assume the full cost. Johns agreed and, acting on behalf of his friend McLeod, he issued a challenge for the Lumsden horsemen to present their Belgian team and pull against the Saskatoon Percherons for the $1,000 prize the Regina

Exhibition was prepared to provide.

McLeod accepted the challenge and undertook to have his team ready for the overnight journey. The Saskatoon Percherons were in Regina early the next morning and by noon everybody in the south seemed to know about the unlisted heavyweight championship and everybody wanted to see it. The afternoon grandstand show was revised to accommodate the heavy horses and by 1:30, the Regina turnstiles were clicking to make Elderkin smile.

Determined by the toss of a coin, the Belgian team would pull first. The Belgians had the advantage of weight and home town support. On their first pull, they registered at exactly 3,000 pounds for the full 27½ feet, not quite as good as they had done the previous day, but the partisan crowd roared approvingly. It was then for the Saskatoon Percherons to show what they could do and they made precisely the same score as the Belgians. The judging committee called for the second pull and both teams started the dynamometer at 3,100 pounds, but neither succeeded in sustaining the forward thrust for the distance. Inasmuch as the McLeod Percherons had moved the 3,100 pound load for the greater distance, namely 18½ feet, they were declared the winners and the cheque for $1,000 was presented on the spot. The Regina fans became silent while the visitors from Saskatoon acted as if they had just won the Grey Cup.

There was still something unsatisfactory about the outcome; although the Saskatoon horses won fairly on the day's performance, the Belgians had made the best pull of the week and were still the world champions. It may have suited Dan Elderkin better than he was admitting and he had something more to say; "There'll be another year," he shouted, "and there'll be another prize of $1,000 for the best pull from the Saskatoon and Regina champions. Don't you people forget to come back. It'll be the biggest show you ever saw!"

The two big teams were taken to their respective homes to be conditioned for the test of 1925. No horses and no athletes in the country were assured of better feed and care, with just enough pulling to keep them fit. Dan Elderkin made sure that everybody across the West knew the dates for the "Battle of the Heavyweights." Weight was important and both teams were heavier in 1925. The Gibbs Belgians weighed in at two tons even, 200 pounds more than the Percherons.

The Saskatoon team pulled first and made 3,200 pounds over the required distance, thereby establishing a new world record for Canadian horses. Sid Johns waved another $10 bill inviting an additional bet and waited only a few seconds to see it covered. Then the Gibbs team pulled—3,300 pounds—a fresh and most convincing world record.

That was it: the Lumsden Belgians were the 1925 champions and their owners collected the $1,000 prize. The Gibbs horses pulled again to see if they could better their own record—and sure enough, they did, pulling 3,350 pounds to make a third world record in one day.

Canadian horsemen representing all breeds were pleased with the demonstration that led to an article in the *Breeder's Gazette*, published in Chicago. The title question was: "Does Canada Have Better Draft Horses Than The United States?" The author offered the opinion that on the strength of the pulling records, Canada did have better horses.

The popularity of the pulling contests rose and fell. When it was presumed that the big and cumbersome dynamometer would not be needed further, it was considerately retired to the Western Development Museum in Saskatoon. But pulling had not lost its appeal. It was still easy to generate enthusiasm, but Canadians had to admit the surpassing records made by American horses in recent times. The report of the National Horse Pulling Contests held at Hillsdale, Michigan, on October 11 and 12, 1949, proved two points: first, a lasting interest on the part of horsemen and, second, the apparent ease with which biological records can be raised and broken. Entries from 11 states and Canada totalled 112 teams battling for $5,000 in prizes. Of these, 68 were in the lightweight category, in which a pair of Belgians from Ohio weighing 2,995 pounds won on a pull of 3,400 pounds for 23 feet, eight inches.

In the heavyweight class, 44 teams from nine states and Canada were in the field. The seven heaviest of them had team weights ranging from 3,960 to 4,950 pounds. Two of the teams—one weighing 4,475 and the other 4,950—pulled the equivalent of the world's record of 4,250 pounds. To break the match tie, the required load was set at 4,275 pounds and both teams moved the load but neither took it the required 27½ feet. Although both teams had equalled the world record, the match decision was made in favor of the team of sorrel Belgians weighing 4,475. They pulled the load for a distance of 20 feet, 11 inches, while the heavier team, also matched sorrel Belgians, pulled the same load 19 feet, two inches.[1]

Canadian horsemen shook their heads and muttered, "Incredible!"

The Moorehouse Herd in Harness

Ralph Moorehouse, better known as "Slim," wasn't born to fame and didn't seek it. But liking horses and having some unusual talent in handling them, he couldn't escape public attention. In the end, his big tandem hitches added substantially to horse history in Canada and his own fame.

Having drifted into the Buffalo Hills district east of Vulcan, Alberta, about the end of World War I, Moorehouse was looking for work as a farm hand. He had experience in handling two- and four-horse teams and hinted that he would like to test his skill with bigger outfits. He became the hired man on the farm of Jim Dew who, like other farmers, complained about the length of time it took to haul grain in the customary two-horse loads over the twenty-two-mile trail to the elevator at Vulcan.

Moorehouse was quick to see the inefficiency and folly in spending two long days and forty-five miles of travel to market a single load of grain at a Vulcan elevator. Instead of hauling one seventy-five-bushel load of wheat, Slim Moorehouse began hooking two or three loaded wagons together and hitching four or six horses to them in tandem fashion, thereby saving the driving time of at least one man. It took expert hands to deal with four or six lines but Moorehouse found that he had them.

He wasn't thinking about getting into a competition with neighbors who were also entertaining ideas about bigger hauling units, but without realizing it, he found himself in a contest with a friend, Joe Whittam, on a nearby farm. After Slim went over the trail with three loaded wagons, Joe did it with four wagons and eight horses. Slim made the next trip with six wagons and twelve horses. People along the route and in Vulcan were thoroughly enjoying the show. Joe Whittam appeared on the road with sixteen horses hauling as much grain as they could handle and Slim Moorehouse was next seen with a twenty-horse tandem hauling more than the equivalent of a half a freight car of Buffalo Hills wheat. And Slim was dreaming about still bigger teams and loads.

The *Farm and Ranch Review*, published in Calgary, graced the cover page of February 5, 1923, with a picture of the most recent Slim Moorehouse train of grain wagons being unloaded at the elevator in Vulcan. The story was inside. This particular Moorehouse delivery, it was reported, consisted of 1,144 bushels of No. 1 wheat carried in eight tank-type wagons. The pulling power was furnished by twenty horses and ten mules. The total length of the train was given as 245 feet. And Moorehouse, without assistance, did the driving.

The day of delivery proved to be one of widespread interest in the prairie town. About fifteen hundred people were present to see the outfit arrive and unload, one wagon at a time. Weighing and unloading took a total of one hour and seventeen minutes.

Officials of the Calgary Exhibition heard about the Slim Moorehouse feat and knew at once that he and his teams and loaded wagons would make an excellent attraction for the next summer show in 1924. They opened negotiations and made a deal. As the following exhibition week drew near, Moorehouse borrowed some additional horses from Glen House of Gleichen, loaded eight big wagons with twelve hundred bushels of wheat and drove away in the direction of Calgary. Burdened with thirty-six tons of wheat, travel could not be very rapid, but after 5½ days on the trail, the horse and mule train halted on the Calgary outskirts, there to camp and rest until the opening day of the show.

The exhibition began with a street parade and Moorehouse and his teams were on hand to take the place of prominence assigned to them. He would know that city streets were sure to present problems but he was fearless. One precaution he did take: he had Don Briar riding beside him on the first wagon, constantly ready to apply brakes if trouble occurred anywhere between the pole team and the leaders.

The signal to start was given promptly at 11 A.M. Moorehouse collected the eight leather reins by which he hoped to control the thirty-two horses and mules and blew a sharp whistle as the signal to his animals to tighten traces. The lead team, Dan and Chubb, being Slim's personal property, had a good understanding of the driver's wishes and responded promptly. It was essential that the foremost teams move first to take up the slack in traces and chains.

Although strangers to city streets, the horses and mules did exactly what they were supposed to do and quietly settled into their collars. The Moorehouse outriders saw nothing wrong and relaxed.

The parade route was planned and fixed far in advance and the Moorehouse men were not denying concern about certain sharp corners to be turned. There was the corner at Seventh Avenue and Tenth Street South West where the parade traffic was to turn east. Skeptics thought they could foresee trouble at that point where horses and mules would be travelling eastward while wagons were still pointed north. But instead of creating an emergency, the teams did exactly what was necessary; lead horses Dan and Chubb, being the first to turn, moved slowly and the teams following did the same. On the entire course, there was nothing more serious than one of the horses stepping over its own trace, but a stranger, spotting the trouble, called to the driver to stop the train and correct the tug. Seconds later Slim Moorehouse blew his whistle and the great herd of horses and mules was moving again.

Spectators, especially farming people, loved the performance and cheered loudly. One remarked that Slim Moorehouse and his well-behaved tandem team "made a worthwhile parade by themselves." When the parade ended, Slim walked slowly down the line of horses and mules as if thanking each member for faithful service and co-operation.

The team returned to its campground in the Manchester district but travelled over a special parade route laid out on city streets for the further display of the celebrated horses each remaining day of the week. At week's end, the cargo of wheat carried as ballast, about twelve hundred bushels, was delivered at a city elevator and Slim Moorehouse and his famous teams turned toward home.

The exhibition management was so pleased with the performance that a request was made for a repeat engagement in 1925. Moorehouse was agreeable but at this point the Canadian Percheron Horse Association entered the act. W. L. Carlyle, secretary of the Percheron association, saw an opportunity to gain valuable publicity for the breed if the driver would harness and drive none but Percheron horses. Moorehouse was agreeable and breeders everywhere promised co-operation in furnishing the needed Percherons. So many Percherons were offered that Chris Bartsch of Gleichen undertook to assemble the required number right in his own district—and did.

Moorehouse was happy with the arrangement and found himself hitching and driving a thirty-six-horse tandem instead of the thirty-two horse and mule team of 1924. This time, too, it was an all-black team with every horse weighing at least sixteen hundred pounds and many individuals weighing eighteen hundred or more.

With more and heavier horses, Moorehouse added a couple of wagons and drove away to Calgary with an outfit that was described as the longest tandem ever hitched—thirty-six horses in eighteen pairs, roughly twenty-nine tons of horseflesh in harness and, altogether, a very bright image. Percheron coats glistened in the sun; polished harness looked like new, and Slim Moorehouse wore a stylish colored shirt, a gift from a Percheron admirer.

This time he was accompanied by a chuck-wagon pulled by four more black Percherons and supported by outriders on black horses. Counting two spare horses, Slim's 1925 outfit showed exactly fifty head, all blacks.

There was another difference in that second year: not all the wheat being transported was in bulk. The last of the ten wagons carried 6,000 miniature bags of wheat for distribution as souvenirs, each bag bearing the words: "The World's Best Wheat, Grown at Gleichen." The bags were tossed out along the parade route and the 6,000 proved to be fewer than enough to meet the demand. Wheat, like the Percherons, was popular.

Percheron breeders were well pleased with their breed's participation in the tandem team display—and they were not through. It being 1925, it was the second year of horse pulling competitions, rejuvenated by the availability of a dynamometer made at the University of Saskatchewan and being shipped around the exhibition circuit. As soon as they could be spared, the lead team and one other from the Moorehouse string were entered in their weight class for the pulling event. There, too, the blacks distinguished themselves, winning their weight classes and adding some championships.

As everybody knew, the growing popularity of tractors was enough to worry all loyal horsemen and the Percheron officers were determined to make the most of every opportunity for promotion. On Saturday night when Slim and his horses were making their final appearance before the grandstand, W. B. Thorne, president of the Canadian Percheron association, came to the platform and presented trophies bearing the inscription: "Presented by the Canadian Percheron Horse Association to the Gleichen Horse Breeding District In Token Of Appreciation For the World's Longest Team, Composed Of Percheron Horses Driven By One Man At The Calgary Jubilee Exhibition and Stampede, July, 1925."

Slim Moorehouse drove away, followed by a knot of men, women, and children who had fallen in love with the black horses and the man who, without knowing much horse history, had just made a substantial contribution to it.

Wit and Wisdom from the Horse Stable

11

Horsemen of all ages loved original humor but like other early humorists, didn't do much to ensure its preservation. They made no prepared speeches and were indifferent about writing. Some were so notoriously remiss about writing that they didn't even answer letters. There were exceptions, like Stanley Harrison of Fort Qu'Appelle whose horse-inspired poetry, essays, and sketches enriched frontier literature.

The horsemen had their own vocabularies; they invented humorous stories, some of which made bold mention of such commonplace barnyard realities as horse manure, constipation and flatulence. They saw no evil in repeating that, "Old horsemen long endure, forking hay and horse manure," or "A farting horse will never tire and a farting man is the man to hire."

Those who would place the physiological facts of the digestive process among the unmentionables might cry, "Crude" or "Vulgar," but to their everlasting credit, the story tellers of that generation past were never so destitute of real humor that sex and profanity were accepted as essential ingredients. It was a sad commentary on the decline of true humor when a modern youth, asked to define humor, replied, "dirty stories about girls."

Horse trading, being an early and popular pastime, invited rather many homespun stories. Leading citizens participated in the swapping. Church parsons who drove horses as they made congregational calls, enjoyed trading more than they generally admitted and many became experts. Even Abraham Lincoln indulged with pleasure and horsemen kept alive his account of one sight unseen trade in which he was dealing with a local court judge with similar instincts.

The very idea of trading horses sight unseen seemed to anticipate unsound and decrepit animals. The judge appeared at the place named for the exchange leading an ancient gelding, thin, lame from multiple unsoundnesses, heaving from broken wind, and altogether not worth more than the value of a green horsehide. Then Lincoln appeared, carrying on his shoulders a roughly constructed sawhorse. When he saw what he was getting in exchange he heaved a sigh, saying, "The judge wins this time; this is the most unprofitable horse trade I've made so far."

An Ontario horseman owned a horse for which he could find no buyer at any price, until he met a farm boy who offered to trade his pocket watch for the animal. The horseman said, "It's a deal," and the boy led his horse away. Everybody who saw the critter laughed and one of the neighbors thought to enlighten the lad by telling him he had been stung. The horse had splints, broken wind, stringhalt, sidebones, curbs, ringbone, thoroughpin, bone spavin, and bog.

The young fellow appeared unimpressed and informed the neighbor: "I didn't get stung because the watch I traded has no mainspring and no insides so it's unsound too."

Unexpectedly, a professor of veterinary anatomy came that way and, upon seeing a horse having every known unsoundness, said: "This is the horse I've been hoping to find, a perfect laboratory model for teaching unsoundnesses, better than a textbook. How much will you take for him?"

The boy replied: "My price is $525 but he doesn't have all the unsoundnesses; I'll be honest and tell you he isn't blind in either eye, so I'll knock off $25 and you can have him for $500."

"I'll take him," the professor said with evident glee. "We've got a blind pig at our college now so we can get along without a blind horse." The boy who had parlayed his useless watch into $500 then bought a purebred draft mare and became one of Ontario's leading breeders and showmen.

Following is a conglomerate of bits and pieces gleaned from the utterances of horsemen:

McGregor and Smith were pioneer Brandon horsemen with a congenital love for trading. They chanced to meet on the First Street Bridge on a Saturday evening. After the usual greeting, McGregor, who was on foot, said to Smith, who was riding: "I could use a horse. How much you want for that one?"

"For you, I'd take $175," Smith responded.

"Not worth it," McGregor replied. "I'll give you $12.50, cash, right here on the bridge."

Smith became silent for an instant and then spoke: "It's one awful come-down, McGregor, but we're coming to Saturday night and I haven't had a deal all week. I've never yet let a week pass without a trade of some kind and if this is my last chance, you've bought a horse."

"Nothing improves the value of a horse like crossing it with a C.P.R. locomotive."
(Attributed to Sir William White)

Alex Galbraith told of the horse exhibitor who believed he had a champion but was placed near the bottom in a class. Later, when questioned about it, he said: "I feel vera' lucky I didna' lose yon horse. I feared for a wee while that those wicked judges who stole ma' prize might be tryin' ta steal ma' whole horse next."

A young Manitoban, who had been preparing himself for the ministry, abandoned that pursuit to become a horse dealer. When the young man's father was questioned about the change of profession, he said thoughtfully: "It may be better because as a horse trader he'll bring more souls to repentance than he could ever do as a preacher."
(As told by Beecham Trotter in *A Horseman In The West*)

"Every horseman needs a good strain of horses, a good hired helper and a good wife. If you don't like your horses, trade them; if you don't like your hired man, fire him; if you don't like your wife, you'd better think again because you picked her when you had the whole world to choose from."
(Wreford Hewson to a press reporter)

"There is something about breeding good horses that makes it the Sport of Kings."
(Stanley Harrison)

"Paul Potter could paint a bull [or horse] but he never bred one."
(Alvin Sanders in the book, *At the Sign of the Stock Yard Inn*)

Somewhere . . . Somewhere in time's Own Space
There must be some sweet-pastured place
Where creeks sing on and tall trees grow
Some Paradise where horses go,
For by the love that guides my pen
I know great horses live again.
(Stanley Harrison)

"When will they make a tractor that can furnish the manure for farm fields and produce a baby tractor every spring?"
(George Rupp, pioneer breeder of Belgian horses)

Believe it or not, one of the early members of the Clydesdale horse association was George Spavin and another was Mr. Dobbin.

Custom breeding was conducted extensively in earlier years at the Lacombe research station where 150 or more outside mares were often bred in a season. Horsemen there could tell of at least one brazen attempt, under cover of darkness, to steal the service of one of the valuable stallions. As it was told and recorded, one of the farm teamsters returning to the station boarding house late at night, caught the outline of a stranger leading a station stallion back to the barn. The worker then obtained the license number of the visitor's truck as it was about to leave with a mare in it.

The police were notified and had no difficulty in locating the truck and the suspected offender, who happened to be well known at the station. But before laying charges, it was necessary to define the offence. There was no precedent for a charge of stealing a stallion's service and the stallion was none the worse for the night's adventure. Hence the charge was forgotten, at least until a sequel to the story appeared in the following summer when the mare's owner demanded the signature of the stallion owner so that he could register the foal from the ill-gotten mating. The demand was refused but the mare owner persisted and complained to the minister of agriculture that the station was in contempt of the Pedigree Act for failure to provide service papers. Only after lengthy correspondence were department officials persuaded to accept the facts as presented by the superintendent of the station. The night prowler was denied his request.

(As related in the anniversary booklet, *Lacombe Research Station, 1907–1982*, written by Dr. Howard Fredeen)

A farmer sold a horse to a neighbor who proved to be slow in making payment. The neighbor was the first to complain, saying the horse would not hold his head up. "There must be something wrong with him," he protested.

"There's nothing wrong with the horse," the seller insisted. "It's just his pride that's hurt. As soon as he's paid for, you'll see he'll hold his head high enough."

(*Percheron News*, October 1949)

A horse with a poor track record won a race. Everybody was surprised and the jockey was asked how he explained the success. "All I can tell you," the jockey replied, "is that I kept whispering in his ear when the race was in progress:

Roses are red,
Violets are blue,
Horses that lose are made into glue."

(*Percheron News*, October 1949)

One of Canada's widely known and well-respected horsemen admitted some difficulty in distinguishing between loyalty and prejudice. He said that if he didn't find Anglicans, Liberals, and Percherons in Heaven, he'd conclude that he was in the wrong place. It had to be the popular Hardy Salter, long-time secretary of the Canadian Percheron association.

"God forbid that I should go to any Heaven in which there are no horses."

(Robert Bontine Cunningham Graham)

Hear this plea, O Lord, for all horses in distress.
Especially for those which have known love and faith in man
And by man have been betrayed;
For those which have grown old in service
And whose simple needs are now begrudged them;
And those which have been used to kind companionship
And are condemned to slavery
And the terrors of the slaughtering pen;
For the over-worked and cruelly treated,
The maimed, the starving, the friendless,
The anguished and the dying,
Forgotten of man.
In their hour of need, O Lord of Mercy,
Remember each whisp of patient life,
And bring to the hearts of the masters who failed them
A saving consciousness of shame.

(Stanley Harrison)

"Somewhere in Chicago, a horse is having a quiet horse laugh. An old Percheron dobbin staged a one-nag rebellion at the Chicago airport and tied up transportation, tight.

The horse, unnamed, unknown, and unclaimed, wandered into the municipal airport and simply by his presence forced the planes that were in the air to stay there and prevented those on the ground from taking off. For fifteen minutes the animal eluded pursuers, then when the game began to pall, he flicked his tail and disappeared into the darkness as mysteriously as he had appeared."
(*Percheron News*, January 1948)

Jim Burnett, when judging heavy horses at North Battleford Exhibition, was asked if he would place the school ponies. "I will," he answered. "I'll judge anything except a baby show; if one of those little cherubs smiled at me, I'd be finished. I couldn't be unbiased. School ponies can't smile so I'll be safe."

A New Brunswick horse breeder remembered when his father had a stack of buckwheat straw which the horses refused to eat, at least until the father made a rail fence around the stack. The horses, revealing a human trait, wanted what they were being prevented from having and immediately broke the fence and showed an appetite for buckwheat straw. By spring the straw was gone.

Like other breeders of purebred draft horses, George Lane was always ready to loan his Percheron teams to haul floats at the Calgary Exhibition and Stampede parade. Asked for such assistance by a Calgary ladies' organization, he assured them of his readiness to furnish the horses to haul the float, provided that he was allowed to identify his Percheron horses with a small banner attached to the side of the float.

The ladies agreed and several of them, wearing stylish and abbreviated clothing, rode on the vehicle on the day of the parade. The float was a success from the beginning of the parade, but there was more interest and more laughter on the part of the spectators than anybody had anticipated. The reason was not clear until the end of the route when one of the ladies read aloud the words on the attached banner: "All bred and raised by George Lane."
(*Canadian Percheron Broadcaster*, December 1971)

"He doth nothing but talk of his horses."
(Shakespeare)

The old mare watched the tractor work
A thing of rubber and steel,
Ready to follow the slightest wish
Of the man who held the wheel.
She said to herself as it passed by,
You gave me an awful jolt
But there's still one thing you cannot do,
You cannot raise a colt.

(Source unknown)

"Another kind of horse story—only it's about a mule, Kate, the twenty-nine-year-old at Colorado Springs that worked long and faithfully in the mines until now—and she is too old. However, a miner's pension was applied for and she is to be on it for the rest of her life."
(*Percheron News*, April 1949)

A farmer drove to town and tied his team to a telephone pole. "Hi, you," shouted the town policeman. "You can't hitch there."
"Well, I've done it," replied the farmer. "And besides, the sign says 'Fine for hitching.'"

Galloping hoofs in Dreamland
Your rhythm rings again
When red flag falls or barrier springs,
Where hope leaps high on magic wings—
O hearts that make of all men kings,
Of all kings simple men!

Galloping hoofs of Memory,
What stirring thoughts you wake
Of swinging stroke and speeding ball,
Of rousing rush to brook and wall!
O hearts that triumphed over all
And strove for striving's sake!

Galloping hoofs of battle,
For this I loved you best
No stable save by grace of name,
No food, perchance, when feed-time came,
But true to service, game—dead game,
Galloping hoofs at rest.

Galloping hoofs! The smudge-smoke
Shrouds o'er the fallow's loam;
On star-lit air where sand-flies hum
I hear a beat like a distant drum—
With dreaming eyes I see you come
Galloping, galloping Home.

(Stanley Harrison)

Notes

CHAPTER 1

1. Grant MacEwan, *Cornerstone Colony* (Saskatoon: Western Producer Prairie Books, 1977), p. 199.
2. *Ibid.*
3. Grant MacEwan, *Hoofprints and Hitchingposts* (Saskatoon: Modern Press, 1964), p. 46.
4. *Saskatoon Star Phoenix*, February 11, 1952.

CHAPTER 2

1. Grant MacEwan, *The Breeds of Farm Livestock in Canada* (Toronto: Thomas Nelson and Sons, 1941), p. 3.
2. James Kilpatrick, *My Seventy Years with Clydesdales* (Glasgow: Henry Munro Ltd., 1949), p. 46.
3. The *Nor' West Farmer*, May 20, 1911.
4. Henry Wade, *Clydesdale Stud Book of Canada* (Toronto, 1886), p. v.
5. Carroll Campbell, *The Story of Douglas Lake* (Vancouver: Mitchell Press, 1958), p. 69.
6. De Witt Wing, "A Tribute to Alexander Galbraith," *Farmer's Advocate*, December 13, 1916.
7. Kilpatrick, p. 49.
8. Kilpatrick, p. 45.
9. *Edmonton Journal*, February 18, 1960.
10. A. E. Arnold, letter to the author, February 22, 1986.
11. Thomas P. Devlin, ed., Clydesdale Horse Association of Canada *Newsletter*, December 1945.

CHAPTER 3

1. Abbé Fret, article translated from the French and published in volume I of the *Canadian Percheron Stud Book*, (Ottawa, 1911), p. v.
2. Sir Merrick Burrell, "History of the Percheron Horse in England," *British Percheron Horse Society Stud Book*, Volume I (London: British Percheron Horse Society, 1922), p. 44.
3. "The Contemporary Percheron in France," *Canadian Percheron Broadcaster*, March 1978.
4. Jean Pelatan, *The Percheron Horse, Past and Present*, trans. John P. Harris (France: Association Des Amis Du Perche, 1985), p. 55.
5. Alvin Howard Sanders, with Wayne Dinsmore, "A History of the Percheron Horse," *Breeder's Gazette*, 1917.
6. Ellis MacFarland, "History of the Percheron Horse in America," *British Percheron Horse Society Stud Book*, Volume I (London: British Percheron Horse Society, 1922), p. 35.
7. Alvin H. Sanders, "At the Sign of the Stock Yard Inn," *Breeder's Gazette*, 1915.
8. *Morning Albertan*, August 24, 1910.
9. Letter from the Secretary of the Canadian Percheron Horse Association, April 4, 1919, to the premier of Saskatchewan; copy in minutes of the annual meeting of the association, July 1, 1919.
10. Letter from the secretary of the Canadian Percheron Horse Association to Dean W. J. Rutherford, University of Saskatchewan; copy in minutes of the annual meeting of the association, July 1, 1919.
11. Bruce Roy, "A Laet Story Little Told," *Canadian Percheron Broadcaster*, June 1984.
12. *Farm and Ranch Review*, January 5, 1921.
13. *Farm and Ranch Review*, April 5, 1922.
14. *Farm and Ranch Review*, May 5, 1922.
15. "Arnold Farms Limited, Grenville, Quebec," *Belgian Review*, 1950.
16. Bruce Roy, "Percheron Paddock," *Horses All*, September 1983.
17. *Ibid.*
18. Grant MacEwan, *The Breeds of Farm Livestock in Canada* (Toronto: Thomas Nelson and Sons, 1941), p. 78.

19. "Drake Farms Chief," *The Draft Horse Journal*, Winter 1983–84.
20. Reginald Black, letter to the author, April 4, 1986.
21. *Canadian Percheron Broadcaster*, March 1983.

CHAPTER 4

1. J. Leyder, extracts of an article in *Le Cheval Belge*, originally published in Brussels in 1905; here taken from volume I of the *Canadian Belgian Draft Horse Stud Book* (Ottawa, 1920), p. XLI.
2. *Ibid*.
3. Arthur J. Paquet, "The Belgian Draft Horse," *Canadian Belgian Draft Horse Stud Book*, volume I (Ottawa, 1920), p. LI.
4. Robert Jones, "The Old French Canadian Horse," *Canadian Historical Review*, vol. 28 (June 1947), p. 152.
5. *Farmer's Advocate*, July 13, 1904.
6. *Echoes From the Prairies* (North Toole County, Montana: Local History Society, 1976), p. 608.
7. *Poet's Corner, A History of Lampman District* (Lampman: Lampman District Historical Committee, 1982), p. 867.
8. George Rupp, "The Changing of the Belgian Type," *Farmer's Advocate*, December 10, 1919.
9. *Farmer's Advocate*, October 15, 1919.
10. *Farm and Ranch Review*, March 20, 1921.
11. *Farm and Ranch Review*, April 5, 1922.
12. Stanley M. Jepson, *The Gentle Giants* (New York: Arco Publishing Co., n.d.).
13. *The Draft Horse Journal*, Summer 1976.
14. *The Draft Horse Journal*, Spring 1983.

15. Grant MacEwan, *The Breeds of Farm Livestock in Canada* (Toronto: Thomas Nelson and Sons, 1941), p. 48.

CHAPTER 5

1. T. B. Franklin, *A History of Agriculture* (London: G. Bell and Sons, 1948), p. 218.
2. *Calgary Herald*, June 8, 1901.
3. Howard T. Fredeen, *Lacombe Research Station, 1907–1982* (Ottawa: Agriculture Canada, 1984), p. 31.
4. F. W. Reed, *Report of the Superintendent*, Dominion Experimental Farm, Lacombe, Alberta, 1930.

CHAPTER 6

1. *Percheron News*, October 1949.
2. *Farmer's Advocate*, August 30, 1911.
3. *Land of the Lakes* (Lamerton, Alberta: Lamerton Historical Society, 1974), p. 79.

CHAPTER 7

1. C. A. Langelier, *The French Canadian Horse* (Ottawa: Dominion Experimental Farms, 1927).

CHAPTER 8

1. *Edmonton Bulletin*, December 13, 1884.
2. *Farm and Ranch Review*, August 1909.
3. Hardy Salter, "Canadian Big Team Hitches, Past and Present," *Percheron News*, October 1949.

CHAPTER 9

1. H. F. Moxley, "Report of the National Horse Pulling Contest," *Percheron News*, January 1950.

Index